RAJENDRA PRASAD

RAJENDRA PRASAD

Edited by

M.K. SINGH

ANMOL PUBLICATIONS PVT. LTD.

NEW DELHI - 110 002 (INDIA)

ANMOL PUBLICATIONS PVT. LTD.
H.O.: 4374/4B, Ansari Road, Darya Ganj,
New Delhi-110 002 (India)
Ph.: 23278000, 23261597
B.O.: No. 1015, Ist Main Road, BSK IIIrd Stage
IIIrd Phase, IIIrd Block,
Bangalore - 560 085 (India)
Visit us at: www.anmolpublications.com

Rajendra Prasad

First Published, 2008

ISBN 978-81-261-3514-1

PRINTED IN INDIA

Printed at Mehra Offset Press, Delhi.

Contents

Preface

The first President of independent India, Dr. Rajendra Prasad was also the President of the Constituent Assembly that drafted India's Constitution. He had participated actively in India's freedom movement. Born on December 3, 1884 in the remote hamlet of Ziradei in Bihar's Siwan district, his father was a renowned scholar of Persian and Sanskrit. He moved to Kolkata for his education. A brilliant student all throughout, he earned a Master degree in Law, going on to complete a doctorate in law. He plunged headlong into the Swadeshi movement and was influenced tremendously by Mahatma Gandhi.

After coming into contact with Gandhiji, Dr. Rajendra Prasad, immersed himself fully into the freedom struggle. He played a active role during Non-Cooperation Movement. Dr. Rajendra Prasad was arrested in 1930 while participating in Salt Satyagraha. In July 1946, when the Constituent Assembly was established to frame the Constitution of India, Dr. Rajendra Prasad was elected its President. Two and a half years after independence, on January 26, 1950, the Constitution of independent India was ratified and Dr. Rajendra Prasad was elected as India's first President.

The presented book covers various aspects on Dr. Rajendra Prasad such as life sketch, on the path of politics, cooperative planning, suffering servant and his achievements as well.

This book is of tremendous significance for the students, teachers and researchers etc.

1

Rajendra Prasad : Life Sketch

Rajendra Prasad was an independence activist and, as a leader of the Congress Party, played a prominent role in the Indian Independence Movement. He served as President of the Constituent Assembly that drafted the constitution of the Republic from 1948 to 1950. He had also served as a Cabinet Minister briefly in the first Government of Independent India.

Early life

Prasad was born in Zeradei, in the Siwan district of Bihar near Patna. His father, Mahadev Sahai, was a Persian and Sanskrit language scholar; his mother, Kamleshwari Devi, was a devout lady who would tell stories from the Ramayana to her son. At the age of five, the young Rajendra Prasad was sent to a Maulavi for learning Persian. After that he was sent to Chhapra Zilla School for further primary studies. He was married at the age of 12 to Rajvanshi Devi. He then went on to study at R.K. Ghosh's Academy in Patna to be with his elder brother Mahendra Prasad. Soon afterward, however, he rejoined the Chhapra Zilla School, and it was from there that he passed the entrance examination of Calcutta University, at the age of 18. He stood first in the first division of that examination. He joined the Presidency College in 1902.His dauntless determination towards the service of nation inspired students like *Bihar Kesari* Dr. Sri Krishna Sinha and *Bihar Bibhuti* Dr. Anugrah Narayan Sinha who came under his tutelage. He passed in 1915 with a Gold medal in Masters in Law examination with honors. He went on to complete his Doctorate in Law.

Dr. Rajendra Prasad was born on December 3, 1884 and died on February 28, 1963. Long before the Gandhian era had set in, there was born on 3 December, 1884, in an obscure village in the Saran district of North Bihar, Rajendra Prasad, whose life was to be an embodiment of the Gandhian principles. He was to Gandhiji, to quote Sarojini Naidu, what John was to Christ. Jawaharlal called him the symbol of Bharat and found "truth looking at you through those eyes". As early as 1922, C.R. Das, the President of the Gaya session of the Indian National Congress, remarked, trial "At the moment Rajendra Prasad appears to be the sole excuse for a further honest trial of Gandhism to solve a political problem". When this view was reported to Motilal Nehru in January 1923, his reaction was almost identical : "Das is certainly correct. We have given a fair trial to Gandhism for over two years. It seems to me that the only good result it has yielded-I do not say it will not yield better or more results-is Babu Rajendra Prasad". Four year later Vithalbhai Patel remarked, "The one argument against the discontinuance of the Gandhian cult is Rajendra Prasad". Gandhiji himself once said of him : "There is at least one man who would not hesitate to take the cup of poison from my hands". No wonder Gunther called him the heart of the Congress organization. Another publicist wrote that Mahatma Gandhi with his uncanny insight picked out and groomed three of his colleagues for important roles in national life. In Jawaharlal he saw the dynamism of youth that never ages and a soaring idealism intent on a synthesis of ethical values and socio-economic objectives of modern revolutions. In Sardar he saw the great pragmatist and the man of iron will who knew how to get things done. In Rajendra Prasad he saw a great deal of himself. Rajendra Prasad's great uncle, Chaudhur Lal, built fortunes of the family, a zamindari income of Rs.7,000/-per year and substantial farm lands. He was the Dewan of the Hathwa Raj, highly respected by all, honest, loyal and efficient. Rajendra Prasad's father, Mahadev Sahay, was a country gentleman, a scholar of Persian and Sanskrit. His hobbies were wrestling and horticulture and he took delight in providing free Ayurvedic and Unani treatment to patients who flocked to him. Rajendra Prasad's mother, Kamleshwari Devi, was a devout lady who would not give up her evening bath and Pooja even though plagued by a cough which eventually proved fatal. Every day she would tell stories from the Ramayana to young Rajendra, as he huddled close to her, eager and receptive, waiting for the light of dawn to peep into the windowless bedroom of the old-fashioned house.

No wonder the Ramayana by Tulsidas became his constant companion, though he loved to browse occasionally on the Upanishads and other scriptures also. The family shunned ostentations, lived simply and mixed freely with the co-villagers. Disparities were not irritating. There was a sense of community, fellow-feeling and kindliness. All shared in the festivals and the Poojas. The flow of village life was quiet and gentle. All this left a deep impression on young Rajendra's mind. The village came to symbolize peace and repose. At the age of five young Rajendra was, according to the practice in the community to which he belonged, put under a Maulavi who taught him Persian. Later, he was taught Hindi and arithmetic. After the completion of this traditional education he was put in the Chapra Zilla School, from which he moved to R.K. Ghosh's Academy in Patna in order to be with his only brother, Mahendra Prasad, who was eight years older than him and who had joined the Patna College. When Mahendra Prasad moved to Calcutta in 1897, Rajendra was admitted into the Hathwa High School. Soon he rejoined the Chapra Zilla School, from where he passed the Entrance examination of the Calcutta University at the age of eighteen, in 1902, standing first in the first division. When it is remembered that the educational jurisdiction of the Calcutta University extended from Sadiya, the easternmost frontier of British India, to a little beyond Peshawar on the north-west, the feat appears truly remarkable. He had been married for five years at that time. His wife Rajbanshi Devi was a true-to-tradition Hindu lady, merging her identity totally in that of the husband. After passing the Entrance examination Rajendra Prasad joined the Presidency College, Calcutta, and both brothers lived together for a time in room of the Eden Hindu Hostel. A plaque still commemorates his stay, for practically the whole of his University career, in that room. Not many from Bihar had joined that metropolitan institution.

But, before long, Rajendra Prasad gained immense popularity. This was demonstrated in a remarkable early moment in 1904 when as a Third year student he won in the first annual election for the post of Secretary of the College Union against a senior student belonging to a rich aristocratic family of Calcutta. Those were days when junior students did not speak to their seniors unless spoken to. Rajendra Prasad had, moreover, neither sought nor worked for the post. Dr. P.K. Roy, the Principal, in whose presence the election had taken place by show of hands, was astounded by the result, more than a thousand against seven, and enquired as to what made Rajendra Prasad so popular. The great scientist Jagadish Chandra Bose and the highly respected P.C. Ray wanted him to offer Science, but he preferred Arts, for though he had topped in I.A. he had not topped in the Science subjects. While his remarkable distinguished academic career continued and he capped it with a First in the M.A. and a First in Master of Law, other ideas occupied his mind and heart. He had been initiated into the cult of 'Swadeshi' by his elder brother, even before his arrival in Calcutta. Now he joined, while in B.A. (Hons.) Class, the Dawn Society run by Satish Chandra Mukherjee, Sister Nivedita, Surendranath Banerjea and many other luminaries gave discourses here. There were debating and essay-writing competitions and he bagged many of the prizes. A new awareness was dawning on him. The anti-partition agitation stirred him. The processions, the slogans, the speeches touched new chords. He collected the Bihari students in Calcutta and they conducted activities similar to those conducted by the Dawn Society. The formation of the Bihari Students' Conference followed in 1908. It was the first organization of its kind in the whole of India. It not only led to an awakening, it nurtured and produced practically the entire political leadership of the twenties in Bihar. At the time he set himself up as a legal practitioner in Calcutta in 1911, apprenticed to Khan Bahadur Shamsul Huda, he also joined the Indian National Congress and was elected to the A.I.C.C. A year earlier, he impressed Sir Asutosh Mukherjee so deeply that the latter offered him a Lectureship in the Presidency Law College.

Gopal Krishna Gokhale, the greatest political leader of India in those days, had met him in Calcutta a year earlier and had exhorted him to join the Servants of India Society in Poona. Due to lack of good management the family estate was in bad shape and Rajendra Prasad was looked upon as the retriever. But had had no doubts about what he should do. Though he could not bring himself to have a straight talk with Mahendra Prasad, his elder brother, he sought his permission and blessing to join Gokhale through a letter in which he gave vent to his innermost thoughts. "Ambitions I have none," he had concluded, "except to be of some service to the Motherland". The shock and the anguish of his brother, however, held him to the family. About that time his mother died and his only sister Bhagwati Devi, fifteen years older than him, returned to her parents' home, a widow at nineteen, and in a way, took the place of his mother. In 1916 Rajendra Prasad shifted to Patna on the establishment of the High Court of Bihar and Orissa. Soon, he succeeded in gaining a marked ascendancy, not only over the clients and his colleagues at the Bar, but even more so on the Judges. His incisive intellect and phenomenal memory were no doubt great assets, but what really established his supremacy, over the minds of the judges in particular, was his innate integrity and purity of character, his inability to stoop to any tactics to score a point, to win a case. Often enough when his adversary failed to cite a precedent, the Judges asked Rajendra Prasad to cite a precedent against himself. Rajendra Prasad had first seen Gandhiji at a meeting held in Calcutta in 1915 to honour him. He was called 'Karmavir Gandhi' in those days. In the December 1916 session of the Congress, held at Lucknow, he again saw Gandhiji. He knew that the Champaran Kisan leader Rajkumar Shukla and Braj Kishore Prasad had requested Gandhiji to pay a visit to

Champaran. The session had also adopted a resolution on the Champaran situation. In the April 1917, A.I.C.C. session, held in Calcutta, Gandhiji and Rajendra Prasad sat very close to each other but he did not know that Gandhiji was to be taken to his residence in Patna on his way to Champaran. He, therefore, left for Puri when the session ended. When Gandhiji reached Rajendra Prasad's residence in Patna next morning, the servant took him to be a client and a villager and showed him the servant's bathroom and the well outside. Barefooted, clad in half achkan, dhoti and Kathiawadi purgree, carrying in a roll his bedding and a few dhotis and some food in a tin box, Gandhiji looked very much an illiterate villager. Gandhiji did not know what to do next, when, hearing of his arrival, Mazharul Haq came and took him to his palatial residence, Sikander Manzil.

There was a similar situation at Muzaffarpur Junction Station where Acharya Kripalani, a Professor in the local College, had come to receive Gandhiji with a large number of students. None had seen Gandhiji. None recognized him. On return to Patna Rajendra Babu learnt all that had happened and hastened to Motihari. He regarded his meeting with Gandhiji as the turning point in his career. He stayed with Gandhiji till his trial was over. Thereafter, things in the country took a different course, by reason of the Rowlatt Act and the Punjab upheaval, and in 1920, even before the civil disobedience and non-cooperation resolution of the special session of the Congress held in Calcutta in September had been confirmed by the regular session held in December at Nagpur, he took the plunge. He openly pledged himself to defy unrighteous laws, and resort to civil disobedience and non-cooperation and thus he constituted himself more or leass as an outlaw in the eyes of the British Government in India. The decades that followed were years of intense activity and heavy suffering. He ceased to be a Senator of the University to the regret of the British Vice-Chancellor. He withdrew his sons, Mrityunjaya and Dhanajjaya, and his nephew, Janardan from the Benares Hindu University and other schools.

He wrote articles for Searchlight and the Desh and collected funds for these papers. He toured a lot, explaining, lecturing, exhorting. He was the life-breath of the constructive programme and a great votary of Khadi. He was the first leading political figure in the Eastern Provinces to join forces with Gandhiji at a time when the latter was without a large and effective following. Another such leader from the West who joined Gandhiji was Vallabhbhai Patel. During the Nagpur Flag Satyagraha Rajendra Babu and Vallabhbhai came closer. Rajendra Babu cherished Sardar's friendship as one of the most pleasant memories of his life. He often went to Sabarmati and toured the country with Gandhiji. He suffered several terms of rigorous imprisonment. He suffered privations for want of a regular income of his own. All the while he suffered from asthma. He would not accept any financial assistance from the Congress or from any other source and depended mostly on his elder brother. He was in jail when on 15 January, 1934 the devastating earthquake in Bihar occurred. He was released two days later. Though ailing, he set himself immediately to the task of raising funds and organizing relief. The Viceroy also raised a fund for the purpose.

While his fund swelled to over 38 lakhs, the Viceroy's fund, despite his great influence, resources and prestige, remained at one third of the amount. The way relief was organized left nothing to be desired. Nationalist India expressed its admiration by electing him to the President of the Bombay session of the Indian National Congress. Mahendra Prasad, his elder brother, had died. The Congress through a resolution remembered his social services and his devotion to the national cause. When the Congress Ministries were formed in 1937, it was the Parliamentary Board consisting of Sardar Patel, Rajendra Babu and Maulana Azad, which really and effectively provided guidance and control. In 1939 when Subhas Chandra Bose had to be relieved of the office of the Congress President, it was Rajendra Prasad who was persuaded to face the crisis and overcome it.

The Congress faced another crisis when Acharya Kripalani resigned and Rajendra Babu had to step into the breach, even though he happened to be India's Food and Agriculture Minister and President of the Constituent Assembly. He realized that industrialism had disrupted the web of village life woven and integrated for centuries. It had to be re-woven into a new pattern. He wanted that pattern to be inspired by Gandhian values; human needs and acquisitiveness to be regulated through self-discipline; agricultural production to be maximized, village industries to be resuscitated and their scope enlarged; the old sense of community to be recaptured. But he found that the country was unable to resist the pull of industrialization, even hurriedly thought-out industrialization, and he was not happy at the development. This was one reason why he declined to accept the Chairmanship of the Planning Commission. This was why, when Wavell informally enquired what portfolio he would choose if he were to choose it for himself, he said that he hardly needed time to think about it. It had to be Food and Agriculture. Wavell was amused and there was an unspoken why. "Well", Rajendra Babu went on, "the subject is familiar to me. He knew all that the best farmer knows about agricultural operations and practices. But he also realized that certain improvements had to be effected on those methods. The slogan 'Grow More Food' was given by him and the campaign was initiated by the Food Ministry under his guidance. He could not, however, continue for long in that Ministry and ensure compliance with the policies initiated by him. But, before he relinquished charge, he did, as Gandhiji wanted, effect decontrol of foodgrains, and though officials and public men alike had prophesied disaster, nothing untoward happened. His stewardship of the Constituent Assembly was exemplary. He guided, regulated, controlled, but did so with such infinite patience, skill, grace and firmness that not only none had a sense of grievance but all felt that the discussions were always full, free and frank and left nothing to be desired. During the very first session of the Constituent Assembly, he had announced that though the Assembly was born under limitations it would outgrow those and function as a sovereign body, recognizing no outside authority.

The proceedings of the last day of the Constituent Assembly read like pages from a book of tributes and, in a way, indicate how loved and respected he was by each section of the House. His elevation to the Presidentship in 1950 came as a matter of course. There were some doubts in some quarters. Could a person who was temperamentally a peasant, who lived and dressed like one, impress in an office where ceremonialism and gilded trappings counted? But nothing else was possible. He was the only choice and there could not be another. As President, he exercised his moderating influence and moulded policies or actions so silently and unobtrusively that many were led to think that, unlike any other Head of State, he neither reigned nor ruled. He never worried about what people said about him. He never looked into the mirror of history. There were occasions when he differed from the Prime Minister. But that was nothing new. They had differred for almost three decades and yet worked together in the Congress. The differences never embittered their personal relations. Perhaps, both realized that they arose out of their differing backgrounds, beliefs, approaches and attitudes. It was in 1960 that he announced his intention to retire, and though there were many regrets and many tried to persuade him to continue for a third term, his mind was made up. Jayaprakash Narayan welcomed the decision, suggesting that his direct guidance might be available after retirement to the Sarvodaya Movement. But the 1961 illness, severed and protracted, shattered Rajendra Prasad's health completely. Many therefore, worried at his decision to go back to the Sadaquat Ashram. How could he guide any constructive movement with that frail body of his? Would not the inconveniences of the Ashram prove too much for his health? His elder sister Bhagwati Devi had passed away in the night of 25 January, 1960. She doted on her dearly-loved younger brother, to whose house she had returned within two years of her marriage, a widow at nineteen.

It must have taken Rajendra Babu all his will power to have taken the Republic Day salute as usual, on the following day, seemingly unruffled. It was only on return from the parade that he set about the task of cremation. Within months of his retirement, early in September 1962, passed away his wife Rajbanshi Devi, whose contribution to making him what he was, though indirect, was considerable. Frail and an invalid for a long time, she was the very embodiment of the spirit of renunciation, selflessness, self-effacement and devotion. She had asked for little and though she had been only partly a companion to him, she had silently encouraged him and never stood in the way. Her husband's will was her will, his pleasure hers. Not many words were exchanged between the two-they would sit quietly together for hours-and yet their silent communion filled the atmosphere with distinct aura. No wonder, his last days were days of agony. The Chinese aggression had shaken him completely. He had apprehended the danger. He had thought of the dreaded possibility. But "perhaps those who thought otherwise knew better". This consolation was shaken away by the naked aggression. His will to live was weakening.

In a letter to one devoted to him, he wrote a month before his death : "I have a feeling that the end is near, end of the energy to do, end of my very existence". And so, when the end came suddenly on 28 February, 1963, he was not unprepared. He died, after a few hours' illness, with 'Ram Ram' on his lips. Ever since the present Contributor came near him in 1933, the bond grew stronger as the years passed. Rajendra Prasad had great affection for him and valued his judgement. Rajendra Babu and the present Contributor were together in the Birla House when the Interim Government was formed in September 1946. Rajendra Babu said, "We must now move to our residences" The present contributor had brought nothing except his clothes, and wondered as to how to go about setting up a home. When he reached No. Queen Victoria Road-now Dr. Rajendra Prasad Road-in the evening, he was pleasantly surprised to find that not only were all provisions and utensils and crockeries there, but even the statue of goddess Lakshmi had not been forgotten. Rajendra Babu shared Gandhiji's great vision, the making of a new man in a new society. His mind was capable of broad sweeps. But it would take in at the same time the smallest details.

As an accomplished lawyer, however, he realized it would be only a matter of time before he would be caught up in the turmoil of the fight for independence. While Gandhiji was on a fact finding mission in Chamaparan district of Bihar to address grievances of local peasants, he called on Dr. Rajendra Prasad to come to Champaran with volunteers. He rushed to Champaran. Initially he was not impressed with Gandhiji's appearance or conversation. In time, however, he was deeply moved by the dedication, conviction and courage that Gandhiji displayed.

Here was a man alien of the parts, who had made the cause of the people of Champaran his own. He decided that he would do everything he could to help, with his skills as a lawyer and as an enthusiastic volunteer. Gandhiji's influence greatly altered many of his views, most importantly on caste and untouchability. Gandhiji made Dr. Rajendra Prasad realize that the nation, working for a common cause, "became of one caste, namely co-workers." He reduced the number of servants he had to one, and sought ways to simplify his life. He no longer felt shame in sweeping the floor, or washing his own utensils, tasks he had all along assumed others would do for him. Whenever the people suffered, he was present to help reduce the pain. In 1914 floods ravaged Bihar and Bengal. He became a volunteer distributing food and cloth to the flood victims.

In 1934, Bihar was shaken by an earthquake, which caused immense damage and loss of property. The quake, devastating by itself, was followed by floods and an outbreak of malaria which heightened misery. He dove right in with relief work, collecting food, clothes and medicine. His experiences here led to similar efforts elsewhere too. In 1935, an earthquake hit Quetta. He was not allowed to lend a hand because of Government restrictions.

Nevertheless, he set up relief committees in Sind and Punjab for the homeless victims who flocked there. Dr. Prasad called for non-cooperation in Bihar as part of Gandhiji's non-cooperation movement. He gave up his law practice and started a National College near Patna, 1921. The college was later shifted to Sadaqat Ashram on the banks of the Ganga. The non-cooperation movement in Bihar spread like wildfire. Dr. Prasad toured the state, holding public meeting after another, collecting funds and galvanizing the nation for a complete boycott of all schools, colleges and Government offices. He urged the people to take to spinning and wear only khadi. Bihar and the entire nation was taken by storm, the people responded to the leaders' call. The machinery of the mighty British Raj was coming to a grinding halt. The British India Government utilized the one and only option at its disposal-force. Mass arrests were made. Lala Lajpat Rai, Jawaharlal Nehru, Deshbandhu Chittranjan Das and Maulana Azad were arrested. Then it happened. Peaceful non-cooperation turned to violence in Chauri Chaura, Uttar Pradesh. In light of the events at Chauri Chaura, Gandhiji suspended the civil disobedience movement. The entire nation was hushed. A murmur of dissent began within the top brass of the Congress. Gandhiji was criticized for what was called the "Bardoli retreat." He stood by his mentor, seeing the wisdom behind Gandhiji's actions. Gandhiji did not want to set a precedent of violence for free India.

In March 1930, Gandhiji launched the Salt Satyagraha. He planned to march from Sabarmati Ashram to Dandi seashore to break the salt laws. A salt Satyagraha was launched in Bihar under Dr. Prasad. Nakhas Pond in Patna was chosen as the site of the Satyagraha. Batch after batch of volunteers courted arrest while making salt. Many volunteers were injured. He called for more volunteers. Public opinion forced the Government to withdraw the police and allow the volunteers to make salt. He then sold the manufactured salt to raise funds. He was sentenced to six months imprisonment. His service on the various fronts of the movement for independence raised his profile considerably. He presided over the Bombay session of the Indian National Congress in October 1934. Following the resignation of Subhash Chandra Bose as the President of the Congress in April 1939, He was elected President. He did his best to heal the rifts created between the incompatible ideologies of Subhash Chandra Bose and Gandhiji.

Rabindranath Tagore wrote to him, "I feel assured in my mind that your personality will help to soothe the injured souls and bring peace and unity into an atmosphere of mistrust and chaos..." As the freedom struggle progressed, the dark shadow of communalism which had always lurked in the background, steadily grew. To his dismay communal riots began spontaneously burst all over the nation and in Bihar. He rushed from one scene to another to control the riots. Independence was fast approaching and so was the prospect of partition. Dr. Prasad, who had such fond memories of playing with his Hindu and Muslim friends in Zeradei, now had the misfortune of witnessing the nation being ripped into two. In July 1946, when the Constituent Assembly was established to frame the Constitution of India, he was elected its President. Two and a half years after independence, on January 26, 1950, the Constitution of independent India was ratified and he was elected the nation's first President. Dr. Prasad transformed the imperial splendor of Rashtrapati Bhavan into an elegant "Indian" home. He visited many countries on missions of goodwill, as the new state sought to establish and nourish new relationships. He stressed the need for peace in a nuclear age. In 1962, after 12 years as President, Dr. Prasad retired, and was subsequently awarded the Bharat Ratna, the nation's highest civilian award. With the many tumults of his vigorous and accomplished life, he recorded his life and the decades before independence in many books, among the more noted of which are "Satyagraha at Champaran" (1922), "India Divided" (1946), his autobiography "Atmakatha" (1946), "Mahatma Gandhi and Bihar, Some Reminisences" (1949), and "Bapu ke Kadmon Mein" (1954). Dr. Rajendra Prasad spent the last few months of his life in retirement at the Sadaqat Ashram in Patna. He died on February 28, 1963. In her first citizen, India had imagined a life of possibilities, and seen an unsurpassed dedication to making them real.

During the Independence Movement : Jawaharlal Nehru, Bhulabhai Desai and Babu Rajendra Prasad (Center) at the AICC Session, April 1939. He was drawn into the Indian freedom struggle soon after starting his career as a lawyer. During one of the fact-finding missions at Champaran, Mahatma Gandhi asked him to come with volunteers. Rajendra Prasad was greatly moved by the dedication, courage, and conviction of Mahatma Gandhi and he quit as a Senator of the University in 1921. He also responded to the call by the Mahatma to boycott Western education by asking his son Mrityunjaya Prasad, a brilliant student to drop out of the University and enroll himself in Bihar Vidyapeeth, an institution he had along with his colleagues founded on the traditional Indian model. He wrote articles for *Searchlight* and the *Desh* and collected funds for these papers. He toured a lot, explaining, lecturing and exhorting. He took active role in helping the affected people during the 1914 floods that raged in Bihar and Bengal. When the earthquake of Bihar occurred on January 15, 1934, Rajendra Prasad was in jail. During that period, he gave the entire responsibility on his behalf to his close colleague and eminent Gandhian Dr. Anugrah Narayan Sinha. He was released two days later. He set himself for the task of raising funds. The Viceroy had also raised a fund. However, while Rajendra Prasad's fund collected over 38 Lakhs (Rs. 3,800,000), three times of what the Viceroy could manage. During the 1935 Quetta earthquake, when he was not allowed to leave the country, he set up relief committees in Sindh and Punjab.

He was elected as the President of Indian National Congress during the Bombay session in October 1934. He again became the President when Netaji Subhash Chandra Bose resigned in 1939.

After India became independent he was elected the President of India. As the first President, he was indepedent and unwilling to allow the Prime Minister or the party to usurp his constitutional prerogatives. However, following the tussle over the enactment of the Hindu Code Bill, he moderated his stance. He set several important precedents for later Presidents to follow.

His sister Bhagwati Devi died on the night of 25 January 1960, a day before the Republic Day of India. She doted on her dearly-loved younger brother. It was only on return from the parade that he set about the task of cremation. In 1962, after 12 years as President, he announced his decision to retire. He was subsequently awarded the Bharat Ratna, the nation's highest civilian award. Within months of his retirement, early in September 1962, his wife Rajvanshi Devi died. In a letter written a month before his death to one devoted to him, he said, "I have a feeling that the end is near, end of the energy to do, end of my very existence". He died on 28 February 1963 at Sadaqat ashram,Patna with 'Ram Ram Ram' on his lips.

His legacy is being ably carried forward by his great grandson Ashoka Jahnavi-Prasad a scientist and a psychiatrist of international repute who introduced sodium valproate as a safer alternative to lithium intreatment of bipolar disorder and a member of the elite American Academy of Arts and Sciences.

Because of the enormous public adulation he enjoyed,he was referred to as Desh Ratna or the *Jewel of the country*. He wrote a number of books including "Satyagrah at Champaran", "Bapu ke kadmon mein", "India divided" and "Atmakatha".Dalai Lama in his autobiographical book *Freedom in Exile* described him as a "true Bodhisatva" and said that his humility brought tears to his eyes.

Dr. Rajendra Prasad, being the youngest in a large joint family "Rajen" was greatly loved. He was strongly attached to his mother and elder brother Mahendra. In Zeradei's diverse population, people lived together in considerable harmony. Rajendra Prasad's earliest memories were of playing "kabaddi" with his Hindu and Muslim friends alike. In keeping with the old customs of his village and family, Rajen was married when he was barely 12 years old to Rajvanshi Devi.

Rajen was a brilliant student; standing first in the entrance examination to the University of Calcutta, he was awarded a Rs.30/month scholarship. He joined the famed Calcutta Presidency College in 1902. His scholarship, ironically, would pose the first test of his patriotism. Gopal Krishna Gokhale had started the Servants of India Society in 1905 and asked Rajen to join. So strong was his sense of duty toward his family and education that he, after much deliberation, refused Gokhale. But the decision would not rest easy on him. Rajen recalled, "I was miserable" and for the first time in his life his performance in academia declined, and he barely cleared his law examinations.

Having made his choice, however, he set aside the intruding thoughts, and focused on his studies with renewed vigor. In 1915, Rajen passed the Masters in Law examination with honors, winning a gold medal. Subsequently, he completed his Doctorate in Law as well.

As an accomplished lawyer, however, Rajen realized it would be only a matter of time before he would be caught up in the turmoil of the fight for independence. While Gandhiji was on a fact finding mission in Chamaparan district of Bihar to address grievances of local peasants, he called on Rajendra Prasad to come to Champaran with volunteers. Dr. Prasad rushed to Champaran. Initially he was not impressed with Gandhiji's appearance or conversation. In time, however, Dr. Prasad was deeply moved by the dedication, conviction and courage that Gandhiji displayed. Here was a man alien of the parts, who had made the cause of the people of Champaran his own. Dr.Prasad decided that he would do everything he could to help, with his skills as a lawyer and as an enthusiastic volunteer.

Gandhiji's influence greatly altered many of Dr. Prasad's views, most importantly on caste and untouchability. Gandhiji made Dr. Prasad realize that the nation, working for a common cause, "became of one caste, namely co-workers." Dr. Prasad reduced the number of servants he had to one, and sought ways to simplify his life. He no longer felt shame in sweeping the floor, or washing his own utensils, tasks he had all along assumed others would do for him.

Whenever the people suffered, Dr. Prasad was present to help reduce the pain. In 1914 floods ravaged Bihar and Bengal. Dr. Prasad became a volunteer distributing food and cloth to the flood victims. In 1934, Bihar was shaken by an earthquake, which caused immense damage and loss of property. The quake, devastating by itself, was followed by floods and an outbreak of malaria which heightened misery. Dr. Prasad dove right in with relief work, collecting food, clothes and medicine. His experiences here led to similar efforts elsewhere too. In 1935, an earthquake hit Quetta. Dr. Prasad was not allowed to lend a hand because of Government restrictions. Nevertheless, he set up relief committees in Sind and Punjab for the homeless victims who flocked there.

Dr. Prasad called for non-cooperation in Bihar as part of Gandhiji's non-cooperation movement. Dr. Prasad gave up his law practice and started a National College near Patna, 1921. The college was later shifted to Sadaqat Ashram on the banks of the Ganga. The non-cooperation movement in Bihar spread like wildfire. Dr. Prasad toured the state, holding public meeting after another, collecting funds and galvanizing the nation for a complete boycott of all schools, colleges and Government offices. He urged the people to take to spinning and wear only khadi. Bihar and the entire nation was taken by storm, the people responded to the leaders' call. The machinery of the mighty British Raj was coming to a grinding... halt.

The British India Government utilized the one and only option at its disposal-force. Mass arrests were made. Lala

Lajpat Rai, Jawaharlal Nehru, Deshbandhu Chittranjan Das and Maulana Azad were arrested. Then it happened. Peaceful non-cooperation turned to violence in Chauri Chaura, Uttar Pradesh. In light of the events at Chauri Chaura, Gandhiji suspended the civil disobedience movement. The entire nation was hushed. A murmur of dissent began within the top brass of the Congress. Gandhiji was criticized for what was called the "Bardoli retreat."

Dr. Prasad stood by his mentor, seeing the wisdom behind Gandhiji's actions. Gandhiji did not want to set a precedent of violence for free India. In March 1930, Gandhiji launched the Salt Satyagraha. He planned to march from Sabarmati Ashram to Dandi seashore to break the salt laws. A salt satyagraha was launched in Bihar under Dr. Prasad. Nakhas Pond in Patna was chosen as the site of the satyagraha. Batch after batch of volunteers courted arrest while making salt. Many volunteers were injured. Dr. Prasad called for more volunteers. Public opinion forced the Government to withdraw the police and allow the volunteers to make salt. Dr. Prasad then sold the manufactured salt to raise funds. He was sentenced to six months imprisonment.

His service on the various fronts of the movement for independence raised his profile considerably. Dr. Prasad presided over the Bombay session of the Indian National Congress in October 1934. Following the resignation of Subhash Chandra Bose as the President of the Congress in April 1939, Dr. Prasad was elected President. He did his best to heal the rifts created between the incompatible ideologies of Subhash Chandra Bose and Gandhiji. Rabindranath Tagore wrote to Dr. Prasad, "I feel assured in my mind that your personality will help to soothe the injured souls and bring peace and unity into an atmosphere of mistrust and chaos..." As the freedom struggle progressed, the dark shadow of communalism which had always lurked in the background, steadily grew. To Dr. Prasad's dismay communal riots began spontaneously burst all over the nation and in Bihar. He rushed from one scene to another to control the riots. Independence was fast approaching and so was the prospect of partition. Dr. Prasad, who had such fond memories of playing with his Hindu and Muslim friends in Zeradei, now had the misfortune of witnessing the nation being ripped into two. In July 1946, when the Constituent Assembly was established to frame the Constitution of India, Dr. Rajendra Prasad was elected its President. Two and a half years after independence, on January 26, 1950, the Constitution of independent India was ratified and Dr. Rajendra Prasad was elected the nation's first President. Dr. Prasad transformed the imperial splendor of Rashtrapati Bhavan into an elegant "Indian" home. Dr. Prasad visited many countries on missions of goodwill, as the new state sought to establish and nourish new relationships. He stressed the need for peace in a nuclear age. In 1962, after 12 years as President, Dr. Prasad retired, and was subsequently awarded the Bharat Ratna, the nation's highest civilian award.

With the many tumults of his vigorous and accomplished life, Dr. Prasad recorded his life and the decades before independence in many books, among the more noted of which are "Satyagraha at Champaran" (1922), "India Divided" (1946), his autobiography "Atmakatha" (1946), "Mahatma Gandhi and Bihar, Some Reminisences" (1949), and "Bapu ke Kadmon Mein" (1954). Dr. Prasad spent the last few months of his life in retirement at the Sadaqat Ashram in Patna. He died on February 28, 1963. In her first citizen, India had imagined a life of possibilities, and seen an unsurpassed dedication to making them real.

The tales of the tenants woes were personally reported to Gandhi. He now requisitioned the support of local lawyers to record their statements. Gandhi had wired to Darbhanga asking Brajkishore Babu to come to his aid. He had at the moment an urgent work in Calcutta. So he sent two junior lawyer friends to serve him as interpreters as Gandhi could not follow the local Hindi of the rural folk.

Besides the day to day troubles of endless varieties the ryots laboured chiefly under two forced agreements. The Tinkathia Agreement compelled a ryot to cultivate indigo on three cottahs per bigha and yield the total harvest to the English planter. But the planters were beginning to find that cultivated indigo could not compete against German synthetic blue. Thereupon they imposed on the ryots the Sharah beshi Agreement which granted them release from compulsory indigo cultivation on payment of 15% enhancement of rent. Men from the villages streamed into Gandhis camp in the town at Motihari. But he also wanted to go out and see villages and the actual trouble spots. As per programme he was one day out to see a ryot at his home in the village which was looted by the agents of the planters. On his way he was served with the Collectors order to leave the district by the first train. He replied in the negative to the Collectors notice dated April 16 :

"Out of a sense of public responsibility I feel it to be my duty to say that I am unable to leave the district but if it pleases the authorities I shall submit to the order by suffering the penalty of disobedience. My desire is purely and simply for a genuine search for knowledge. And this I shall continue to satisfy so long as I am free."

Gandhi sent a detailed wire to Rajendra Prasad which reached him at the court. This was the first direct communication between them. But why did Gandhi think of Rajendra Prasad and wire to him in detail? He had not seen him and known him personally. Evidently then he must have heard so much of him as to consider that he was a person who ought to be informed and used for the country's good. Evidently he had gained this significance in the eye of Gandhi though at the time he was only a rather junior lawyer and could not be said to have attained quite a leaderly standing.

The reason of it all could merely be this that young Rajendra Prasad must have already made a name for honesty and uprightness and for will and ability to do things for the good of others. Having put in just about seven years practice of which about two years were given to the Patna High Court he had already setup such a unique reputation for clean conscience and clear selflessness that the Patna High Court used to admit any Appeal moved by him in the faith that he was not a lawyer who accepted all kinds of cases for the pleasure of gambling in law at others costs and earning fees. Gandhi who had an instinct for knowing men focussed his eye on Rajendra Prasad as much as he knew him from public report without having seen him. It should be helpful to get the background of a person who though unknown had occupied the thought of Gandhi. In his student years in Calcutta he was devoted to his studies scored top places in examinations and yet interested himself in public causes. His moral mind was built under the influence of the Dawn Society a society for bringing up young men on high and patriotic ideals. Contact with Dawn Society gave a kind of definiteness to several of his soaring emotions and a pointed direction to his stray thoughts on serving the motherland. Still and that is general with a noble minded but inexperienced youth he had but equivocal ideas of what to do. And even then these ideas that sprang upon him from time to time subsided silently under the pressure of this or that domestic difficulty. It was thus again in 1910 while preparing for the B. L. Examination that he could not join the Servant of India Society after weeks of restless and almost tearful struggles to embrace this dedicated life. His elder brother shielded him from many earthly troubles. Himself in difficulties he protected his younger brother from breakdown. For instance relying on his protection young Rajendra Prasad having stood first in B. A. Examination did not care to go in for a ready job of a Deputy Magistrate and took to the more distant and ambitious prospect of the High Court Bar. He was a student when the Partition Agitation !swelled up in Bengal. He was emotionally and intellectually stirred by it but could not throw himself head long into its stream of action. But that was his habit of the mind. The man who could not just speak to Gandhi while sitting by his side for hours feasibly could not be one to take any big step like leaving College and giving himself up to active movements. He took the vow of Swadeshi alright. Indeed it was no trial for him as he was already habitual to wear Swadeshi clothes. Merely once when he was about to sail for England he had got clothes made to order from English shops. But he happened not to wear them at all as his programme for foreign education was altogether cancelled. A friend of his had the advantage of his English tailored suits when he went to England. It was an amusing incident that both of them had seen an old astrologer who predicted that such would be their fate. But on the way back to the hostel in his absence they made fun of the old man since at the time Rajendra Prasad had about full preparation for leaving for England while there was not the remotest talk of his friends going out. There is however one solitary example of Rajendra Prasads having slipped into buying a foreign article. It was a stylo pen. He used to take notes from lectures in class room. He could ill resist the temptation of having a pen then just new in the market that would save him from doing it with a pencil. His friends in the Hindu Hostel of the Presidency College poked fun at him. He promised to do without it. But then he demanded that All his friends must open their trunks and discard all foreign contents. Probably this was only once in his life that the shy Rajendra Prasad in great grief overcame —his habitual diffidence and challenged a whole hostel. He also disclosed his own while others did so. He poured out his belongings and all were found to be Swadeshi. Some friends had foreign clothes and goods of other descriptions. Out of the big display foreign materials were collected into a pile and all friends willingly lit a bonfire of these. While he was studying Law and M. A. it occurred to him that students in Bihar should be filled with Swadeshi spirit as those in Bengal were. He talked about it at the Bihari Club in Calcutta. Its members students as well as ex students all responded to his idea. He had composed a song to encourage the men of his Province (now State) and the song worked its way into their mind. He was sent by the Club to popularise the plan in Patna. This was his first action in public life and he gave his first public speech at the Patna College Hall. The Bihar Students Association was established. Mr. Sachchidananda Sinha and Babu Mahesh Narayan were among its patrons. His life at Eden Hindu Hostel was pleasant and profitable. Between him and his Bengali hostel mates there was perfect goodwill and memories of sweet relations still haunt him. Not a harsh word he says was exchanged. After graduation he left this Presidency College hostel and lived in a private mess. In due course he was enrolled as an article clerk of a practising lawyer. He was Khan Bahadur Syed Samsul Huda who later was taken in as a Member of the Bengal Governors Executive Council. Mr. Justice Digambar Chatterjee at whose house he took up private tuition for a while had prophesied that he would get poor clients to begin with but if he worked hard he would make his mark and prosper. The prophecy came true for that was exactly how he began his career and secured his rise to reputation and prosperity in practice. He had another singular triumph. He had distinguished himself by obtaining the M. L. degree while doing his profession. And then by sheer intelligence and industry he extracted the appreciation of no less a hard critic and acute lawyer than Dr. Rash Behari Ghosh.

In 1912 he was Secretary of the Reception Committee to the All India Hindi Conference in Calcutta and could not attend the Congress at Patna that year. In 1916, when Bihar had its own High Court Rajendra Prasad left Calcutta to join the Bar at Patna. That year he had been elected Vice President of Bihar Provincial Congress Committee. Soon he became a figure at the Bar and in the Province. So much in brief outline of Rajendra Prasad who at the Court received Gandhis wire. He in turn wired to Brajkishore Babu to hurry back from Calcutta. In the mean time Mazaharul Huq Saheb and Mr. Polak had come to Patna. Shri Anugrahnarayan and Shri Sambhunarayan also joined. And the whole party reached Motihari to meet Gandhi. By this time the case had already been heard by the S.D.O. before whom Gandhi read his statement :

"Amidst the conflict of duty I could only throw the liability of removing me on the administration. I am fully conscious of the fact that a person holding in the public life of India a position such as I do has to be most careful in setting examples. It is my firm belief that in the complex constitution under which we are living the only safe and honourable course for a self respecting man is in the circumstances such as face me to do what I have decided to do that is to submit without protest to the penalty of disobedience." The village folk learning that their deliverer was in problem for their sake rushed in thousands to the town and thronged the court house while Gandhi was pleading disobedience to the court and obedience to conscience. The police failing to control the crowd sought his help to pacify them and the mob obeyed as they listened to the Master. On the arrival of the party from Patna Rajendra. Prasad was introduced to Gandhi. This was the first meeting between the Master and the disciple. But the impact of the very first moment was no where near overwhelming. In fact Rajendra Prasad had come more with a mind to assist Brajkishore Babu in his task of serving Gandhi than for the sake of Gandhi directly.

At the time of introduction Gandhi said smilingly : So you are here. I had been to your house. Remembering the type of reception he had at his house Rajendra Babu felt a little embarrassed. The good natured way of the words struck him but again the effect was hardly quite such as would overwhelm him. That overwhelming effect was upon him when shortly afterwards he heard Babu Dharnidhar and Babu Ramnawmi from whom he got Gandhis fuller details while Gandhi himself was presently immersed in a discussion with Mr. Polak. They were the two junior lawyers whom Brajkishore Babu had sent to work as Gandhis interpreters. Dharni Babu the elder of the two did most of the talking to Rajendra Babu. He said Gandhi kept awake one whole night making ready letters to the Viceroy and to the leaders of India as also his statement to the Court.

Thereafter he asked them what they would do when he would be arrested. He said he replied almost in joke – Well then interpreters work would be gone and we should be free to go back home.

A gloom settled on Gandhi. He again inquired would they have the heart to reject the work and leave the country folk to their fate in that type of chaos? Thereupon he said he realised the seriousness. Taking some thought he told Gandhi that they would continue the recording. When he would be threatened with jail he would leave work replacing another at the post; likewise a chain of men would retire and work. Gandhi he said appeared happier if not very happy. They too were no better. At night they thought it over again. And in a flash they saw their way. In the morning as they accompanied Gandhi to the Court they told Gandhi that they would follow him to the jail if the work at any moment would need them to. Gandhi he said to Rajendra Prasad beamed in a mysterious manner as he heard this and exclaimed : Now we have won the case!' This dramatic part of the narration revealed Gandhi in a light that Rajendra Babu had never seen. And in this light he saw as well his own duty. It had never crossed his mind even in a dream that no sooner he would meet Gandhi than itself before him in such a startling reality. But he and his party made up their mind and definitely gave Gandhi their word that they were getting ready for jail. Thus, they got ready. Huq Saheb and Brajkishore Babu went away only to return having fixed up matters at home in readiness for jail. Others awaited their turn to speak to their family and came back to court arrest. So they all out of their own free will permitted themselves to be caught in the snare of Gandhi. And Gandhi in his strange business like manner put pen to paper and wrote down the names of the prospective jail goers and divided them in batches so that they would march into jail according to programme and with picturesque precision. The dramatic tension grew more tense. Malaviya had hastened to Patna to be as near the scene as possible and give as much help as he could readily give. Andrews rushed right to Gandhis camp at Motihari. The Bihar party requested Andrews to stay and assist them He would stay he said if Gandhi wanted him to. But Gandhi did not. He told them : "You think that in this unequal fight it would be helpful to have an Englishman on our side. This shows the weakness of our heart" The cause is just and you must rely on yourselves to win the battle." (Louis Fischer : Gandhi :" His Life and Message) So Andrews next day started for Fiji. But before he left he saw) the" District Magistrate and carried the news to the camp that Gandhi would be set free. Rajendra Prasad observed : Mahatmaji told the right thing and read our minds correctly that fear complex inclined us to depend on Andrews. The work of recording statements of sufferers went on Over 25000 cases were recorded." Gandhi spoke apparently to the lawyers who had come to help him that beyond careful recording he did not need any legal advice. The Vakils were asked to become clerks and they agreed But faithful and intelligent understanding of duty had its scope even in clerical work and it could not go unrecognised. Gandhi was soon to realise : "Brajkishore Babu and Rajendra Babu were a matchless pair. Their devotion not made impossible to take a single step without their help." (Gandhi My Experiments with Truth) Steadily and surely; Rajendra Prasad was coming under the shadow of the Mahatma. Here he relates how he tuned his conduct according to the teaching of the Master. Once an intimate colleague of Gandhi in social service came to see him at Motihari. At the time he was engaged in discussing peasant problems with local lawyer colleagues. He sent him word to wait. But he got impatient even wounded. He took it ill that a good worker and a familiar friend like him could be kept out like that. But Gandhi called him only when the discussions were over. He told him that he should not mind being outside when there was something going in the room in which he had no support to offer and no business to enter though in other matters his cooperation would be so desirable and valuable. "Since then" Rajendra Prasad comments "I have personally never felt cut up when I have been required to retire from a Committee or discussion where for some reason my presence was not considered necessary or helpful". One day a police officer kept sitting and watching the lawyers and the ryots as statements were recorded. The lawyers realised perplexed. They approached Gandhi that he might find out a way of removing the intruder. That he did but he also gave the lawyers a lesson in courage of conviction. He said : If there were hundreds of villagers and statements taken down in that crowd could be alright how should it hinder if besides one police officer remained there? First they should not think that anything was secret. Secondly they should take a policeman as a part of the countrymen there. It hurt the police officers vanity that his personality could be unfelt and that a member of the police could be supposed to be lost in the crowd. Gandhi gathered facts about the planters with a view to see how the ryots lived or if they could really live in the circumstances. The ryots recorded their statements openly and with great risks of molestations by their planter landlords. That courage is rigid which grows in calmness.

An atmosphere of excitement may well make a hero of a coward. Gandhi avoided sensationalism. He himself banned public meetings. Bravery generated under the heat of oration may lead to bravado. Stress on propaganda may produce resentment and counter propaganda. So Gandhi instructed that though informations must be kept ready they should not find their way to the press before the last moment of necessity. And the necessity did not arise. Nor did he like to dissipate money and energy of^ the peasants over litigations. That was the kind of help that the peasants had so far been given by Brajkishore Babu and Rajendra Babu. And now they listened to Gandhi saying : "I have come to the conclusion that we should stop going to law courts....where the peasants are so crushed and fear stricken law courts are useless. The real relief for them is to be free from fear." To be free from fear they naturally required to be free from ignorance to some extent. So Gandhi paid great attention to give them elementary education. As soon as the tension with the Government was over he used the breathing time with endeavours for educating the country folk. As teachers of the Gandhian pattern were not available locally they were indented from Gujrat. Among them came Mahadev Desai with his wife. Still later Gandhi raised money for national college in Bihar. In February 1921 he opened the Bihar Vidya Pith. On April 21 1917 the judgement was delivered, permitting Gandhi to carry on his search for knowledge even offering Governments co-operation in his investigations. On June 4 Sir Edward Gait the Lieutenant Governor invited him to an interview at Ranchi. The Government set up a Committee to redress the wrongs of the ryots and took him in as one of its members. For a time he left on August 14 for Ahmedabad leaving Rajendra Prasad in charge of Champaran.

The Committee eventually published its report on 18th October. The Champaran Agrarian Bill was sponsored by the Home Member in the Bihar Legislative Assembly. And in five years from now the planters were liquidated by the force of changed commercial circumstances. Gandhi won the indigo war. But his strategy was one that was till now unknown and its efficacy unsuspected. His technique was to grow in the oppressed the moral strength to resist the oppression rather than to launch a frontal attack on the oppressors themselves. His thinking to the remedy was a treatment of the constitution rather than utilising only drugs to put down the manifest disease. He moved away to the philosophy behind the political issues. (Rajendra Prasad notes that Gandhi would not yield an inch on principles but would go a long way to meet planters in questions of details. Mahatma Gandhi and Bihar). So in Champaran he concentrated on vitalising the tenants instead of seeking directly to defeat the planters. This was the originality of the Gandhian generalship and Rajendra Prasad in Champaran like the good student he was in college years assiduously learnt the strategy and devotedly imbibed the spirit.

2

Dr. Rajendra Prasad : A Unique Personality

Long before the Gandhian era had set in the country a true Gandhian was born in a small village in North Bihar. Jawaharlal Nehru, life long associate of Rajendra Prasad both in the struggle for independence and later in the Government after attaining independence described him as 'Bharat". Gandhiji, speaking of him said, "There is at least one man who would not hesitate to take the cup of poison from my hands." Such was this man of extraordinary qualities. Despite a peasant background, Rajendra Prasad had a brilliant academic career. He obtained First class First in all the examinations he took. He started his legal career in Calcutta as junior lawyer to Khan Bahadur Shamsul Huda. Impressed by his brilliance, he was offered a teaching assignment in Law College in Calcutta. But he plunged wholeheartedly into freedom struggle and the service of the people. He was earning as much as Rs.4000 every month when he gave up legal practice in 1920 at the call of Mahatma Gandhi. Rajendra Prasad was in jail when on January 15, 1934 a devastating earthquake rocked Bihar. He was released two days later.

Though ailing he immediately undertook the task of raising funds and organizing relief. The fund sponsored by him more contributions than the Viceroy's fund. Never in the history of India had a single individual had organized relief to earthquake victims on such a grand scale in an efficient and effective manner. Rajendra Prasad became the President of the Congress party twice before independence. His stewardship of the Constitution Assembly was exemplary. At its very first meting, he had announced that though the Assembly worked under limitations it would outgrow them and function as a sovereign body that recognized no outside authority. His elevation as the first President of India in 1950 raised doubts in some quarters- could a person who was temperamentally a peasant, who lived and dressed like one, impress as the Head of the state of a big country like India? His performance as President received admiration of one and all. He lived a life of utter simplicity. During his visits to the holy places like Varanasi, he bathed like a common man. Without any hitch, he could sit down on the floor with people and at times share their food. He was common man's President. R. Venkataraman in his "My Presidential Years" said, "Dr. Rajendra Prasad continued the practice of the Viceroys and visited Simla for one month every year. Not only this he started the practice of sojourn in Hyderabad to give an opportunity to the people in the South to meet him. Dr. Rajendra Prasad never mixed religion with public life. He embodied the true Hindu concept of life.

On the wall of his study and his bedroom in Rashtrapati Bhavan had his favourite couplet from Tulsi Ramayan –

'Hariyai na himat visariyai Na Hari Ko Nam. Jahi Vidhee Rakhiyai Rama Vahi Vidhee Rahiyee' (Have courage and do not lose touch with God, whatever role, he allots to you that you must fulfil)". Rajendra Prasad's devotion to duty was unparalleled. Way back in 1947, he could not attend the funeral of his son's wife, because his presence was required at Patna to curb communal riots. He put his grief aside and tried to stop further killing of innocent people. Similarly on January 25, 1960, when his sister who has been both a sister and a mother to him passed away, he sat near her death bed, numb with grief. The following day on January 26 he went to Janpath to take the Republic Day salute. Private grief gave way to public duty. Returning at noon, he took the body of his sister to the banks of the river Yamuna for the last rites. In the evening he was present again for the' At Home' hosted by him at Mughal Gardens. After completing two terms in Rashtrapati Bhavan, Rajendra Prasad moved to Sadaqat Ashram in Patna. His last days were days of agony. The Chinese aggression shattered him completely. 'I have no doubt in my mind that he who is a devotee of God, who is brave and who is a servant of the nation can become the first President of India'-so wrote Mahatma Gandhi, the Father of the Nation, in 1947.The description could not have applied more fittingly and more faithfully to any other person than the man who was elected to that august office in 1950.If it can be said that the life of Dr. Rajendra Prasad, crowded as it is with momentous events, is inextricably interwoven with the history of modern India, it can be even more truly said that the period of his Presidentship has been one of outstanding achievement and progress for the country.

Born on December 3, 1884 at village Zeradai in Bihar, Rajendra Prasad, popularly known as Rajen Babu, was educated in Bihar and Bengal.Throughout his educational career, he showed exceptional brilliance.In 1915, he secured the M.L. degree of the Calcutta University; his professional practice established him as a legal luminary of a high order, first at the Calcutta High Court and later at the Patna High Court.

The Champaran Satyagraha in 1917 was a turning point in his life; it was also the opening chapter of the country's Freedom Struggle.It was during those days that Mahatma Gandhi discovered in Rajen Babu and Brijkishore Babu a matchless pair whose devotion made it impossible for him to take a single step, without their help.Little wonder, therefore, that Gandhiji chose Bihar as the place for launching his first experiment in civil disobedience, named by him as Satyagraha.With the Champaran Satyagraha began for Rajen Babu a period of long and unbroken association with the Father of the Nation, for whom he showed matchless and unsurpassed loyalty.He found in Gandhiji-'the beau-ideal of meekness of spirit and passion for humanitarian service', of which he himself is such an outstanding example. Rajendra Prasad took an active part in the Non-Cooperation Movement through which he saw that the people of India had 'rediscovered their soul'.As a result of the national renaissance which swept the country, a number of educational institutions were established.One of these was the Bihar Vidyapith which was inaugurated by Gandhiji in Patna and Rajen Babu became, first, its Registrar and later, its Vice-Chancellor.About this time was also founded the Sadaquat Ashram which was to become his permanent residence during 1924-46.

Rajen Babu was imprisoned several times during the Freedom Movement.In jail, his health broke down and he was in hospital when Government found it necessary to release him on January 17, 1934, two day after the disastrous Bihar earthquake.This calamity brought to light further the many qualities of the man who had always been associated with Bihar 'as its most devoted public servant'.Rajen Babu as Chairman of the Central Relief Committee worked ceaselessly for the relief of distress and the reconstruction of devastated Bihar.

Rajendra Prasad was elected President of the Indian National Congress in October, 1934.He was subsequently re-elected in 1939 and again in November, 1947.His affability and gentleness won him universal love and esteem.During the troubled days of 1946 and 1947 when there was a great deal of communal unrest, he worked hard in his home province to restore it to the position of grace from which it had fallen.On the 2nd September, 1946, Rajendra Prasad joined the Interim Government as Minister of Food & Agriculture.He was elected President of the Constituent Assembly on the 11th December, 1946 and he discharged that responsibility with great tact and ability.In harmonising conflicting interests and in bringing unanimity of view to bear on discussions, he made a highly fruitful contribution to the labours of that august body.In 1950, when the country became a Republic, the mantle of Presidentship rightly fell on his shoulders.For a decade and more he has held this high office, with dignity and humility, wisdom and humanity which have distinguished him always as a man among men. To his many qualities of head and heart which ensure him a permanent place in the hearts of his people must be added his gift as a writer.Among his books, which make an outstanding contribution to the understanding of Indian History in the first hall of this century, are 'At the Feet of the Mahatma', 'India Divided',

'Mahatma Gandhi and Bihar', 'Satyagraha in Champaran' and 'Atma-katha (an autobiography). There can be no greater tribute to the First President of the Indian Republic than that he has always been the First servant of the Nation.

It seems to have been taken for granted that by acquiring certain material resources we can raise the standard of living of human beings. Following this principle, all the countries of the world are set upon acquiring and multiplying their resources. It is no doubt right that a hungry man cannot think of praying. Mahatma Gandhi himself once said that the hungry man sees God only in the form of bread. But even then we should think how far this kind of material prosperity can lead to real happiness. I have also heard that the countries, which are known to be prosperous and resourceful, are not blessed with mental peace, whereas, on the other hand, we find lots of poor people, who excite our pity, leading a happy and contented existence.

The truth is that the source of real happiness is in one's own inner self and not in the outside world. We equate happiness with the world of external things and that is why there is a scramble for acquisition and accumulation of things. The fact is that these things are, at best, no more than the means to achieve happiness and not happiness itself. One can experience happiness even without them. Apart from this, it is worthwhile considering what is real happiness. I think real happiness or peace of mind means the complete freedom from extraneous pressure or restraint or inhibitions. One basic fact, which must be recognized, is that any kind of inhibition or restraint is irksome. It ceases to be irksome only when it becomes something voluntarily accepted or adopted without restraint or coercion. It is this voluntary adoption of any line of thought or action without restraint or coercion from outside which brings real happiness. Any subtraction from complete freedom is loss of freedom to that extent and implies dependence on something else. Man as a member of society or even as an individual has long ceased to be fully free, if he ever was or can be free. All that can be aimed at or achieved is the reduction or minimization of this restraint or coercion and increasing to the maximum the freedom which man enjoys.

His material requirements can be satisfied, it is obvious, only by subjecting himself to some curtailment of this freedom. His mental satisfaction and possibly his spiritual aspiration becomes reduced in quantum and perhaps also in quality by the amount of material satisfaction which in the very nature of things implies restraint. What is generally termed progress has tended more and more to restrict man's freedom. In every department of life and activity man has to submit more and more to external restraints and inhibitions. It follows that there must be consequential and proportionate diminution in the mental satisfaction and spiritual endeavor even though man may not feel that restraint or realize the ever-growing restraint being put on him from day to day. It is thus clear that real happiness lies in freedom from restraint, which in turn, implies man's capacity to carry on with as little dependence on others as possible. We cannot escape from the conclusion that what is generally called high standard of living has served to increase our dependence on others and to that extent has removed us further from real happiness. We see in the world of today that distance between country and country has almost been eliminated and nations living far apart from one another have come closer so that if something happens at one place it has its repercussion far and wide.

It does not hold good with regard to only dreadful things like war but also of beneficent activities. One of the results of this progress has been that man is now dependent for his daily necessities of life on far off countries. An example will clarify the point. Many of us present here today have known the days when the railway system in India not expanded to the present extent, when there were no automobiles of any kind and when we had not even heard of the aeroplanes. At that time also food was as important as it is today. Then every community depended for its food on itself and on the land, which it cultivated. True, if there was failure of a crop on account of natural calamities like floods or drought, the community suffered. But otherwise it managed to live on what it produced and learnt in course of time the wisdom and the prudence to save food for emergencies. On account of the improvement in the means of transport today food grains can be easily supplied from one part of the country to another. We saw recently that food had to be dropped by aeroplanes on areas, which were rendered inaccessible, by flood. All this sounds so nice, but we have to see whether these developments have enhanced or restricted our freedom. My feeling is that by increasing such needs, as he cannot fulfill himself man has necessarily restricted his freedom. By giving the example of food imports, I have tried to show our dependence on other countries. That is not all. If far off Argentina, Canada or America has a bumper wheat crop, it results in the falling of wheat prices in India. Because of the improved means of transport, the availability or otherwise of things does not depend on local conditions but on the overall world conditions. If food cannot be imported from other countries because of some natural calamity or as a result of the out-break of war, the needy country will have to suffer untold misery. We saw during the last war how even people of neutral countries had to suffer because of the restrictions on export and import of certain articles from overseas. So, there are two aspects of this, progress. One promises plenty during peacetime, the other threatens to release a rich harvest of sufferings and privations in case communications are dislocated on account of hostilities. It is necessary to remember that even if all of our requirements are satisfied, we are bartering our freedom for that satisfaction. For instance, whenever there is disease in an epidemic form in the country, we have to depend on other countries to supply us with medicines. Similarly, whenever there is a famine, others can save us from its dire consequences, but at the same time, if they like, they can also starve us by withholding the supply of food grains. If war breaks out today the belligerents need not resort to deadly weapons in order to kill others. They can do it equally effectively by disrupting the system of transport. Therefore, while on the one hand, we are endeavoring to raise the standard of living; those very efforts might result in the curtailing of our freedom and independence. In spite of this all-round progress we have not yet reached a stage when we could produce an article in sufficient quantity so as to meet the requirements of all the peoples of the world. When we cannot say this about food, which tops the list of man's needs, it is no use talking about other things which are produced in still lesser quantities. That is why the standard of living of all the countries is not uniformly high and presents an unpleasant contrast. Those who possess more are anxious to extort more and more from those who do not possess much. The result is naturally conflict between man and man and country and country. The fear of this conflict has become a nightmare for the modern man.

It is, therefore, necessary to realize that what we have assumed as axiomatic truth, namely, that increase in material prosperity also means the attainment of happiness, is neither quite correct nor so self-evident. This assumption is true only up to a certain limit and the more we transgress this limit the more remote become our chances of being happy. This limit has to be fixed by man himself. This is undoubtedly beset with countless difficulties, but I do think that it is not altogether impossible for man to achieve happiness without the usual paraphernalia, which passes for his everyday necessities. This is exactly what is meant by the adage, 'simple living and high thinking'. It was by practising this truth that Mahatma Gandhi could enjoy that happiness which a humble follower of his is unable to have even in the palatial Rashtrapati Bhavan. I do not suggest that ambition or high aspirations or desire for progress should be discouraged. But let us be sure that our will to progress and rise high will materialize in the true sense only after we have realized that the source of our happiness does not lie outside us but is enshrined within our own hearts. Our happiness will vary directly in proportion to the degree of our faith in the above truth. The more we try to achieve happiness, basing it on the outside world, the more we shall be inviting conflicts and depriving others of their happiness.

•

3

Rajendra Prasad : On the Path of Politics

Rajendra Prasad with patriotic zeal in his views, made himself available for any kind of political or social cause. In spite of his serious occupation in the legal Profession, he found time to do work for the welfare of the common masses. He felt much concerned at the grinding poverty of the millions of people living in the villages of Bihar and elsewhere and very often discussed this social and economic problem with the Congress leaders. At a fairly young age he understood that the panacea for all these ills was the fight for Swaraj and end of the colonial rule from the Indian sub-continent. To achieve this goal, he chose Mahatma Gandhi as his political guru and joined the Satyagraha movement. Suddenly, when Gandhi visited Champaran in Bihar along with Rai Kudiar Shukla, Rajendra Prasad helped him wholeheartedly in seeking the solution of the problems being faced by the Indian labourers in the indigo fields.

The solution signed after some time was satisfactory and this kind of success generated a new spirit in Rajendra Prasad and several other Satyagrahis who from now onward, did not hesitate to take up any problem the solution of which could help them to attain Swaraj for our country. The chance at the national level came before the nation 11 in 1920, after the ghastly tragedy in the Jallianwala Bagh at Amritsar in April 1919. A new spirit of patriotism was generated by the prominent Congress leaders who gathered at Amritsar to participate in the historic Congress session presided over by Pandit Motilal Nehru.

Next year the programme of the Non-cooperation Movement was chalked out at the Calcutta and Nagpur sessions of the Congress. It was decided to launch a boycott movement against councils, courts and educational institutions. Whereas the programme of picketing of foreign cloth shops, wine, opium, ganja and toddy shops was to be carried on by non-violent satyagrahis, they were advised to promote swadeshi and carry on spinning regularly. Besides the cause of the Khilafat was to be supported with all sincerity, Hindu-Muslim solidarity was to be achieved. The Punjab wrongs were to be rectified and the guilty should be punished and above all, the Swaraj was to be achieved in one year. Gandhi was to initiate and organise the movement and the satyagrahis participating in the movement were to function in a non-violent way. They were to behave in a perfect disciplined way. More details of the Satyagraha movement were as follows.

It was at the historic annual session of the Congress at Nagpur in December 1920 that the exact details of the non-cooperation programme were finally drawn up. I was unable to attend it owing to reasons of health. Believing that there would be a battle royal between the opposing sections there was a record attendance at the session, but such expectations were belied and the session reached a compromise, with minor changes to the original programme. The final plan was as follows :

Four boycotts constituted the main Programme : (1) surrendering of titles and distinctions conferred by the Government (2) severance of connections with Government and Government-aided schools and colleges, (3) boycott of Legislative Councils, and (4) boycott of courts, that is, avoiding litigation and giving up legal practice.

To this programme, giving up of Government service was later added. On ad hoc instructions being received people were asked to start no-tax campaign. Establishment of national schools, setting up of panchayats to settle disputes, propagation of the use of the spinning sheel, boycott of foreign cloth and propaganda for prohibition also formed part of the movement. The session laid great emphasis on Hindu-Muslim unity and non-violence. After the Nagpur session, even waverers became staunch supporters of non-cooperation. Mahatma Gandhi told the people that if they carried out the programme faithfully Swaraj would be theirs within a year. People then set out assiduously to implement the programme. The movement was catching the popular imagination in Bihar as elsewhere when Maurice Hallett, Secretary of the Bihar and Orissa Government (who later retired as the Governor of U.P. during the Second World War), sent out a circular directing the members and employees of the Municipalities and District Boards not to participate in the non-cooperation movement.

The people resented this order. The title of Rai Saheb had been conferred on my brother for his work in the cooperative movement and he was Vice-Chairman of the Chapra Municipality as also an honorary magistrate. He renounced his title and resigned his magistrateship. But he said he would continue to work in the municipality as before as he had been elected by the people. His action was voluntary and I had not made any request to him to join the movement. His son Janardan, had just then joined the Engineering College of Banaras Hindu University. My elder son, Mrityunjaya, was studying in the Matriculation class but was not allowed to sit for the University examination on account of being under-age. My younger son, Dhananjaya, was studying in a lower class. We withdrew all the boys from the institution. They never entered any Government institution. Janardan worked as an apprentice in the Kirtyanand Iron and Steel Works and after a year got a scholarship for training in metallurgy in London where he was able to carry on his own. Mrityunjaya joined the Bihar Vidyapith from where he graduated. Dhananjaya studied in the national school at Chapra as long as it existed and then continued studies at home. Our family was thus able to implement the non-cooperation programme to the full. The Congress was not well-organised at that time in Bihar.

There was a Provincial Congress Committee whose secretary was Sarfraz Hussain Khan to whom I gave all possible help. There were district congress committees also but there was no regular membership and there were no proper elections. One had only to pay Rs. 10 as fee and get a certificate from the secretary of the district or provincial committee to become a delegate to a Congress session. These delegates elected the members of the A.I.I.C. But it was almost taken for granted that those who paid Rs. 100 as membership fee would be elected members of the A.I.I.C. The Bihar Provincial Congress Committee had to pay Rs. 1,500 as subscription every year to the Central Committee. But we were not generally able to fulfil our quota and in 1920 Bihar was in arrears of several thousands of rupees.

The Nagpur session of the Congress changed all this. New rules and regulations were framed making enrolment of members compulsory. Each province was authorised to send to the Congress sessions one delegate for every 100,000 of its population. Delegates had to be now elected at regular meetings of the congress committees, A list of the elected delegates had to be sent to the office of the A.I.I.C. some days prior to the Congress session. Without sufficient reasons a change in the list was not to be accepted. The Provincial Congress Committees were directed to change their rules in accordance with the Nagpur Constitution. Fresh elections under the new rules were also to be held. Many old Congressmen had left us because some of them were unable to accept the new creed and programme of the Congress and others, while accepting the creed, were unable to support the programme. In order to re-organise the whole structure, the Bihar Provincial Congress Committee set up a Reorganisation Committee, with Mazharul Haq as president and me as secretary, to report before the next provincial Congress elections. The committee had also to enrol members as well as carry on propaganda for the non-cooperation programme. Public meetings were the order of the day in Bihar. There was not one little corner of the province where the Congress message did not penetrate. Congress workers were active every day explaining the Congress programme.

The whole province was agog. I toured the entire length and breadth of Bihar in 1920 and for the first time I saw the whole province and made innumerable contacts. I became an adept at public speaking. Hitherto I had not had much opportunity to address public meetings though my practice at the Bar had given me considerable experience in the art of speaking. Now I had to address meetings every day and I got over my natural shyness and began to speak with the utmost confidence. I spoke in Bhojpuri in the Bhojpuri areas; in other places in Hindi. I even remember to have addressed meetings in Bengali in Purulia but that was probably much later. Meetings of 5,000 to 10,001 were quite common and I was able to make myself quite audible to such audiences. But at meetings of 20,000 people or over, I had to make special efforts to be heard, loudspeakers not being in then in vogue, with rather unhappy results for my stomach.

Once in Hathua, in Chapra district, where I was to address a meeting, somehow word had gone round that Mahatma Gandhi would address it and people gathered in their thousands. There were over 50,000 people present and, try as I might, my words could not reach them all. The duration of my speeches depended on the strength of the audience. Where the Crowd was large I had necessarily to limit my speech to half an hour at the most. At smaller meetings I spoke for even 90 minutes At such times, my speeches were comprehensive, covering the history of the Congress, the Khilafat agitation, the Punjab atrocities, the non-cooperation programme and the demand for Swaraj. I could sense the mood and the reaction of my audience and was quite effective in my presentation of the nationalist case. In March 1921, the A.I.C.C. met at Vijayawada. It decided to collect a crore of rupees before June 30 as a memorial to the late Lokamanya Tilak the Tilak Swaraj Fund to be spent on Swaraj work. It was also decided to enrol one crore primary members and put into use 20 lakh spinning wheels. Gandhiji has been touring the country before leaving for Vijayawada. I joined him in Orissa which was in the grip of a famine. He had known about it earlier and had rendered instant help. New when he saw the ravages of the famine personally, his heart bled for the sufferers, who hearing of his arrival, flocked to Cuttack from far and near. He had been put up in a biggish house and elaborate preparations had been made to welcome him.

The contrasting pictures of the grand temple of Jagannath, with its pandas and pomp and splendour, and the rich people of Orissa leading a life of case and plenty as also the preparations for giving Gandhiji a grand welcome on the one hand; and the utter misery and the enunciated appearance of the poor people who came in their thousands to see him on the other, affected him so deeply that he was moved to tears. He described graphically the sufferings of the people in an article in the newspapers and appealed for food and clothing for the victims of the famine. At one of the meetings in Orissa, Gandhiji was asked why he was so much against English education when men like Raja Ram Mohan Roy, Lokamanya Tilak and he himself, who were the products of that very education, had risen to great heights. Gandhiji, in his characteristic manner, replied : "I am a mere nonentity. But as for Lokamanya, he would have been a much greater man had he riot been forced to study through the medium of English, a foreign tongue. Where do Raja Ram Mohan Roy and Lokamanya stand in comparison with Shankaracharya, Guru Nanak, Guru Gobind Singh and Kabir ? They had in their days none of the communication facilities that we enjoy today. Even they were able to revolutionise the world of thought." He said that it was our ill-advised attachment to English education that led us to give it credit for the country's progress. To learn English was not bad but it could not obviously be the medium of instruction in the schools. Then we left for Vijayawada The scenes of enthusiasm. We witnessed in Andhra are indescribable. We saw mammoth meetings where full-throated patriotic slogans rent the air. At every railway station there were crowds of people. They even lined the track though the train passed through at full speed without stopping. At Vijayanagaram, where we detrained at three in the morning, we saw the town illuminated, which reminded us of a Diwali night. While returning from Vijayawada, the Bihar representations to the A.I.C.C. conferred among themselves in the train and decided on the exact programme to be followed in their province.

On our return we set about collecting money for the Swaraj Fund. To obviate the need of writing a receipt every time a subscription was paid, we got receipts printed for various amounts, the smallest amount accepted being four annas. Moving about was quite a strain and there were many interesting incidents. I was to cover Bundu, Khunti and Lohardaga. We left Ranchi early in the morning after breakfast, seven of us including the driver and the cleaner, in a ramshackle car. After covering some distance the car developed some defect and we were stranded for hours on end in the midst of a jungle, reaching Bundu only at 6 p.m. after the big gathering had dispersed. The village meting was, however, very encouraging and we collected eight hundred rupees. As we had only tamarind fruits for our lunch the villages persuaded us to stay on dinner. We again left at 11 p.m. and after honour found that the car which it had taken hours to repair had again suffered a break-down.

For some time we sat quietly in the car listening to the roar of a tiger and expecting it to appear any moment.

When the roar was heard no more, we took shelter in a Dak Bungalow which happened to be near by. We could reach Ranchi just in time for our Patna train and had to skip both Khunti and Lohardaga. Congressmen worked so enthusiastically and the response of the middle class was so generous that by June 30 we were able to collect seven to eight lakhs of rupees. It took us several months to complete the work of reorganisation of the provincial Congress. By the end of June 1921, the district Congress committees had elected members of the Provincial Congress Committee and shortly afterwards the provincial committee was able to hold the election for membership of the A.I.C.C. The leaders who left the Congress founded a new party called the Bihar Provincial League. The moderate press of the country welcomed it but the party made no headway and after a short period nothing more was heard of it. In spite of differences in viewpoints, however, the old and the new leaders maintained their social contacts and no serious conflict ever arose in Bihar. The violent posture shown by satyagrahis at Chauri Chaura, near Gorakhpur made Gandhi to announce the suspension of the movement. About twenty policemen were burnt alive by a mob.

Gandhi condemned this kind of goondaism and hooliganism as he felt much injured. He found his creed of non-violence being violated and discipline of the party being tarnished. Several prominent leaders of the party like Motilal Nehru, C.R. Das, Jawaharlal Nehru, Lajpat Rai and others did not approve of Gandhi's action. Rather they were much critical of his decision at a time when they were still in jail. When these leaders came out of jails, they decided to form a new party, later on known as the Swaraj Party. Their main programme was to enter the councils and oppose the government resolutions and bills presented from time to time. Indeed the Swaraj Party did well in the Bengal Council under the leadership of C.R. Das and in the Legislative Assembly of India under the leadership of Motilal Nehru. With this kind of their performance the British bureaucracy had the realization that their was such force in the arguments of the prominent leaders of India. At this juncture that the A.I.C.C. met at Patna on the 21st September, 1925. When we remember that it was at Patna in 1934 (May) that Civil Disobedience was withdrawn, this meeting of 1925 does not fall to strike us as particularly interesting, because at this meeting three outstanding changes were effected in position of the Congress. Khaddar was divested of all political significance.

Yarn franchise only became an alternative to four-anna membership of the Congress which was once again restored, and finally, political work was made over to the Swaraj Party. The Party was no longer a wing of the Congress, a protestant wing,-a minority receiving concessions a bare majority anxious to take the rest with it. It was the Congress itself. Thereafter elections would be run not by the Swaraj Party but by the Congress. The members of the Assembly of this persuasion would be not the 'Swarajists', any longer, bet the Congress members in the Councils. The Yarn franchise was to be no longer the sole franchise not because the response was inadequate-for there were 10 :000 members on the rolls,-but because the Swaraj Party did not like it. Gandhi made up his mind to meet the Swarajists more than half way, as a reply to Lords Birkenbead and Reading. When the Swaraj resolution on Gopinath Saha in 1924 jeopardised the position of Das and his liberty, and was followed up by the Bengal

Ordinance Act, Gandhi decided to stand by Das. This year Das passed away and Birkenhead's bluster was in the air Gandhi made up his mind' to wind up the remnants of N.C.O. and render all assistance to the Council front. He had no answer to give to the Secretary of State and, therefore clothed the Council Party with the full authority of the Congress to deal with the political situation.

Thus, was the country taken through a series of sudden and startling changes; the latter half (clause B) of the Patna resolution, making over the political work to the Swaraj Party, was not before the informal sitting of the A.I.C.C. on the 21st September, but was sprung upon the Working Committee itself on the morning of the 22nd September, and considered by it for a bare five minutes. Here is clause B of the resolution passed at Patna :

"Whereas the Congress in the 39th session held at Belgaum, endorsed an agreement entered into between Mahatma Gandhi on the one hand and Deshbandhu C.R. Das and Pandit Motilal Nehru acting on behalf of the Swaraj Party on the other, whereby the Congress activity was restricted to the constructive programme mentioned therein and it was provided inter alia that the work in connection with the Central and Provincial Legislatures should be carried on by the Swaraj Party on behalf of the Congress organisation, and that for such work the Swaraj Party should make its own rules and administer its own fund; and whereas subsequent events have shown that this restriction should not continue under the altered circumstances that face the country and that the Congress should henceforth be a predominantly political body; "It is resolved that the Congress do now take up and carry on all such political work as may be necessary in the interests of the country, and for this purpose do employ the whole of the machinery and funds of the Congress, save and except such funds and assets as are specially earmarked and belong to the All-India Spinners' Association started by Mahatma Gandhi as an integral part of the Congress organisation, but with independent existence and full powers to administer these and other funds for the fulfillment of its object. "Provided that the work in connection with the Indian and Provincial Legislatures shall be carried on in accordance with the Policy and Programme laid down by the Swaraj Party under the constitution framed by the Party and the rules made thereunder, subject to such modifications made by the Congress as may be found necessary from time to time for the purpose of carrying cut the said Policy." When an amendment was tabled to the main resolution handing over the Congress to the Council Party, to the effect that clause B be replaced by a clause saying "Provided that the work in the Indian and Provincial Legislatures shall be carried on in accordance with such policy and programme laid down by the Congress as may be found necessary from time to time for the purpose," instead of allowing the Council work to be done with the Swaraj Party as an intermediary, the very thought of an amendment to a resolution agreed upon, and a remark made in moving it that the Swaraj Party had "betrayed its trust", set Panditji ablaze and there was a general conflagration in the House.

Gandhi assuaged the feelings by asking the mover of the amendment not to proved with his diatribe against the Swaraj Party at such a juncture. In the mood in which we found Gandhi at the time, all that Pandit Motilal had to do was to ask and it was given forthwith, and given wholesale. Gandhi as President of the A.I.C.C. would not allow the House even to examine the record of the Swaraj Party in the Assembly-that would disturb the harmony of the situation and deprive the gift of its grace as well as its value. When Rajendra Babu asked Gandhi whether there was a pact between him, and Nehru and Das, Gandhi replied in the negative and added that with him, personally; it was a point of honour to concede what the other side demanded. It was a point of honour too with his following to concede to Gandhi what he demanded of them, for they trusted his judgment as the instinctive judgment of a pure-hearted person in all times of doubt or difficulty. The question at and after Patna was whether it was a partition or partnership that the Patna decisions had brought about. The. Congress changes had been kaleidoscopic in character. Each shift of the panes and pieces in the tube had brought about during the previous two years new disposition. A new play of colours, new scenes and sights.

At Juhu, affairs were amorphous. When we met it Ahmedabad in June, 1924 Gandhi was still trying to bold on to the fundamentals of his position. He was in a mood to assert himself. He had tightened the rigour of khaddar and compelled the Executive to spin everywhere. The threats of the bureaucracy against Das, following the Serajganj resolutions, impelled him to close up the ranks of the Congress. When an inch was given, usually an all would be taken. So it was here. The equities of Belgaum were set at naught at Patna, for at Patna, the Council wing took the whole prestige of the Congress and took away the spinning franchise as well. It was, therefore, a partition of the Congress between the apostles of the Councils and those of khaddar. Whatever show of unity there was externally, people could not fail to perceive the discontent of the latter wing. For one thing, The demand of the Swaraj Party "for a Round Table Conference or other suitable agency" was considered inadequate. People began to feel that the

Attorney went beyond or below the instructions of the Principal, but Gandhi would not countenance such arithmetical calculation. When he gives, he gives unreservedly, wholly, and without regret in himself, or generating regret in his recipient. This is what Bhishma of old prescribed in respect of all gifts. Accordingly, at Kanpur, we had only to register what at Patna be held decreed. The Congress Committee (1925) was ahead. We are in the month of October. Shrimati Sarojini Devi was elected President according to the Constitution. Gandhi had said at Belgaum that he was stepping in where really Shrimati Sarojini should have been. Early in October the President-elect published her message for the new year : "Mine, as becomes a woman, is a most modest, domestic programme merely to restore to India her true position as the supreme mistress in her own home, the sole guardian of her own vast resources, and the sole dispenser of her own hospitality.

As a loyal daughter of Bharata Mata, therefore, it will be my lovely though difficult task, through the coming year, to set my mother's house in order, to reconcile the tragic quarrels that threaten the integrity of her old joint-family life of diverse communities and creeds, and to find an adequate place and purpose and recognition alike for the lowest and the mightiest of her children, and foster-children, the guests and the strangers within her gates." That was a fine ideal, especially for a lady to lay down. What should the no-changers do to bring about such a harmony ? Gandhi exhorted them to fall in with the Patna resolution or to resign from the Congress. They had to hibernate or extinguish themselves. Gandhi's position was that he recanted his programme for the time being, while reiterating his principles. The people are there, the mass that may develop momentum at any time as they once did, but they can develop that momentum only on the impact of a dynamic force, a living idea, convulsing programme which must be carried to them by a body of 'educated' people. But these have failed. While, therefore, the material remained, the momentum has disappeared. The sparks from the centre would not explode the air in the chamber. The passage for the jet of petrol is occluded somewhere, and in the absence of petrol, more air and electricity cannot cause the first explosion that starts the motor.

When a motor does not start by the ordinary process, an ingenious method resorted to is to push it from behind. Within a few yards, the engine begins to work until the next halt necessitates a repetition of the process. Even so, when the dynamic force of Civil Disobedience was for the time being held in suspense, all sorts of devices began to push themselves to the fore. The capture of Local Bodies became more and more attractive. Though the elders of the Congress might have enough legitimate preoccupations and public activities, it was a problem how to divert the energies and the enthusiasm of the younger folks. With the wine of elections before them, with the consciousness and confidence of success in their own minds and hearts, they could not be easily restrained. And too, the Mayoralty of Calcutta held with such lustre by Das and later by Sen Gupta was captivating to a degree. Already four big corporations were captured by Congressmen. Vallabhbhai J. Patel had for sometime been President of the Ahmedabad Municipality and was the only person who would occupy that position till 1928. Vithalbhai was adorning the Mayoralty of Bombay, and when interviewed on the subject as to how he would discharge his duties if he became the President of the Assembly', said in reply, with his wonted wink in the eye and mischievous smile on the lips, "Just as

I have done the duties of the President of the Bombay Corporation." Jawaharlal had become the President of the Allahabad Municipality, but did not take long to discover that he was a round man in a square hole, and that Local Bodies were not for Congressmen. Babu Rajendra Prasad become President of the Patna Municipality and was not only pleased with his experiences and cleared out after about 15 months. But the alphabet of life, like that of letters, should be learnt by every one and will not be taken on trust.

Most people would learn by their own experience, not by others. And the lessons of Local Bodies must be learnt by Madras toe. It was at this time, i.e., about May, 1925, that the Madras Congress Committee began to take interest in the capture of seats in the Madras Corporation, and after an arduous campaign in which neither energy nor expense was spared, it succeeded in capturing 7 seats out of 10. The object of one and all in thus capturing Local Bodies, was to get power with which to push the constructive programme through those bodies. It was a laudable idea and, throughout the campaign, we had the advantage of conceiving our ideas and planning their execution much in advance of Governmental preparations to resist our plans or rebut our ideas, The wheels of Government grind slow, but grind steady. Within a short time Government made it impossible for the Local Bodies to engage the services, as teachers or otherwise, of those who had gone to jail, to buy khaddar, to teach Hindi, to introduce the charkha into schools, to give addresses of welcome to national leaders or to raise the national flag over the corporation schools or offices. Anyway, there were reasons for interest in Local Bodies, and the same reason brought out Mr. Srinivasa Iyengar in Madras from his comparative quiet into the maelstrom of politics. He assumed command in the city, spent lavishly out of his purse, being never a niggard in public or private life, and in a moment installed himself as the head of the Congress Party.

New programmes bring new leaders, and must bring them. When old leaders cannot trim their sails to the new winds or disappear altogether from the winds and the boat alike. Under the influence of Gandhiji, who had re-entered the field of politics, the Congress at its Calcutta session, held on December 29, 1928, passed a compromise resolution, which, while "adhering to the resolution relating to complete independence passed at the Madras Congress (1927)", was ready to adopt the constitution recommended by the Nehru Committee if it was accepted "non-acceptance by that date or its earlier rejection" the Congress was to "organise a campaign of non-cooperation by advising the country to refuse taxation and in such other manner as may be decided upon".

Rajendra Prasad had opposed the resolution about independence at the Madras session of the Congress. Influenced by the views of Gokhale during his contact with him in Calcutta in 1910 about the equal status of all the members of the British Commonwealth and then "equal share I in shaping its policy" and as "an admirer of the British Constitution", Rajendra Prasad then felt that Dominion Status could be the "right goal" and that "complete independence would only add to our difficulties." The Congress at its Calcutta session also emphasised the furtherance of the constructive programme.

A foreign Cloth Boycott Committee was formed in 1929 and the Congress Working Committee resolved that "on Sunday, March 17, and thereafter on the first Sunday of every month special attention should be paid to the propaganda for the boycott of foreign cloth and Khadi should be hawked." Rajendra Prasad was then one of the Secretaries of the Bihar Provincial Congress Committee, and he sought to facilitate the work regarding boycott of foreign cloth in various ways. He prepared a scheme according to which the workers in each district were to select respective areas and to visit every home. He himself explained the scheme to the workers of the four districts, Saran, Champaran, Darbhanga and Bhagalpur. There were two exciting events in Bihar at that time-one was a strike in the Tata Iron and Steel Works at Jamshedpur from June I to September 12, 1928, which ended in a compromise with the intervention of Subhas Chandra Bose, President of the Mazdoor Sangh, and the other was a strike in 1929 among the workers of the Tinplate Company at Golmuri, a suburb of Jamshedpur. Subhas Chandra Bose came here also and at his request Rajendra Prasad visited the area several times to study this matter. Prof. Bari took a leading part in conducting the strike which continued for ten months. Rajendra Prasad pleaded to the Government that, under the Trade Disputes Act, the matter should be placed for adjudication. In this connection, he met the Chief Secretary and a member of the Governor's Executive Council. But despite all his efforts, the Government did not agree to any such settlement. In pursuance of the programme of constructive activities Rajendra Prasad addressed a meeting at Barhi in the Monghyr district on April 12, 1929, with an appeal for enlistment of volunteers to be employed in propaganda for boycott of liquor and foreign cloth. The same day Rajendra Prasad presided at a meeting organised at Jagdamba Pustakalaya at Barhya, also in the Monghyr district. On May 13, 1929, he addressed a meeting at Gopalganj in the Saran district where he advised the people "to take lesson from Bardoli", that is, from the successful peasant Satyagraha at Bardoli. On the release of Jagat Narayan Lal from the Hazaribagh Jail on July 13, 1929, Rajendra Prasad addressed a meeting of the citizens of Patna at Gulabbagh on July 14. He boldly criticised what was then known as the law of sedition.

The police advised Government to prosecute him for this. But the Government thought that as it was, "the prosecution now of a man who has won the respect of the Moderate Party and is reputed to be one of the honest men of his own party, it would cause a great deal of unnecessary bitterness." Rajendra Prasad toured the district of Chapra from September 16 to 18. He addressed meeting at different places and urged people to use Khaddar and to work for Swaraj. In November 1929, Rajendra Prasad visited Burma accompanied by his Secretary, Mathura Prasad, at the invitation of Hariji and also in response to a request from the tenants of Kyantaga to settle their dispute with their zamindar, Mylne, who was originally an indigo planter in Shahabad, Bihar. Hariji's zamindari in Burma was called Ziyawadi. Rajendra Prasad was pleased to see many Biharis in Rangoon and one of his old servants met him there. Nageswararao Pantulu of Andhra Pradesh had also come to Burma at that time. Both he and Rajendra Prasad were given a reception by leading Burmans and Indians. While returning from, Burma, Rajendra Prasad had a bad attack of asthma on board the ship. Reaching Calcutta he went to the house of his friend Jogendra Narayan Majumdar, a barrister. He thought of leaving Calcutta for Monghyr where he was to preside over the 28th session of the Bihar Provincial Conference.

At the request of his friend, he placed himself under the treatment of a homeopath, which ultimately did him good. The Conference was held on December 9, 1929. On reaching Monghyr, Rajendra Prasad again fell ill and the Hindi translation of his Presidential speech was read out. In his speech he advocated Dominion Status. "My conception of Dominion Status", he said, was one of partnership on equal terms dissolvable at the will of any of the partners". But the Conference passed a resolution for independence.

Rajendra Prasad was then elected President of the Bihar Provincial Congress Committee. Sardar Vallabhbhai Patel attended the Conference at Monghyr and toured the Province of Bihar which added to the enthusiasm of the people for constructive work and for the impending national struggle? Events were moving fast in all parts of India, adding momentum to the national movement. Besides the factors mentioned above, the post-1924 period was marked by recrudescence of revolutionary activities, and those who had organised a new revolutionary party, called the Hindustan Socialist Army, were active at various places. On April 8, 1929 two of its leaders, Bhagat Singh and Batukeshwar Dutta, threw bombs from the visitors' gallery on the floor of the House of the Assembly "to make a noise and create a stir, and not to injure", as they stated later. A large number of other persons were also arrested in connection with what came to be known as the Lahore Conspiracy Case. Along with Bhagat Singh and Batukeshwar Dutta, many other accused persons went on hunger strike as a protest against the treatment meted out to the undertrial prisoners.

All the strikers except Jatindra Nath Das, took food after a prolonged hunger strike. Jatindra Nath Das ultimately died on September 13 which was the 64th day of his hunger strike. This caused intense grief and excitement among the people all over the country. While celebrating the Political Sufferers' Day on August 10, 1929, Rajendra Prasad led a procession at Patna, presided over a meeting held at Gulzarbagh and addressed another meeting in Patna. The British Government realised the gravity of the situation These were "critical days", observed the Viceroy, Lord Irwin, when "matters by which men are duly touched" were "at issue". So, after consulting the Labour Cabinet in England of which Ramsay Macdonald was the Prime Minister, and Wedgewood Benn, Secretary of State for India, be made an announcement on October 31, 1929, the effect that "the natural issue of India's constitutional progress", implicit in the declaration of August 1927, was "the attainment of Dominion Status". He also made a mention of the meeting of a Round Table Conference in England to consider the future constitution of India. But the Viceroy's statement was criticised by a section of the Press and many statesmen in England, and after an interview with Gandhiji and Motilal Nehru had with the Viceroy on December 23, it became clear that Dominion Status was far away. "For us", writes Rajendra Prasad in his autobiography, "it served as a warning that all pronouncements of the British Government should be read and re-read, scanned and analysed in a dispassionate and realistic manner." The country was forging ahead and there was an intense fervour all around when the Congress met at Lahore on December 29 to 31, 1929, with Jawaharlal Nehru as President. It passed a momentous resolution for complete independence as the goal of India. Besides appealing to the "nation zealously to prosecute the constructive programme", this Congress authorised the All India Congress Committee, whenever it deems fit, to launch upon a programme of Civil disobedience including non-payment of taxes, whether in selected areas or otherwise, and under such safeguards as it may consider necessary. At midnight of December 31, Jawaharlal Nehru unfurled the Tricolour, the flag of Indian Independence, amidst of 'Inqilab Zindabad'. "Long Live Revolution". Rajendra Prasad could not attend the Lahore session of the Congress due to his illness. He spent about two months in his village home, Zeradel, with his friend Satish Chandra Mukherjee.

When the Congress was in session at Lahore Bihar lost one of its noblest patriots, Mazharul Haque, who passed away in his village of Faridpur in Chapra district. Very much pained on hearing this, Rajendra Prasad went to Faridpur and offered his condolence to the Begam Saheba and other members of the bereaved family. In its meeting held on January, 2, 1930, the Congress Working Committee fixed January 26 to be celebrated as Independence Day when the country was to take the pledge of independence. In Bihar the Provincial Congress Committee issued on January 20, 1930, a definite programme for celebration of the Independence Day and it was followed with due colemnity on January 26. Rajendra Prasad got several calls to address meetings on that day. But he could not respond to any of these as he was then convalescing in his village home following his illness. He addressed only two meetings in his village and another at Siwan. The Congress Working Committee passed a resolution at Ahmedabad on February 15, 1930, to launch Civil Disobedience. Meeting at Ahmedabad on March 21, 1930, the All India Congress Committee authorised Gandhiji and others, who believed in non-violence as an article of faith, to start it as and when they decided to do so.

Gandhiji thought of launching Civil Disobedience by breaking salt laws. Salt was an article of prime necessity for all and the salt monopoly affected all. Gandhiji argued : "There is no article like salt, outside water by taxing which the State can reach the starving millions, the sick, the maimed and the utterly helpless. The tax constitutes, therefore, the most inhuman poll tax the ingenuity of man can devise." Rajendra Prasad was not hopeful about the success of this plan in Bihar, an inland area where people manufactured salt only at some places as a by product while preparing saltpetre out of earth. So he sought Gandhiji's permission to start Satyagraha in Bihar by non-payment of the chaukidari tax, which everyone had to pay and against which there was much discontent among the people. But Gandhiji did not agree to this. "Let us first break the salt laws", he observed, "and then we shall be able to launch other no-tax campaigns if popular enthusiasm is aroused." Rajendra Prasad then decided to abide by Gandhiji's directive. Gandhiji's plan was to start Satyagraha on April 6, 1930, by breaking the salt laws at Dandi, a village on the sea-coast, about 322 kilometres from the Sabarmati Ashram. He left his Ashram for Dandi on March 12 with seventy-eight volunteers. Many delegates including Rajendra Prasad, who had gone to attend the Congress meeting at Ahmedabad, proceeded to Jambusar and met Gandhiji. They accompanied him for some distance and then came back. There was a wave of enthusiasm and preparation for Satyagraha in Bihar as in other parts of the country. At the request of Rajendra Prasad, Jawaharlal Nehru toured the Saran, Champaran and Muzaffarpur districts and his speeches greatly inspired the people there.

The Searchlight of April 9, 1930 observed : "The thrill of a new hope, the surge of a new inspiration, the pursuit of a noble ideal and romance of a new sacrifice surcharge the atmosphere." 'Salt Satyagraha' was soon launched in different parts of Bihar, the districts of Champaran and Saran being the first in the field. Rajendra Prasad moved from place to place propagating the message of Satyagraha, for which he issued suitable instructions as President of the Bihar Provincial Congress Committee." Rajendra Prasad's views as to how the policemen were to be treated is contained in the following extract :

"I hear that in the areas where Satyagraha operations are going on, the members of the police are not getting foodstuffs or quarters for residence. I want to make it known to the public that we have no enmity with the men in the Police Service, although we are making all possible efforts to remove the Government of which they consider themselves the servants. Therefore, if a policeman in uniform demands food or shelter authoritatively as a member of the Government, he should on no account be provided with it. But in case he claims it as a matter of courtesy and obtains permission from the Satyagraha Camp Officer or the local Sardar, he should be supplied with all the necessary articles so that he may not be put to any trouble." From the year 1928 certain factors generated a new impulse throughout the country and there was a tremendous stir in the minds of the people leading to a formidable challenge to alien domination. The Government's policy of manipulating India's currency to suit its own interests, the measure of its Finance Member Sir Basil Blackett, stabilising the rupee, two pence above the traditional exchange ratio, and its decision on the Skeen Committee's Report containing a plan for complete Indianisation of half of the cadre of the Indian Army in twenty-five years were considered by some to be anti-national measures. The publication in England of Miss

Mayo's 'Mother-India' during the summer of 1927 wounded national feelings as it presented an untrue, biased and damaging picture of India's civilisation, calculated to prejudice her case for freedom.

The 'no-revenue' campaign conducted in Bardoli by Sardar Vallabhbhai Patel in 1928 with much tact and courage infused a new spirit of boldness into the minds of the people of Gujarat and presented a stirring example of Satyagraha to the country as a whole. The announcement by the British Government on November 8, 1927, of the appointment of a Statutory Commission on constitutional reform to be presided over by Sir John Simon without any Indian as a member on it greatly shocked Indian national sentiment and evoked' 'universal condemnation" all organisations representing different shades of opinion in India "as a negation of the fundamental right of self-determination which is inherent in every nation." The Indian National Congress in its two annual sessions in Madras and Calcutta in December 1927 and December 1928, respectively, strongly condemned this step on the part of the Government. The Commission was boycotted with the cry of "Go back, Simon" by the Congressmen, the Liberals and important sections of the Muslim Community on its arrival at Bombay on February 3, 1928 and during its visits to other parts of India. Under the guidance of Rajendra Prasad and some other leaders, Bihar too made an enthusiastic response to the determination of the country as a whole to boycott the Simon Commission. In this province there had already been a wide-spread agitation at the time due to an ill-advised step on the part of the Government in superseding the District Board at Gaya and removing Anugraha Narayan Sinha, a prominent national leader, from its chairmanship.

A public meeting was held at Gaya to protest against the high-handedness of the Government and Rajendra Prasad delivered a speech strongly denouncing it. He pointed out that proper enquiries had been made by the Congress into the allegations made against Anugraha Narayan Sinha and these were found to be baseless. Rajendra Prasad and some other Congress leaders addressed meetings at other places in the Gaya district about this matter till January 10, 1929. Rajendra Prasad could not attend the meeting of Nawadah in this district due to an attack of Asthama. A meeting of the Bihar Provincial Political Conference was held at Patna on December 6, 1928, with Anugraha Narayan Sinha as President and Sachchidananda Sinha as Chairman of the Reception Committee. Here also the Government's policy regarding the Gaya District Board was bitterly criticised. Most of those who had come from different districts to attend the Conference joined the demonstration against the Simon Commission when a special train, carrying its members reached the platform opposite the Hardinge Park, near the Patna Junction Railway Station, on December 12, 1928. In this enthusiasm against the unwanted Commission, about 30,000 people reached there on the chilly morning of December and', holding black flags in their hands, shouted "Go back, Simon". Rajendra Prasad advised the students and others "to avoid conflicts and remain quiet even if the opposite party becomes aggressive." The demonstration was peaceful and was not marked by anything like what had happened in the Punjab and the U. P. where the police had treated leaders like Lala Lajpat Rai, Jawaharlal Nehru and Govind Ballabh Pant with wanton cruelty and Lala Lajpat Rai succumbed to the injuries inflicted upon him. Boycott of the Simon Commission was a clear indication of the country's awakening. The people here also proved their constructive statesmanship and formulated a scheme of constitution. A committee for this purpose had been formed with Pandit Motilal Nehru as Chairman at a meeting of the All Parties Conference held at Bombay on May 19, 1928.

In its Report, published in August 1928, the Nehru Committee recommended Dominion Status on the basis of the constitution for India. It was not in favour of separate electorates, the only communal safeguard being reservation of seats for the Muslims where they were in a minority. The recommendations of the Nehru Committee were accepted with certain amendments at a meeting of the All-Parties Conference held at Lucknow on August 28 and 29, 1928. But the Muslim League was opposed to these. In March 1929, M.A. Jinnah formulated his fourteen-point scheme on behalf of the Muslims. The Calcutta Congress presided over by Motilal Nehru in 1928 decided for Dominion Status. But in the next year, the Congress met on the banks of river Ravi at Lahore under the presidentship of young and dynamic leader, Jawaharlal Nehru. Has presidential address was indeed historic in contents. He talked about socialism and gave his verdict against the ruling princes. He declared complete independence for India instead of the creed of Dominion Status decided earlier. It was also decided that twenty-sixth January should be celebrated as the Day of Independence in every nook and comer of the country. The regional leaders were advised to organise a disciplined soldiers of freedom who should take the vow of complete dedication and behave in a non-violent way. Mahatma Gandhi was given sometime to apprise the Viceroy of the main constitutional demands of the Congress party and in case of refusal, Satyagraha at all-India level should be started.

Gandhi indeed tried to negotiate with the Viceroy, Lord Irwin on certain issues. The Viceroy refused and soon after, Dandi March of 78 satyagrahis was commenced from the Sabarmati Ashram. At the end of this march on 6 April 1930, Gandhi gave a call for salt Satyagraha and Civil Disobedience Movement. From April 16 to 21, 1930, many worthy sons of Bihar inspired by the motto of 'do or die' carried on Salt Satyagraha at Patna with heroic determination and courage in the face of ruthless police violence.

Selecting Nakhas Road, situated about three kilometres east of Mangles Tank in Patna City, as the place for violating salt laws, the Satyagrahis marched from the Patna Congress office at 9 a.m. on April 16 under the captainship of Ambika Kant Sinha, Manager of The Searchlight and Secretary of the Town Congress Committee, for their destination. Undeterred in the least by police atrocities, the precisionists squatted on the ground at the junction of the main road leading to the Bihar College of Engineering. Following the arrest of the leaders of this batch, another batch of volunteers wanted to proceed under the leadership of Pandit Ram Briksh Sharma Benipuri, who too was soon arrested. These volunteers were obstructed near the Sultanganj police station. But they did not leave that place and remained there till late in the night.

The people of that area supplied them food and also some mattresses on which they slept. On receiving the news of what had happened at Patna, Rajendra Prasad rushed there from Chapra on April 16 and proceeded to the scene at about 12.30 in the night along with Anugraha Narayan Sinha, Acharya Kripalani and Mathura Prasad. He saw the volunteers sleeping on the street and the police standing at a short distance. Early next morning Rajendra Prasad again visited the site, asked the volunteers to remain where they were before and to be non-violent in the face of assaults. He presided over a meeting held nearby. Acharya Kripalani, Professor Abdul Bari and Mathura Prasad also spoke. After briefly tracing the progress of the Salt Satyagraha Bihar till then, Rajendra Prasad made an appeal for recruitment of a large number of volunteers, exhorted the people to be ready for greater sacrifices and "to be perfectly peaceful and non-violent even when they witnessed scenes of horror and excitement and to regard him as the traitor to the motherland who induced them to throw brickbats and to commit any similar violence." At the request of Cousins, the District Magistrate of Patna, Rajendra Prasad saw him after the meeting. He thus reported the result of this meeting in an interview with The Searchlight : "Mr. Cousins, the District Magistrate, told me that if I withdrew the volunteers he would treat the matter as closed. I told him that volunteers had been assaulted on the previous day without provocation and without justification and it was not possible for me to give any such instruction. He said be agreed there was no counter-attack but they were an unlawful assembly and had to be dispersed by force after they had been warned more than once. He further said that it was not in our present programme to disobey the Police Act and it was not our present intention to precipitate any action against the Police Act but after the previous day's assault I could not withdraw them. He then told me that I was taking a very serious responsibility and that he would take very drastic action and use force to disperse them. I told him I understood that and as then advised I could not withdraw them but before finally deciding I would like to consult other friends. He said that he would wait for an hour and wanted me to regulate my watch according to his. I told him that was not necessary and if no reply came before the end of the hour, he should take it that none was coming.

After consulting friends and before the hour was over, I told him on the phone that as it was not our intention to start Satyagraha against the Police Act, I was prepared to advise the volunteers not to go in a regular formation as a procession but to walk in the streets as others were walking provided he or anybody else responsible for yesterday's assault expressed regret. He suggested at first that they might go one or two together but on my saying that the number would be larger, he suggested that they should not carry emblems. I told him so many people were going with flags in the streets that it could not be said to be a procession unless they went in a regular formation. He said it was a question of fact as to whether the effect produced on the public would be that they were going in a procession. He ultimately expressed his unwillingness to discuss the previous day's happenings for which he was responsible. I told him that on that view, I was afraid, he would have to do what he thought best and I would do what I considered best for me." The policemen engaged against the Satyagrahis were Muslims from Baluchistan under the command of two Englishmen, Churcher, Assistant Commandant, M.M.P., and Walker, Assistant Superintendent of Police.

Considering the Satyagraha to be "a religious war", which "should not stand in the way of others attending to their religious duties", Rajendra Prasad wrote to the District Magistrate of Patna that as Friday next besides being a Good Friday also a day of congregational prayer for the Muslims, volunteers would not be sent out on that day. On receiving this letter in the evening, the District Magistrate felt some doubt if its writer was serious and if what he had suggested was not a face-saving device to extricate himself from a difficult situation. So, he telephoned Rajendra Prasad to see him next morning. Rajendra Prasad met him at the appointed time and convinced him about the seriousness of his proposal. The District Magistrate suggested alternative routes for the volunteers, but Rajendra Prasad did not agree to it. Rajendra Prasad and others of the Satyagraha at Patna planned to send Satyagrahis to Sultanganj in batches, four times in 24 hours, at fixed times, informing the District Magistrate accordingly. In the morning of Saturday, August 19, a batch of five Shahabad volunteers proceeded towards Sultanganj police station to offer Satyagraha. They were arrested, but they prevented one European police officer from snatching away their flags. Some Satyagrahis who came later were ignored; but many were mercilessly assaulted and seriously wounded. A crowd had naturally gathered in a wide area extending from Sultanganj to the front of the Patna College. They were peaceful but the police, led by English Sergeants on horseback, sought to disperse them with terrible atrocities, "belabouring all and sundry, kicking, listing and battening." A Police Officer made a "savage attack" on Prof. Abdul Bari when he was trying to control the crowd in front of the Patna College and dealt three blows with batons upon him which were followed by strokes with a hunter. Acharya Kripalani, while standing near the gate of the T.K. Ghosh's Academy, opposite Patna College, was assaulted by some policemen with lathis. The policemen charged "the crowd with their horses and whipped them right and left." After the police had dispersed the crowd on the road, Rajendra Prasad, Acharya Kripalani, Abdul Bari and Badrinath Varma began to move on the road from cast to west when one of the Police Sergeants pressed Prof. Abdul Bari from the back with his horse. Another Police Officer pressed against Rajendra Prasad and the officers shouted 'get along' by poking them with their batons. Prof. Bari was hurt also the hoofs of the horses. Still both the leaders moved on quietly and pacified the people who "received blows with courage and determination and there was no attempt at retaliation. But the outrages perpetrated by the police shocked the sentiments of all classes of people at Patna, whether they were Congressmen or not. To protest against these, a mammoth meeting of persons of all classes and communities and of all shades of opinion was convened by the eminent citizens of Patna on Tuesday, April 22, at Bhanwarpokhar ground (Patna), under the presidentship of Hasan Imam, who had been very much moved when Mrs. Hasan Imam, an eye-witness on the day of police atrocities, had reported these to him.

While proposing Hasan Imam to the Chair, Sachchidananda Sinha observed that "they were united in their condemnation of those outrages. Such outrages were indefensible and could not be tolerated." Probably this state of public feeling led the Government executive to withdraw the mounted police on April 23 and a batch of volunteers proceeded without obstruction to Nakhas Pond and manufactured salt calmly." This work progressed in other parts of the province due to the enthusiasm and courage of the local leaders and other Satyagrahis, many of whom were subjected to intense Governmental repression.

In Bihar even a patriot like Shrikrishna Sinha, "loved and respected all over the Province, was seen handcuffed with one of his co-workers while they were being removed from one jail to another." Leaders of the movement were arrested at other places, too. Hearths and pots used for salt manufacture were forcibly destroyed by the police at different centres and at some places they assaulted the Satyagrahis, for example, in Dhanha thana of Champaran. But still the number of volunteers increased and they did not slacken their activities. Vithalbhai Patel, who resigned the Presidentship of the Legislative Assembly, significantly wrote to the Viceroy on April 25, 1930 : "Thousands are prepared to lay down their lives and hundreds of thousands are ready to court imprisonment." Rajendra Prasad did not himself manufacture salt but he led the movement in Bihar by touring the districts, supervising the activity, addressing public meetings and giving encouragement to the Satyagrahis. In all areas people vied with one another in manufacturing salt. Rajendra Prasad auctioned the salt manufactured by the Satyagrahis wherever he went and utilised the amount to meet their expenses. After watching events for some time, the Government arrested Gandhiji on May 4, 1930 and took him to Yervada jail. This caused much indignation among the people which found expression in hartals and strikes from one part of the country to another. On the evening of May 6, a large number of people assembled in a meeting at which Rajendra Prasad made a stirring speech. Rajendra Prasad decided in consultation with other leaders of the province to continue the Salt Satyagraha till the month of June, as after the commencement of rains salt manufacture would not be possible. In conformity with a decision at a meeting of the Working Committee of the Congress held at Allahabad from May 12 to 15, 1930, which Rajendra Prasad had attended, he asked the people of Bihar to carry on the programmes for boycott of foreign cloth and prohibition also and to be in readiness for non-payment of the chaukidari tax. A circular was issued by the President of the Bihar Provincial Congress Committee on May 3, 1930, with a direction to the subordinate committees to start picketing of foreign cloth and liquor shops from May 16. Since then propaganda for such work was carried on vigorously and with much success by Rajendra Prasad and other leaders. Thus, he, along with Prof. Abdul Bari, went to Bhabhua and Sasaram towards the end of May to encourage the foreign cloth boycott and prohibition movements. The traders cooperated with them. In Bihar most of the foreign cloth dealers in the district towns or in smaller towns or bazars agreed to place no further orders for foreign cloth, packed their stock and got the same scaled by Congress Committees in their respective areas.

Picketing of shops became necessary only in rare cases. Women also contributed their mite to the success of the movement. While inaugurating the Satyagraha, he had issued an open letter to the women of India asking them to foster the cause of nationalism by participating in the activities for boycott of foreign cloth and prohibition of intoxicants. In Bihar there was a grand response to his call. At Patna particularly many ladies, headed by Mrs. Hasan Imam, involved through the streets requesting people not to purchase foreign cloth. Vindhyavasini Devi organised such activities with much enthusiasm. During this Satyagraha, the situation in Bihpur in the Bhagalpur district had taken a very serious turn with many shocking incidents. Here the Governmental machinery out Heroded Herod and perpetrated cruelties on Satyagrahis with ruthlessness in disregard of human feelings, honour and life, which exceeded in their severity even the Patna outrages of April 1930.

Some of the Congress volunteers, who lived in an Ashram near the Railway Station, had begun picketing liquor and ganja (hemp) shops. At this on May 31, 1930, A.R. Toplis, the District Magistrate of Bhagalpur, went there, accompanied by the Superintendent and the Assistant

Superintendent of Police, and a body of armed and ordinary policemen. The volunteers were severely beaten by the police, who snatched away from them the national flag and burnt it and raided and got possession of the Congress Office, the Khadi depot and the Charkha Sangh by turning-out their inmates.

With a view to recovering the Ashram and other buildings, the volunteers offered peaceful Satyagraha by going there in batches of four or five from June 2 to 6. But the police belaboured them so furiously that some fell unconscious as a result of gruesome injuries. This caused a sensation in and around the locality and many people assembled in a meeting in a mango orchard near the Congress office. Policemen, headed by a European officer, indiscriminately assaulted the crowd both on that day and the day following. On hearing this tale of police terrorism in Bihpur, Rajendra Prasad hurried to that place accompanied from Patna by Baldev Sahay, Abdul Bari, Gyan Saha, Secretary, Bihar Provincial Seva Dal and Murli Manohar Prasad, Editor of The Searchlight and from Bhagalpur by Anant Prasad and Kamaleshwari Sahay, two Bihar M.L.Cs., Upendranath Mukherjee, President of the Bhagalpur District Congress, an ex-Member of the Legislative Assembly. A crowd of about twenty thousand assembled there. Under the advice of Rajendra Prasad, it remained peaceful and non-violent amidst grave provocation. After a meeting addressed by Rajendra Prasad, Abdul Bari and Yakub Arif was over at 5 p.m, a procession of volunteers proceeded towards the Congress office which had been already seized by the police, but they were arrested and kept in custody in a primary school building.

The people, who had been watching the events from a short distance, were furiously and indiscriminately charged by the police with lathis under the orders of the Superintendent of Police. Having thus cleared the road, the Superintendent of Police with his party rushed towards the bazar where Rajendra Prasad and some others were standing, and asked his men to charge them also though they had done nothing and they dealt lathi blows on such respectable persons. Most of them including Rajendra Prasad were injured. Prof. Abdul Bari was hurt seriously and he was bleeding profusely. A local doctor dressed their wounds before they took a train for Bhagalpur where Rajendra Prasad stayed for two days. The police arrested Upendranath Mukherjee, President of the Bhagalpur District Congress Committee, Mewalal Jha, Secretary, Bhagalpur District Congress Committee, and Satyadeva Roy, President of the Bihpur Thana Congress Committee, on the charge of joining unlawful assemblies. Satyagraha was resumed at Bihpur on June 21, 1930, and continued till it was stopped according to the instructions of the Congress as a result of the Gandhi-Irwin Pact in March 193 1. Everyday batches of volunteers went to the Ashram, and were arrested, beaten and tortured in other ways.

Government's policy of ruthless repression, instead of suppressing the Satyagraha, gave additional impetus to it. The report of the Bihar Provincial Congress Committee for the week ending June 13, 1930, noted : "The spirit which was attempted to be crushed has steadily grown with every attempt at suppression, and now there is no more enthusiastic area in the province bubbling with life and energy as the locality round Bhagalpur." The Bihpur Satyagraha "electrified Bhagalpur", wrote Rajendra Prasad. Public sentiment in Bihar was deeply shocked by the police outrages at Bihpur particularly for the attack on Rajendra Prasad and his party.

Anant Prasad and Kamleswari Sahay resigned their seats in the Legislative Council and there were resignations by some other legislators also, chaukidars 22 numbering 216, six sarpanchs and some dafadars" also resigned their posts under protest. Considering the unique position of Rajendra Prasad as the most revered national leader of the province, the Government had proceeded rather cautiously in arresting him, and instructed their officers on April 17, 1930 that "he should not be arrested without reference to Government." By the middle of June the Government's view was that "proceedings may be taken against him and he may be arrested without reference to Government, if there is clear case against him, under the provisions of the Prevention of Intimidation Ordinance or the Unlawful Instigation Ordinance or the Police (Incitement to Disaffection) Act (Act XXII of 1922) or for a substantive offence under the Indian Penal Code.... The arrangements for his arrest and trial will require care, but the District Officers must use their own discretion about them." For sometime when Rajendra Prasad was constantly touring the districts, rumours were afloat about his impending arrest. On June 30, 1930, Vithalbbai Patel visited Patna and in the evening a public meeting was held there in his honour. Hasan Imam attended this meeting for the first time in a Khadi dress. When Rajendra Prasad expressed to him his feeling that he might be arrested soon, he replied that work would not suffer even after his arrest. Rajendra Prasad then went to Chapra district on a three-day tour programme. When he was proceeding to Garkha he was arrested on the way on July 5. After meeting his relatives at his village home, he followed the police to the Chapra jail, where he was offered a "tumultuous welcome" by about 400 Satyagrahi prisoners, and a big crowd outside the Jail gate had to be dispersed by the Warder's firing in the air.

The Magistrate, who was ordered to try Rajendra Prasad's case, was known to him as one of his old clients while he was practising at Patna. As he did not offer anything by way of defence, the Magistrate sentenced him to six months' imprisonment. After a few days, Government arranged to send him the Hazaribagh jail by a round-about journey via Banaras and Moghal Sarai to avoid popular demonstrations. But inspite of this precaution on the part of the Government, the news of Rajendra Prasad's arrest spread like wild fire and produced a tremendous stir throughout the province, adding to the determination and enthusiasm of the people to carry on the movement for boycott of foreign goods and non-payment of the chaukidari tax. At Rajendra Prasad's suggestion made before his arrest, Deep Narayan Singh of Bhagalpur accepted the leadership of the movement. As a matter of fact, national discontent had been mounting high in all parts of India.

The issue of the Indian Statutory Commission's Report in the month of June 1930 did not allay it, as its recommendations were considered to be reactionary and unsatisfactory by Indian leaders of different schools of thought. But in view of the extremely grave situation in the country, the Viceroy mooted on July 9, the idea of convening a Round Table Conference in London in October next and efforts were made by leaders like M.R. Jayakar and Tej Bahadur Sapru to evolve a compromise by a high-level talk with the Congress leaders.

So, Motilal Nehru and Jawaharlal Nehru were transferred from the Naini jail to the Yervada Jail, Poona, for a meeting with Gandhiji. A joint interview of Jayakar and Sapru with the Congress leaders took place oil August 13, 14 and 15, 1930. But the compromise negotiations failed to produce any result. Several other national leaders of Bihar had been kept in the Hazaribagh Jail. The Jailor, Narayan Prasad, knew Rajendra Prasad from his school days as his elder brother was a classmate of Rajendra Prasad and he often went to their house in Chapra. He arranged for Rajendra Prasad's accommodation with his friends, like Ram Dayal Singh, Shrikrishna Sinha and Bepin Behari Varma, Deep Narayan Singh, and Swami Bhawani Dayal of South Africa joined him later. Rajendra Prasad spent his time mostly reading and spinning. After some time, with permission from the Jailor, he learnt weaving by joining the jail workshops. "We suffered no inconvenience at all", writes Rajendra Prasad, "in the jail. Friends in other wards used to meet us often with the permission of the jailor. We had some difficulty in getting books which were not given to us unless they were passed' by the police or a Magistrate" as 'safe'.

A compilation, containing some writings of Gandhiji prepared by Rajendra Prasad with an introduction, had already been published by Natesan & Co. of Madras. He now compiled another volume of Gandhiji's writings under various heads like Nonviolence, Swaraj, Satyagraha, Education, and Khadi with a brief introduction for each. The manuscript of this work was just complete when he was released from jail and Gandhiji himself approved of the idea of publishing it. This idea appealed to one of Rajendra Prasad's intimate friends, Nibaran Chandra Das Gupta of Purulia, also a selfless patriot of high character, who, in the words of Rajendra Prasad, "looked upon Gandhiji's agitation not merely as a political struggle but also as a religious renaissance." He made some suggestions which were accepted by Rajendra Prasad.

But the manuscript could never be printed. It was in the Sadaqat Ashram, Patna, and from there it was lost when the police seized it in 1932. Study of religious literature also kept Rajendra Prasad engaged for some time in the jail. Pandit Bharat Misra of Chapra and Pandit Vishnu Dutt Shukla recited to him and his friends the Ramayana and other scriptures. The principal Upanishads were studied by him for the first time. But he could not attend Swami Sahajananda's discourses on the Gita for a lack of time. Along with Nibaran Chandra Das Gupta, he studied Patanjali's Yoga Sastra. Among the inmates of the jail some produced a monthly magazine in manuscript called Qaidi and some got out another monthly called Karagar. Both contained articles about the national movement. The chief contributors and organisers of these magazines were Swami Bhawani Dayal, Mathura Prasad Sinha, Ram Briksh Benipuri and Mahamaya Prasad. Some issues of these had pictures and cartoons prepared by Kumar Kalika Sinha of Gidhaur in the Monghyr district. Supply of newspapers in the jail was strictly limited to the overseas edition of The Statesman containing matter for which the 'political prisoners' did not have much interest. In this jail Rajendra Prasad developed greater intimacy with persons than what he previous had. "I shall ever cherish", he recorded, "the memory of those contacts I had in the Hazaribagh jail. Swami Bhawani Dayal, Nibaran Chandra Das Gupta and Thakur Nawab Singh (of Sitamarhi sub-division in the Muzaffarpur district who joined the non-cooperation movement with his sons, nephews and grandsons) were some of them." Rajendra Prasad was released on December 14, 1930, and the progress of the Civil Disobedience Movement was accelerated in spite of uninterrupted repression in various ways and counter-propaganda on the part of the Government. Immediately after returning from Hazaribagh, Rajendra Prasad proceeded to Bombay to meet Sardar Vallabhbhai Patel and some other Congress leaders.

From Bombay he went to Allahabad to see Motilal Nehru, who had been released from jail on grounds of illness and just come back from Calcutta after medical treatment. In spite of this bad health, he wanted to guide the movement. Meanwhile, the Round Table Conference had met in London on I November 12, 1930, without any representative of the Indian National Congress attending it, but it was adjourned sine die on January 19, 1931, though its work was not complete. On that day the British Prime Minister, Ramsay Mcdonald, delivered a valedictory address in which he observed : "The view of his Majesty's Government is that responsibility for the Government of India should be placed upon Legislatures, Central and Provincial, with such provisions as may be necessary to guarantee, during a period of transition, the observance of certain obligations and to meet other special circumstances and also with guarantees as are required by minorities to protect their political liberties and rights. In such statutory safeguards as may be made for meeting the needs of the transitional period, it will be a primary concern of His Majesty's Government to see that the reserved powers are so framed and exercised as not to prejudice the advance of India through the new constitution to full responsibility for her own government.... His Majesty's Government, in view of the character of the Conference and of the limited scope of its disposal in London, has deemed it advisable to suspend its work at this point so that Indian opinion may be consulted upon the work done and the expedient considered for overcoming the difficulties which have been raised. His Majesty's Government will consider, without delay, a plan by which our cooperation may be continued so that the results of our contemplated work may be seen in a new Indian constitution. If, in the meantime, there is a response to the Viceroy's appeal to those engaged at present in Civil

Disobedience, and others wish to cooperate on the general lines of this declaration, steps will be taken to enlist their services." The Congress Working Committee met at Allahabad on January 21, 193 1, with Rajendra Prasad in the chair.

With regard to the declaration of the British Prime Minister it expressed the opinion that "it was too vague and general to justify any change in the policy of the Congress." At the suggestion of Rajendra Prasad the publication of this resolution was postponed till the next morning. But the same night Motilal Nehru received a cable from V.S. Srinivasa Sastri, Tej Bahadur Sapru and M.R. Jayakar for withholding the publication of the resolution till their return to India. This was done. As a conciliatory measure for solution of the constitutional problem, the Viceroy, Lord Irwin, released Mahatma Gandhi unconditionally and also the other members of the Congress Working Committee "to give an opportunity for them to consider the Premier's statement at the Round Table Conference." As there was growing deterioration in the health of Motilal Nehru, Jawaharlal Nehru was released on parole.

During Motilal Nehru's last days Rajendra Prasad stayed with him at the Swaraj Bhawan, Allahabad. Motilal Nehru's condition grew serious and he was shifted to Lucknow for treatment but passed away immediately on reaching there on February 6, 1931. On the same day, a group of Indian delegates to the Round Table Conference landed at Bombay and expressed the view that the ','attainment by India of Dominion Status is no longer in dispute." Srinivasan Sastri, Tej Bahadur Sapru and M.R. Jayakar met Gandhiji at Allahabad and persuaded him to negotiate with the Viceroy.

All the members of the Congress Working Committee, including Rajendra Prasad, went to Delhi with Gandhiji and stayed there with Dr. Ansari. Gandhiji had discussions with the Viceroy for several days and as a result of this, the Gandhi-Irwin Pact was signed on March 5, 193 1. Thus, as Gandhiji observed, the Congress "embarked deliberately, though provisionally, on a career of cooperation." The Government lifted the ban on the Congress Committees and the Congress Working Committee immediately issued instructions to stop Satyagraha. Rajendra Prasad, President of the Bihar Provincial Congress Committee, then at Delhi, sent telegraphic instructions to this effect to his friends at Patna. He soon returned to Zeradei for the marriage of his younger son Dhananjay. On April 14, 1931, he toured the districts of Champaran, where he visited places like Bagha, Piparia, Bettiah, Segowli, Dacca and Motihari. At each of these places he addressed public meetings which added to the enthusiasm of the people who had suffered much from unmitigated governmental repression. The next day he visited the villages where indiscriminate and wholesale looting by the police and military had taken place. The broken locks, chests and doors and grounds dug up were still eloquent witnesses of what terrible days the people of Champaran had to pass through. On his way back he addressed a meeting on the Tilak Maidan at Muzaffarpur. At a crowded public meeting of the citizens of Patna held in the Bhanwar Pokkar Park on April 15, 1931, Rajendra Prasad observed : From today the Hindus and Musalmans of Patna must take a vow that they would never quarrel with each other and would never break each other's heads. There were bound to be differences of opinion but that was no justification for breaking each other's heads. Baldwin was the leader of the Conservative Party but he would not think of assaulting his son because he belonged to the Labour

Party. Lord Curzon would not kill his daughter for difference of opinion in matters political, but in India even without any difference of opinion they were massacring each other on account of ignorance and folly." He appealed to the people to control their temper even under the greatest provocation. Rajendra Prasad presided over the fourth session of the Manbhuni District Conference held on April 25 and 26, 1931, at Hutmura, a village near Purulia, and delivered a highly inspiring speech referring to various aspects of the national struggle and for observance of the terms of the truce. After a reception at Adra he visited Raghunathpur, where an address of welcome was presented to him at a highly enthusiastic reception. The next day Rajendra Prasad was taken to Purulia where three addresses were presented to him, the first two by the local Sahitya Sabha and the local Hindi Pustakalaya and the third by the Purulia Municipality on April 29. In his reply to the last, he referred to the historic role and sacrifice of the Purulia in the freedom struggle. He advised them to continue it with unflinching determination and to observe the truce terms. Rajendra Prasad left Patna on May 1, to tour the districts of Darbhanga and Purnea. Accompanied by Abdul Bari, he visited Supaul on May 16, 1931, Bihpur on May 18, addressed meetings at these places and opened a Khadi Depot at Sombarsa.

From May 19 to 22, they went to Bhagalpur, Sabour, Nathnagar, Rajaon, Banka, Sultanganj, Amarpur, Belbar, Panjwara and Colgong and appealed to the people to use Khaddar, boycott foreign cloth and enrol volunteers. In the next month, for six days they toured the district of Santhal Parganas. He was also present at the Political Conference of the Jehanabad sub-division of the Gaya district, where in his speech, he asked the people to observe the terms of the Delhi Pact and to follow the instructions of Gandhiji for attainment of 4 complete Swaraj through their self-governing institutions.

Referring to India's non-violent Satyagraha, he observed that it was an ideal fight for the whole world. The people of other countries were looking towards Indians with surprise that these disarmed people were fighting with such a great power, and in case they were successful, the weapon of Satyagraha would be useful for the whole world. The tours of Rajendra Prasad in the Shahabad district in the months of August and September were followed by "increased activity on the part of the Congress workers in regard to picketing of foreign cloth shops" and formation of panchayat. He opened a Khadi exhibition at Arrah on August 30 and addressed a meeting there next day. He again went to Arrah on September 26, 1931, accompanied by Shri Krishna Sinha and Baldev Sahay, and unfurled the national flag in a meeting there. He went to Bhagalpur district in November. 1931 with Abdul Bari and addressed several meetings there, including one held at Lajpat Park, Bhagalpur, on November, 28. He also spent two weeks with Sardar Vallabhbhai Patel during the enquiry into the affairs regarding confiscation and auction of land in the Gujarat villages during the Satyagraha. While Jawaharlal Nehru was addressing the last meeting of his Bihar tour at Maharajganj, in Chapra district, we received intimation that Gandhiji had given the signal and salt Satyagraha was to be offered everywhere from April 6. This was rather sudden, fer, we had not yet finalised our plans. Jawaharlal left the same day for Allahabad and we sent messengers in the night to all places giving the go-ahead signal. In Champaran, Bipin Bihari Verma had decided to march from Motihari to Jogapatti to offer Satyagraha, there.

Muzaffarpur came next. Then within a few days the movement spread to the whole province. I reached Jogapatti on the day Bipin Bihari Verma manufactured salt but before I could see him I was told that he had been arrested and taken to the improvised court at Jogapatti for a summary trial. I made my way to the court. On the way I found that the entire route of Bipin Bihari's march and the place where the satyagrahis were camping were gaily decorated with buntings, festoons and archies. The whole place went wild with enthusiasm,. At the court I found that the magistrate was an old non-cooperator, who had left the Patna College in 1921 and had joined us in the National Mahavidyalaya but who had, after sometime, pressed by his family, gone back to the Patna College. I noticed that while hearing the case he never once raised his head. With his eyes glued to the papers on the table, he wrote his judgement and read it. Sentenced to a term of imprisonment, Bipin Bihari Verma was taken to Motihari Jail. Meanwhile satyagraha was being offered throughout the country and people were being arrested in thousands. Gandhiji had not been arrested. After a visit to Motihari I left for Patna.

From there I went on a tour of the province to propagate Satyagraha. After a hurried tour of some places I returned to Patna by steamer at midnight. At the jetty I was told that Satyagraha had been started in Patna just that day. People from Bakarganj were moving to the city with flags in their hands with-the intention of manufacturing salt but they were stopped opposite the Sultanganj police station. The police formed a cordon round them, preventing them from proceeding further. I went straight to the place and witnessed a strange sight. With the police round them in a circle, the satyagrahis were sleeping in the middle of the road. The people of the neighbourhood had given them food and bedding. When I arrived, most of them woke up and narrated their story to me. After a while I went to the Sadaqat Ashram to rest for the night. Early next morning I returned to the spot. I found a large police force mustered there. The District Magistrate and the Superintendent of Police were also there. A large crowd of people had gathered to watch developments. I thought that the satyagrahis might arrested or let off after a beating. Suddenly a man approached me and said that the District Magistrate was in the police station and would like to speak to me. I followed him.

The Magistrate told me to ask the satyagrahis to disperse as otherwise he would have to take action against them. I told him that he could arrest them. He said that he wanted the crowd to disperse and that if the place was not cleared quickly the consequences might be serious. When I refused to withdraw the volunteers, he replied that the responsibility for the consequences would be mine. I thought it advisable to consult my colleagues and the District Magistrate gave me half an hour to give him an answer. When I was leaving the police station, he took out his watch and asked me to adjust my time to him. I resented this and refused to do so, saying that he could do what he liked if he did not hear from me in half an hour. I drove to Sadaqat Ashram and consulted my friends. They were all of the view that we should do nothing and let the District Magistrate take any action he thought fit. I conveyed this decision on the telephone to the police station. Then I returned to Sultanganj. On the way my car crossed the District Magistrate's and I saw him smiling. At Sultanganj I was told that on the satyagrahis' refusal to disperse, the District Magistrate had ordered the mounted police to make a charge. The police came riding towards the satyagrahis who had laid themselves prostrate on the ground and stopped short. Then the satyagrahis had been bodily lifted and placed in lorries which left for an unknown destination. Now we decided to send satyagrahis in batches of five to Sultanganj. As soon as a batch was arrested another took its place. This went on day and night. April was coming to an end and it was getting very hot. The satyagrahis had to stand in the sun the whole day waiting to be arrested. So in order to reduce the inconvenience I changed the plan. I sent batches at fixed times, four in 24 hours. On the first day, only the satyagrahis were arrested, but from then on, when the crowd of spectators began to swell, the mounted police was ordered to charge at them too.

The satyagrahis were sometimes arrested, sometimes ignored, but the people were invariably the victims of police violence. The police attacks occurred generally in the mornings and afternoons. I was sometimes in the crowd, a witness to the police atrocities and though I escaped their attention, Abdul Bari was badly injured. The Satyagraha lasted several days and it attracted more and more people and the area covered by the Satyagraha went on expanding till it touched the Patna College premises. The people remained peaceful but the police became more and more aggressive. One day while the police were attacking the spectators, Mrs. Hasan Imam, who happened to be passing that way, witnessed the tragic scene. Many heads were broken. Moved deeply, she rushed back home and told her husband the story, expressing great anxiety about the future. Hasan Imam, of whose interest in our activities I was till then not aware, sent for me.

On my meeting him and giving him an account of the police atrocities, Hasan Imam, impulsive and impetuous by nature, flew into a rage and assured me of all help that he could give. As the days passed, his enthusiasm for the movement grew. Meanwhile, the Easter holidays intervened. I hoped upon Satyagraha as a religious war and so I thought that it should not stand in the way of others attending to their religious duties. I wrote a letter to the District Magistrate saying that, as there were some Christians in the police force, no batch of satyagrahis would be sent on Easter Day. For the same reason, we had not offered Satyagraha on the afternoon of the previous Friday because of the employment of a number of Muslims in the police force. The District Magistrate, on reading my note, telephoned to me to confirm if I really meant it. When I said, "Yes", he asked me to meet him so that we could find a way out of the impasse. I had a long talk with the District Magistrate. I said that it was a minor matter and that it would be settled amicably if batches of five were allowed to pass unchecked and arrested according to law when they manufactured salt. The Magistrate suggested an alternative route but I would not agree to his suggestion and the talks broke down. The next day, the satyagrahis who marched in front of the Sultanganj police station were arrested by the Assistant Superintendent of Police and after the arrests the crowds melted away. The mounted police was conspicuous by its absence.

The arrested satyagrahis were taken to court. While the case was being heard, another batch passed near Sultanganj police station but 'it was not stopped by the police. At the court the satyagrahis were sentenced to imprisonment till the rising of the court, which synchronised with pronouncement of the sentence. It was now clear to us that the satyagrahis would not be barred by the police. Our view was confirmed when a third batch was also not interfered with. Then we stopped sending batches of satyagrahis via the Sultanganj area and began manufacturing salt. But those who broke the salt law were not spared. Thus, the number of arrests in Patna as well as the whole province began to mount." The Government had a salt depot at Dharsana, in Gujarat, where large quantities of salt were stored in the open. Congress volunteers led in turn by Abbas Tayabi and Sarojini Naidu marched to the depot in defiance of Government orders and were severely beaten. The leaders were arrested one after an other. The police were almost brutal. Satyagrahis were beaten till they became unconscious and were dragged about in that condition. Badly injured men were taken to Congress hospitals on cots.

The lurid accounts published in the newspapers instead of scaring the people brought more and more volunteers to the scene in a renewed endeavour to continue the violation of law. But the lathi charges continued mercilessly and hundreds were arrested. The Satyagraha was carried on till the rains set in, rendering the approaches to the Dhirsana salt depot impassable. Early during the movement Jawaharlal Nehru was arrested and Motilal Nehru took over the presidentship of the Congress. He was not arrested till the end of June though he too manufactured salt in his own house, and showed it to us with pride. The Congress Working Committee met frequently at Allahabad and issued regular instruction to satyagrahis and offered them whatever help it could give. The Government did not slacken a bit in their repressive policy which had by now become a settled pattern throughout the country. Wherever salt was manufactured the police went to the spot, broke the pots, destroyed the ovens, arrested some volunteers and beat up the rest. But, undaunted, people renewed their efforts, with the same results. In Bihar salt was manufactured from saline earth. I did not manufacture salt myself but wherever I went I auctioned the salt manufactured by satyagrahis, using the money collected to meet our expenses. Though the sale of salt without a licence was also unlawful I was not arrested for a long time. I learnt that in the beginning the Government had no intention of arresting me. It was later that I discovered that at a conference of officials, the District Magistrates had been authorised to arrest me if it was thought necessary. I was mostly engaged in touring the districts, seeing to the manufacturing of salt, encouraging the satyagrahis and addressing public meetings. A sense of rivalry prevailed in the countryside.

Every village wanted to have the honour of getting the largest number of people arrested. The villages which for one reason or another could not manufacture salt felt sorry about it. None broke the law clandestinely because it was an open Satyagraha. During my tour of the countryside I often saw the villagers gather in open places decorated with buntings and plantain leaves and manufacture salt with great ceremony. In consultation with other leaders, I decided to continue the salt Satyagraha till June, when the rains would set in, making the manufacture of salt impossible, and thereafter to take up the boycott of foreign cloth and prohibition propaganda. In my speeches and informal talk I told the people of the significance of the salt satyagraha, the boycott of foreign cloth and the prohibition programme. I told them that just then the salt Satyagraha took precedence over the others but when the time came the others would be taken up and, therefore, they should keep themselves in readiness for them. In answer to their questions, I said that anti-chaukidari tax and no-rent campaigns could also be taken up later. Though the salt Satyagraha had the priority, boycott of foreign cloth and propagation of prohibition were also carried on in towns and in the countryside. We learnt of the progress of these campaigns at the time of the Working Committee meeting in Allahabad. We then took up the boycott of foreign cloth in Bihar also.

Even traders co-operated with us with great enthusiasm. The spirit of healthy rivalry which marked the salt Satyagraha spread to the foreign cloth boycott movement too, each town trying to seal up a larger quantity of foreign cloth than the others. It became a routine for stockists to pack up foreign cloth and have the bundles sealed by Congressmen to be opened only if the Congress allowed them to. In some places businessmen formed their own committees to organise this work and the committee imposed fines on errant traders. Shops of recalcitrant traders who defied the committees were subjected to picketing. But in Bihar, most of the traders sealed their stocks willingly and only in rare cases had we to picket shops. Leading businessmen of Kanpur, Delhi and the Punjab often met Motilal Nehru and discussed with him how best to make the picketing of foreign cloth and liquor shops a complete success and how to enlist the help of the mill owners. Printed pledges were widely distributed for the public and traders to sign. In some places greater emphasis was laid on prohibition, and it resulted in large-scale arrests and even shooting. In the North-West Frontier Province where the police resorted to shooting, many Pathans were killed. Vithalbhai Patel, first elected President of the Central Legislative Assembly, resigned his office in protest and went to that province to conduct an inquiry. The Government confiscated his report and it could not be widely publicised but what had come out in the papers electrified the whole country. The picketing of foreign cloth shops was entrusted to women by Gandhiji and they responded with great enthusiasm. No prospective buyer dared to come near a shop outside which woman was picketing, and even the shopkeepers, faced with delicate situation, behaved well. Picketing in Bihar, though it had not to be done on a large scale, was organised by Vindhyavasni Devi. Male volunteers used to go round houses, and bring the women picketers to the bazar and post them in front of the shops and assort them all back to their homes in the evening. One incident which occurred in Patna may interest readers. One day a newly-married girl went out to picket a shop. In the evening, the volunteers forgot to take her home.

The husband of one of the picketers who had come in his car to take his wife home saw the girl outside a shop. When she said she was waiting for the volunteers to escort her home. The gentlemen said that the volunteers must have forgotten to pick her up and offered to take her home in his car. But the girl did not know her address nor, she said, would she be able to recognise her house, not having ever seen her house from outside. The couple took her in their car, thinking that they would be able to locate her house by some clue that they might get from her on questioning. They fruitlessly ran about here and there and when they did not succeed in finding her house asked her to write the name of her husband as, according to custom, women do not pronounce the names of their husbands. But the girl wrote it out in the Kaithi script which the couple did not understand. With some difficulty they were able to find a man who knew the script and succeeded in locating the girl's house late in the evening. This little incident will show the straits to which women were reduced on account of the custom of purdah though, at the same time, it is an example of the great enthusiasm with which the women of Bihar responded to the Congress call.

The custom of purdah prevails among nearly all strata of society in Bihar. When I was away in England an agitation was started to end the custom. A young man of Darbhanga, Ramnadan Mishra, took his wife unveiled to Sabarmati Ashram. Gandhiji sent Radha, daughter of Maganlal Gandhi, to Bihar to educate the women and help remove purdah. Maganlal then came to Bihar to see his daughter and find out how she was progressing. He took ill and died in Patna. Somehow this occurrence led to the acceleration of the drive against the evil system in the province. A provincial anti-purdah conference was held, in which Braj Kishore Prasad took a leading part. Though there was an awakening in this direction in the province it was during the 1930 Satyagraha campaign that the purdah system began losing its hold." On his return from Allahabad after attending the Working Committee meeting, he learned that a peculiar kind of Satyagraha had been started in Bihpur, which was a small railway junction, the starting station of the train for Bhagalpur Ghat.

The genesis of the trouble was that some Congress volunteers who lived in an ashram near the railway station picketing a ganja (hemp) shop situated a few yards away. Soon, the police arrived on the spot, threw away the stocks of cotton, yarn and cloth, beat up the Congressmen, turned them out of the ashram and took it into their possession. Congressmen began offering peaceful Satyagraha in an effort to retrieve the ashram from the police. Volunteers in batches of four or five with small flags in their hands would arrive at the place and try to enter the ashram. It was obvious that these unarmed satyagrahis could not displace the armed police force which was in numbers and that it was just a pretext for offering Satyagraha. The police thought likewise. The batch would march every afternoon and court arrest. The news of the Satyagraha spread and people started collecting at the place. I went to Bihpur accompanied by Anant Prasad and Kamleshwari Sahay, Bihar M.L.As. Baldev Sahay and Murli Manohar Prasad of Patna, and Patel Babu, a well-known advocate and a Congress worker of Bhagalpur. Hearing of our arrival, a crowd of about twenty thousand collected. I appealed to the crowd to be peaceful and maintain perfect non-violence. When the usual time when satyagrahis marched towards the ashram and courted arrest arrived, the people stood on the road and all around to have a view of the events. I was viewing the scene from a place in the market. At that time a batch of volunteers arrived and marched towards the ashram and when they neared the place, the police quietly arrested them. The crowd now began to disperse. Just then the Superintendent of Police came out of the ashram and gave an order to charge the crowd with lathis. That was the signal for an indiscriminate and wild lathi charge. The road was soon cleared, and then the Superintendent with some of his men came towards the bazar where I was standing along with the other leaders and, on seeing us, though we had done nothing, asked the police to attack us too using abusive words. I received four or five lathi blows but Ramgati Singh, a young volunteer, had rushed forward and interposed himself between me and the policemen and taken on many of the blows himself. Thus, my injury was not as serious as it might have been. Baldev Sahay and Murli Manohar Prasad, who were near me, were hurt. Abdul Bari, who was standing a little farther off, was hurt badly and began to bleed profusely. The Superintendent and the policemen retraced their steps to the ashram. By now the crowd had dispersed, leaving only those of us who had come from other places. We sat down in a meadow awaiting the even train for Bhagalpur. A local doctor came to us and dressed our wounds. Suddenly we saw the Superintendent and his men coming towards us. We were expecting more trouble but he stopped short and sent a police officer who arrested Patel Babu and took him away. Then we took the train to Bhagalpur where I stayed for two days. Bhagalpur was the biggest centre for the foreign cloth trade in Bihar. While foreign cloth stocks were being sealed in other places, Bhagalpur had not stirred. Now the news of the Bihpur satyagraha electrified Bhagalpur too women volunteers began picketing foreign cloth shops. The traders came to me and expressed their willingness to seal their cloth stocks. A committee was formed and in a few days the entire stock with the business community there had been sealed and put away in a godown. Our aim was accomplished without any trouble, thanks to the Bihpur Satyagraha. The two M.L.As., Anant Prasad and Kamleshwari Sahay, who had come along with me to Bihpur, though they escaped the attentions of the police, were pushed about a great deal. They were outraged by the fact that the police had attacked a crowd which had started dispersing and anyway would have dispersed in a short time. Further, they said that there was even less justification for attacking us. In protest they resigned their seats in the Assembly. This was followed later by some more resignations. A more surprising development was a rift in the police force. While one section of them did not require to be told twice by the Superintendent to wield the lathis, another section was of the view that such action was unnecessary and, while seeming to obey orders, only flourished their lathis without hitting anyone. When Abdul Bari had fallen almost unconscious and a policeman raised his lathi to strike another blow, it was parried by the lathi of another policeman. A third policeman then came on the scene and hit the policeman for having dared to raise his lathi against prostrate Abdul Bari. This was later confirmed by Abdul Bari himself. I shall narrate another incident here.

The Police Inspector who came to arrest Patel Babu in Bihpur was a resident of Chapra district and a school-mate of mine. We were together for four years in school and passed the Entrance Examination together. When I went to Calcutta for further studies he joined the police service. He had aged somewhat prematurely and his hair had turned grey. When he came to arrest Patel Babu, he had quietly raised his hand to wish me but I kept silent as I did not recognise him. It was later that I learnt his name. The next day I sent a Khadi worker, Rambilas Sharma of Bhagalpur, to Bihpur to request the police officer there to allow him to collect the spinning wheels, cotton yarn and other things from the ashram and bring them to the Bhagalpur Khadi Bhandar. Rambilas Sharma had come to know that the Inspector of Police was my school-mate. When he went to the Bihpur police station and found that the Inspector was the officer in-charge, he approached him with his request.

The Inspector, it appeared, was somewhat sorry for the previous day's happenings. Sharma was bluntly sarcastic. He said that I was sorry that I did not recognise him the previous day when he saluted me. The Inspector's face lost colour and he asked Sharma politely not to say anything more on the subject. A few' minutes later, Sharma again reverted to it and stated that I was very sorry not to have had an opportunity of a talk with an old class-mate whom I had met after such a long time. The Inspector was very much moved and again cut Sharma short. He saw that the Police Inspector's eyes were wet. Even after this lathi-charge, the Bihpur Satyagraha continued. The volunteers continued to march in batches to the ashram every day, get beaten up and arrested till the Satyagraha was called off as a result of the Gandhi-Irwin Pact some eight months later, in March 1931. This demonstration of non-violent practice by the people of that area was for me a pleasant surprise.

Like other people, they are a brave and determined sort. Long ago when a Britisher hired a number of Gurkhas and terrorised the locality, the people had killed all of them, about 25 in number, in one night and their bodies thrown in the swollen Ganga could never be traced nor the culprits apprehended." After conviction during the Civil Disobedience Movement, Rajendra Prasad was lodged in Chapra and Hazaribagh Jails. There were several other satyagrahis from various parts of Bihar. In his Autobiography, he mentioned about jail life, daily routine, the names of prominent satyagrahis with him, the lack of basic facilities, the behaviour of District Magistrate, Superintendent of Jail, police and other officials. Even newspapers were not supplied. He mentioned how, one day, he received the transfer orders from Chapra jail to Hazaribagh jail. He was not told by the District Magistrate of Chapra where he was being taken. In fact the bureaucracy was well-aware of the mass popularity of Rajendra Prasad and feared that there could be reception, slogans and hooliganism, on the way, beyond the control of police.

It therefore wanted that nobody should get the news of his transfer. So it was arranged secretly and in a zig zag way via Banaras. The journey performed was by rail and car and he was asked not to speak to anyone on the way. In Hazaribagh jail, the Superintendent of Jail was known to Rajendra Prasad. Therefore he had no difficulty in having the basic amenities in the jail. But still the bureaucratic behaviour and arrangements in the-barracks were subject to periodical checking by higher authorities. Rajendra Prasad spent his time in reading and writing, and this kind of work made him very busy. He also used to have occasional discussions with his colleagues on various aspects of the movement, but he was always keen to see that the discipline of the jail was well-maintained and nobody should get the idea that the Congress satyagrahis misbehaved in any way. The 'C' class prisoners were accorded shabby treatment in terms of the supply of foot-stuff and cleanliness. But still satyagrahis passed their time with a tinge of smile on their faces. Indeed they did not complain about the non-availability of the basic amenities and above all maintained discipline required of them by the jail authorities. Thus, they bore all the vicissitudes of jail life and contributed their share of patriotism with patriotic zeal. On my return from Bhagalpur I heard in Patna that a warrant of arrest had been issued against me. Unconcerned, I continued my tours as before and nothing happened. I was constantly on the move and the District Magistrates felt somewhat relieved when I left their districts as none of them wanted to take the responsibility of arresting me. Then Vithalbhai Patel came to Patna. He had endeared himself to the people by his resignation of the Central Assembly Presidentship. A public meeting was called in the evening to which Hasan Imam came, for the first time, in Khadi dress. When I told him that I somehow felt that my arrest would not be long delayed, he assured me that the work would not suffer even if I were to be arrested. Only that morning had Motilal Nehru been arrested. I then left Patna on a three-day programme in Chapra District. After spending the first night in Zeradei and fulfilling my second day's schedule, I arrived in Chapra at midnight. I heard that my brother was not in town and that the police had been waiting for me at my brother's place till eleven in the night. I knew that my turn had come. I had my dinner and went to bed.

The next morning I left for a place called Garkha where I was to address the day's first meeting. The police were apparently aware of my plans because on the way a car overtook mine and stopped it. A police officer got down and informed me that I was under arrest and that if I wished I could meet my relatives before I was taken away. So I went home, informed my people and in half an hour was ready to follow the police. I was taken to the Chapra Jail. There were about 400 satyagrahis in the Chapra Jail. Somehow they appeared to have heard of my arrival and when I entered the outer gate they rushed to the inner gate, shouting slogans. The embarrassed jailor would net open the inner gate to let me in. When I told him that they might calm down once I was in, the jailor, a stickler to rules, replied that it was against regulations to open the inner gate when the prisoners were nearby. It took some time to persuade the jailor to open the gate. When I entered, I had a tumultuous welcome but the satyagrahis calmed down soon and after accompanying me up to my barracks, they took leave of me. Meanwhile we heard a great uproar outside the jail. There was a double-storeyed barrack and we went to the upper floor to see what the trouble was about. We saw a big crowd surging towards the jail. In his nervousness, the jailor ordered the warders to open fire on the crowd.

The warders, did so, but as they only fired in the air, none was hurt and the crowd only went round the jail and dispersed. We learnt later that the District Magistrate took the jailor to ask for having run the risk of precipitating a major disturbance by opening fire on the crowd-and that without the permission of the Magistrate. This way my first experience of jail life. At that time there was no classification of prisoners, and no instructions had been received about me. I was served my food on an iron plate and I accepted it without a demur. My brother sent my meals from home and the jailor told me that since I was only an under-trial prisoner I could take meals sent by outsiders provided that I took them at the gate. In any case, I would have declined the offer but his condition made me to say "No" instantly.

The next day, some of my friends came to me in connection with my trial which was going on inside the jail. They brought some mangoes sent by my family. The jailor insisted that I go to the gate and eat them there. I refused and sent the mangoes back as he would also not agree to giving them to anyone else. The Magistrate to whom my case went up for hearing was known to me. He had been my client while I practised as a lawyer in Patna. As I had nothing to offer by way of defence, he sentenced me to six months imprisonment under a section of the Penal Code. After the trial, for five days my position was uncertain. I did not know where I was to be lodged but I knew that prominent leaders of the province were kept in the Hazaribagh Central Jail. Then one evening the jailor came and told me while I was strolling in the courtyard that the District Magistrate had come and wanted to see me at the gate. When he saw me coming, the District Magistrate turned and moved to the outer gate. When I approached it, that gate was opened to let me pass and was closed behind me. The Magistrate was there and he told me that I should get ready to leave at once. When I wanted to bring my kit he replied that it would not be necessary and asked me to get into the waiting car. I stepped into the car and we set off at a rapid pace.

The blinds were drawn and I had the experience of travelling in purdah. The Magistrate directed the driver to go westwards. When I asked him our destination, he replied that I would soon know. The car apparently passed the railway station and after some time the blinds were lifted. I saw that we had passed the city limits. The Magistrate then told me that I was to go to Hazaribagh Jail by rail and car. He apologised for the rough journey I might have to undertake but he said that they had tried to reduce my inconvenience by arranging for a saloon for the railway journey. He then outlined the route I was to take. We reached Manjhi on the banks of the Saryu on the Chapra-Banaras line. I found there that a Deputy Magistrate had followed us with my kit. The Superintendent of Police was waiting on the platform for me and took me to the saloon. He asked me not to speak to anyone or disclose my identity. I said I would not certainly do so myself but what was I to do, I asked, were I to be recognised, at which he merely laughed. Anyway he had not much to be worried about as our saloon was at the tail end of the train. The train moved on and the Superintendent began conversing with me in a friendly manner. We reached Banaras in the small, hours of the morning and we detrained there and took a car-that was waiting for us to Mughal Sarai.

There the Superintendent took me to the Refreshment Room but I declined to have my breakfast as I was not yet ready for it. Then the train arrived and in the saloon I had my bath and then breakfast. At the Sone East Bank station, the Superintendent of Gaya District took over. He put me in a car and placing me under the charge of an Inspector of Police, left. The Inspector and I motored to Hazaribagh, reaching there at one in the afternoon. In Hazaribagh Jail I was billeted with some friends. They were somewhat surprised to hear about my round-about journey. I told them that the District Magistrate of Chapra told me that it was meant to avoid crowds at Chapra, Sonepur, Patna and Gaya stations, further, I repeated what the Inspector of Police had told me regarding his instructions not to stop the car anywhere and to speed up the car in Aurangabad where the road passes through the town. After I left Chapra Jail, the other inmates came to know of my transfer when the Deputy Magistrate came to collect my kit and began demonstrating against my being taken to some unknown place. Somehow they sent word to my brother, who immediately took his car and went to the Chapra railway station. When he was told that I had not taken the train there, he motored to Sonepur station and getting no news of me returned home disappointed. How was he to know of my route and that I had travelled westwards to Banaras instead of going eastwards ? When he later learnt that I was in Hazaribagh jail, he came to see me there. The jailor of Hazaribagh Jail, Narain Prasad, a fine and intelligent man, was known to me from school days. His elder brother was my classmate and I had often visited their house in Chapra. He lodged me with friends like Ram Dayal Sinha, Sri Krishna Sinha and Bipin Bihari Verma, Deepnarain Singh and Swami Bhawani Dayal of South Africa came later joined us. I spent my time mostly in reading and spinning. Some time later, with the jailor's permission, I joined the jail workshop and learnt weaving. In the six months I was in jail I wove about 200 yards of nawar", which I brought out with me when I was released, and 15 yards of cloth. We suffered no inconvenience at all in the jail. Friends lodged in other wards used to meet us with the permission of the jailor. We had some difficulty in getting books which were not given to us unless they were 'passed' by the police or a magistrate.

The officer who was entrusted with this job did not appear to be a well-read person and had a unique criterion for 'passing' a book as safe. He would not pass a book which had either the word 'politics' or 'political' on its cover. On the other hand, even those books which would be considered by knowing police officers as very "objectionable" were passed on to us if they did not have on the cover these words To give an instance, which was joked about, somebody asked for a college textbook of economics, entitled Textbook of Political Economy. The authorities refused to pass it because of the word "political" in the title. But they saw no objection in approving A.B.C. of Communism and Theory of the Leisure Class. I do not know on what grounds they not approved the first book, but I have a shrewd suspicion that the second was possibly approved because the censor thought that it dealt with matters of interest to the leisured classes. I wanted to compile a book of all the articles written by Gandhiji at various times on various subjects in the newspapers. Such a work had already been published by a Madras publisher with a foreword by me but I thought it would be better if I could publish separate books on different subjects, with short introductions. I classified the writings under different heads like Non-violence, Swaraj, Satyagraha, Education, Khadi and then prepared brief introductions for each. I then selected the articles which my friends kindly copied out for me.

When the manuscript was just ready I was released. 1, however, got no time to publish the volumes, although Gandhiji approved of the idea, saying that a similar work had been published in Gujarati. Many friends like Nibaranchandra Das Gupta of Purulia liked the idea. He made some suggestions in this behalf which I accepted. But the manuscript never went to press. It lay in the Sadaqat Ashram and when in 1932 we were arrested and the Ashram was attacked and taken possession of by the police, it was lost for all time. Besides learning cottage industries in jail, we got time to read a lot of religious literature. Pandit Bharat Mishra of Chapra and Pandit Vishnu Dutt Shukla, who were with us, recited the Ramayana and other scriptures to us. For the first time I read the principal Upanishads. Swami Sahajanand lectured on the Gita but I could not attend his lectures for want of time. With Nibaranchandra Das Gupta, with whom I developed an intimacy, I studied Patanjali's Yog Sastra, which made me realise how scholarly he was and how he had tried to follow the yogic principles of life. A simple and self-sacrificing man, he looked upon Gandhiji's agitation not merely as a political struggle but as a religious renaissance. Unfortunately, he contracted tuberculosis and died some time after his release. There were occasional friendly competitions among the inmates. Some people brought out a hand-written monthly journal which they called Qaidi. Some others then published another monthly called Karagar (prison), in which the editor made the point that while prisoners came and prisoners went, the karagar went on for ever. Article connected with the political movement formed the main content of these journals. Some issues contained sketches and cartoons prepared by Kalika Kumar Sinha. Once a special issue was produced in which all the prominent prisoners were asked to give an account of the progress of Satyagraha in their respective districts. I should think that these hand-written journals would provide excellent material for a history of the national movement in Bihar. I wonder if it is possible to trace these journals today. Among the contributors and organisers of the journals were Swami Bhawani Dayal, Mathura Prasad Sinha, Ram Briksh

Benipuri, and Mahamaya Prasad. In the beginning we were not supplied with newspapers. But in the jail one somehow got anything one wanted, provided one knew the trick. One or two secured some newspapers which they would read and then pass on the news to the others by word of mouth. Every day we used to wait for the human newspapers; we were never starved for news. Soon after I came in, however, Government began to supply us with newspapers. But the concession was one that was grudgingly given and hence what we got was the overseas edition of the Statesman. It contained only material that was of interest to foreign readers and none that interested political prisoners like us. Despite the fact that I have toured my province a great deal and thus had opportunities of meeting many people from all walks of life, I should say that I never came to know people as intimately as I did in the jail. I shall ever cherish the memory of these contacts I had in the Hazaribagh Jail. Swami Bhawani Dayal, Nibaranchandra Das Gupta and Thakur Nawab Singh were some of them.

The Thakur joined the non-cooperation movement under the Mahatma's influence in the district of Muzaffarpur, with his sons, nephews and grandsons. A prominent man in Sitamarhi sub-division, he took over the direction of the movement there. Though without modern education, he was a very intelligent and sharp-witted man. He and his son were my constant companions in jail. At this stage, we may appropriately refer to a sympathetic fast by Gandhi on 2nd December, 1932, for S.P. Patwardhan of Ratnagiri. Sgt. Patwardhan had asked for scavenger's work in jail but it was refused by the authorities. Gandhiji wrote to the Bombay Government in the matter but to no effect. Consequently Sgt. S.P. Patwardhan started a starvation fast by reducing his diet. Gandhi had agreed, in the truce period, to go on fast with Sgt. Appasaheb Patwardhan if his demand was not granted, and so Gandhi in sympathy with him commenced his fast. But within two days the authorities gave assurance to consider the demand and the fast was given up. Within about a week, the Secretary of State made the necessary amendments in jail rules and the bar against giving scavenging work to caste Hindus was removed and the Satyagraha thus became successful. We have described the developments of the Civil Disobedience movement in the year 1932, as well as the episode of the Poona Pact. The public response to Gandhi's call for the removal of untouchability did doubtless affect the progress of the Civil Disobedience movement. In spite of that, the Congress Programme was carried out. There was another reason for, the slackening of the Civil Disobedience campaign. As things stood and as already stated, it could be conducted mainly by practising methods of secrecy which are not only abhorrent, but even opposed to and subversive of the fundamental principles of Satyagraha. The meeting of friends at Poona in connection with Gandhi's fast must have given an opportunity for exchange of thoughts on the subject amongst leading Congressmen who were then free, and accordingly two circulars were issued. The first pointed out the supreme claims on Congressmen of Civil Disobedience, work in connection with the removal of untouchability being primarily entrusted to nationalist non-Congressmen and such Congressmen as, for some reason or other, were unable to court imprisonment. The second insisted on the desirability of terminating secret methods which had crept in during the progress of the Civil Disobedience campaigning. The 4th January was the day on which the Government offensive had started in 1932, and the Acting President, Rajendra Prasad who had succeeded,

Rajagopalachari, issued instructions to all provincial offices that the anniversary should be observed on that day by reading a special statement which had been sent out and which gave in a short compass the progress of the movement and a survey of the problems holding the foremost place in the thoughts of the country at the time.

Meetings were held at numerous places and the statement was read in the midst of arrests and lathi-charges followed by the arrest of the President himself on the 6th January, 1932. Thereafter, Mr. Aney became the Acting President. When the fight commenced in January, 1932, Vallabhbhai Patel was the President of the Congress. The Working Committee had decided that unlike in 1930, vacancies in the Working Committee should not be filled up and Vallabhbhai drew up a list of persons who were to succeed him and act as President one after another during his absence. Rajendra Prasad, Dr. Ansari, Sirdar Sardul Singh Cavceshar, Gangadharrao Deshpande, Dr. Kitchlew, Rajagopalachari, Rajendra Prasad and Aney acted between January 1932, and July 1933, when the Congress organisation ceased to function. Amongst those who acted as Secretaries during this period and on whom fell the burden of carrying on the office work in the midst of indescribable difficulties may be mentioned the names of Jaya Prakash Narayan, Lalji Mehrotra, Girdhari Kripalani, Ananda Choudhary and Jugal Kishor Agarwala." Thus, it is quite evident that there was national upsurge not only in Bihar, but all over India. The prominent leaders of the Congress including Rajendra Prasad generated the spirit of sacrifice by participating in various phases of the freedom movement. The spontaneous participation in the Satyagraha was considered as an act of honour and respect for satyagrahis who belonged to various strata of our society.

They did not mind to suffer in jail or to lose property for non-payment of land revenue. With an ardent faith in the efficacy of the movement and the patriotic action undertaken by Rajendra Prasad, a common man of Bihar always showed much reverence for him and made himself available for any non-violent act at his bidding. Undoubtedly this region produced a rich crop of devoted and ardent followers of Mahatma Gandhi whose representative was Babu Rajendra Prasad.

Rajendra Prasad had developed a habit of depending on Gandhis advice. "We are accustomed" he writes "to accept whatever he says so much that we do not at any time consider it necessary to apply our own intelligence and judgment." For him it became all the more difficult that Gandhi retired just when he in his new office as President of Congress needed his guidance most. Still Rajendra Babu resolved not to disturb him in his retirement. The benefit of his presence at the session of Working Committee and All India Congress Committee would be great. He would then give his direct advice in the light of the first hand knowledge of the situations that might really arise in the course of debates and discussions.

But Rajendra Babu was prepared to forego this benefit and would be content with obtaining his instructions on reports made to him so that he might be spared from personal attendance as also from day to day attention to Congress work. It, however so happened that Gandhi came to Delhi on this own at a time when the Working Committee met there to talk over and plan out the policy and programme of Assembly business which was to start from January. And it was a meeting that in an exceptional way awaited his instructions for Congress was now to embark on a venture which was new to it. The task in this Assembly was not that of fighting the government as on last occasions but of running it of which they had no early experience. They were needed to tackle the machinery of government both as an immediate service to the nation and as preparation for self government in a realistic manner. It was a matter calling for imagination for vision into the future. Congressmen needed very much to draw on Gandhis imagination and prevision. Such a vital need was met just by chance. The great difficulty in Indian politics at the time Rajendra Prasad had become Congress President was the composition of Hindu Muslim ill will. Rajendra Prasad made a great contribution to the endeavour at building up goodwill in his capacity as Congress President by means of negotiations that were based on what was known as Rajendra Jinnah formula. Later, on in his individual capacity as a thinker he sought to give an intellectual lead to the issue by means of his well known book : India Divided written while in jail during 1942 45. The problem is so very complicated that it is necessary in the interest of clear understanding to go over the background against which Rajendra Prasad was called upon to act as a mediator. For it should be remembered that the problem was so desperate that a settlement could not be helped forward even by Mahatma Gandhi with his ubiquitions moral force and remarkable command over the technique of persuasion.

Gandhi specialised as a man of compromise and his failure at the Round Table Conference must have made the problem ever more desperate. Rajendra Prasad as Congress President as well as a man of goodwill was loyally backed by two outstanding Indians Vallabhbhai Patel and Ghanshyamdas Birla both men of great strength and exceptional organizational acumen. But to no tangible result.

Now let us have a look back. Mahatma Gandhi before to his taking part in the R.T.C. began a preparatory work in India. He said he would accept any terms provided these had the sanction of all the Muslim organisations. Accordingly he conferred with different Muslim parties in various parts of the country at different periods of the year. But these conferences at Bombay Ahmedabad Bhopal Delhi and Simla did not prove much profitable. The Nationalist Muslims held an All India Conference at Lucknow on 18th April. Sir Ali Imam presiding over the gathering made an inspiring appeal. "So much is said about the share of the Indian Moslem in concession loot. I do not believe that this share can be fixed by statute. His share Will be in proportion to the contribution he makes towards the obtaining and maintaining of India's freedom." Dr. Ansari sketched a scheme of joint electorate which he further supplemented at the All Bengal Muslim Conference at Faridpur on 27th June. The Congress Committee in Bombay meeting in June 1931 authorised Mahatma Gandhi to go to London although the communal compromise was not effected. In July again further efforts were made and ultimately was drawn up a "compromise between undiluted communalism and undiluted nationalism"; It was formulated that joint electorate was to be the basis of representation in the Federal and Provincial Legislatures in proportion to population with extra right to win additional seats in any province where any minority was less than 25 p.c. of the population.

But this would not do. In the U.P. Muslim Conference held on 8th August Maulana Shaukat Ali wanted "ten clear years for internal organisation with separate electorate". About this time the second Round Table Conference met. Practically the main subject before it were the two unities : Hindu Muslim and Hindu Harijan. The situation soon became intriguing. An All India Federation seemed to have been brought within the sphere of practical politics. Its implications started to disconcert many parties in whom federation as a political philosophy had not yet taken roots. Particularly the Moslem minority of some seventy millions prepared themselves to hold up all advance until their claims to security against Hindu majority were granted. Their claims comprised a demand for a clear majority of the seats on the Councils of the Punjab and Bengal the creation of a new province in Sindh separated from Bombay and the establishment of complete self government in the North West Frontier Province claims which if granted would make the Moslems masters of North West. The Princes became more nervous about their own position within the Federation the more they examined its implications. Congress regarded with alarm the prospects of a Federation in which it was likely that the conservative forces of the Princes and the Moslems would in many ways be combined against them. Gandhi who was Chairman of the Minorities Sub committee would be not willing to think of any separate representation to the Depressed classes since they have a history that disproves any separation from the Hindu community. The second session was staged as if chiefly to show that communal differences could not be harmonised by Indians themselves. There was something in the air that rendered it not possible even to conduct a peaceful approach to the problem.

If the Hindu Mahasabha was largely to be blamed in the starting of the first session the Moslem Conference was mainly responsible for the final break up. Speaking at the Round Table Conference as the sole representative of the Congress Mahatma Gandhi said : "I would like to repeat what I have said before that while the Congress always accepts any solution that may be acceptable to the Hindus the Musalmans and the Sikhs it will be no party to special reservation or special electorates for any other minorities. In my humble opinion the scheme sponsored by Sir Hubert Carr is the very negation of responsible Government the very negation of nationalism. Heaven help India if India have representatives elected by these several specially cut up groups... I say it will be much better for us that we should remain without so called responsible Government than that we should accept this scheme put forward by Sir Hubert Carr and others." It may be noted that the Award is practically drawn on the lines advocated by Sir Hubert Carr and the representatives of the British Commercial interests in India. These interests are more insatiable than the mere political interests. It may be relevant to quote from a letter (March 1932) from Birla to Sir Samuel Hoare : "As regards closer co-operation between the two communities I regret to have to say that I have not been given much encouragement by Mr. Benthal."

Even today these interests have a malignant influence. These interests grew at the expense of Indian industry. Upto 1800 for example there were no import of cloth. On the contrary India utilised to export fine textiles to the tune of one and a half crore. By 1850 India started to depend on not only for cloth but also silk wool paper steel. Gandhi in his broadcast from London to America said that he would prefer not to describe the means by which Indias home industry was destroyed by the British. Mahatma Gandhi told the Conference that all negotiations to reach a communal settlement "had unfortunately proved entirely abortive". A document representing the Congress scheme for a solution of the communal problem was circulated. It was thrown out not only by Muslims and the Scheduled classes but also by Hindus. Memoranda were submitted by Dr. Moonje and Raja Narendranath and others. The Mahomedans did not differ amongst themselves. Jinnah had not yet irrevocably gone to the extreme length of disunity. He was still nursing a possibility of unity through understanding of common destiny But he was not helpful at the Round Table Conference. Besides he was at the time not the dominating figure in Muslim politics. The leading Muslims of the Punjab and the Aga Khan were the key figures of the day. However, after the second Conference was over at a public meeting held in the Central Theatre of the Kings College. Jinnah said with vehemence that only to side track the central question of self government the conveners of the R.T.C. introduced the Hindu Muslim conflict which was "exaggerated in England by various interested parties".

"And to make matters worse the question of Hindu-Muslim settlement is brought over and over again. In all sincerity I want to ask if you think that we can possibly get an agreement on a question like this without there being any sanction behind it or any instrument with which you can enforce the decision arrived at. Do you think if tomorrow your people are asked if they will have tariffs or no you will get unanimity of opinion? Do you mean to say they are not patriots? And yet they do not agree... It is not the voters on your electoral roll who decide the questions or the question of tariffs. It is the machinery that is behind your Government in power.. When we met in the second Conference the differences were only confined to the Punjab and Bengal and about the Central Legislature whether Muslims should have 27 or 13 seats in that legislature. And what do you notice? The settlement fell through because of one seat here or another seat there. And once again I repeat my question to the British public why do you go about talking of Indian Communal question when you yourself cannot settle the much vexed tariff question?" Later, as the Second World War began Gandhi mentioned that it was a British technique that the minority argument was "flung in the face of a credulous world." The Premier MacDonald pleaded before the Round Table Conference : "Believe me the British Government has no desire to use your disagreements for any ulterior purpose." Curiously it is a British Journalist who expressed doubts : "The action of the Muslims in playing their cards with such joy and confidence is giving India more than a glimpse at their triumph cards held by the Government in reserve". Contrarily Sir Samuel Hoare maintained : "It must be the aim of Indians themselves to remove these divisions just as it should be our aim to help Indians in their task. So far are we from wishing to divide and govern that we regard these divisions as a calamity and are ready to do our outmost to remove them. We have shown our good faith in the matter. We showed it when we made the Communal Award." So then the Award was the gesture of goodwill!

All the different minorities however were planning a pact among themselves. Sir Samuel Hoare it was pointed out in a speech of Sir Tej Bahadur Sapru in the Conference manoeuvred to dismiss the Indian delegation with the offer of mere Provincial Autonomy. It is suggestive that the communalist section of the Muslim delegates persistently refused to discuss the constitution of the Central Government until their claims were not fully accepted. The following rejoinder to a speech of Mr. Jinnah in the Muslim League meeting in Delhi from Sardar Santsingh M.L.A. indicates what happened behind the schemes. He says :

"My feeling is that Muslims are not free agents to make any serious effort at mutual settlement. I would like to warn those who believe in reviving these talks that they should remember what happened here recently. The Aga Khans mission here led to an exchange of views between himself Sir Fazli Hussain and other Muslim leaders which again led to a general understanding among them that they must at all costs stand by Sir Samuel Hoare who was reported to have told certain Muslim leaders that if they joined opposition to the White Paper they would be discredited as a community and that everything including the communal Award would go into the melting pot. Unless therefore some Muslim leaders openly commit themselves to denunciation of the White Paper irrespective of the fate of the Communal Award there can be no honest unity in the common endeavour to build up nationalism." The Award was published on the 17th August. 1932. As Sir N. N. Sircar later at a meeting of the non party leaders conference pointed out it was not in the nature of an arbitral award. It was just the decision of the British Government imposed on Indian people. An agitation against the Award was at the time got up by Pandit Malaviya who convened an all leaders conference known as the unity conference at Allahabad. It seemed to make history at the commencement while in conclusion it failed to make any.

The Congress could not make up its mind for months and after long cogitation it was finally declared in June 1934 that Congress neither accepted nor rejected it. As protest against this "half hearted tactics" and 66 weak kneed compromise" a new party called the Nationalist Party was formed by Malaviya and he claimed that it was a Party "within the sheltering bosom of the Indian National Congress". Also the British Joint Parliamentary Committee had published in November 1934 their Report on the White Paper of March 1933. It was at this stage that Rajendra Prasad became President of the Congress. Also by now the Muslim stalwarts of the Punjab were gone leaving the leaders role only to Jinnah. In the circumstances the Congress President was to meet the League President. Thus, Rajendra Prasad met Jinnah. He met him at Dr. Ansaris place. For a long week there were talks. Ansari Naidu and Kripalani were helping him but to no result. He wrote to Patel and to the Mahatma for instructions. Yet after all talks fell through. Hereafter Rajagopalachariar and then the Mahatma himself tried to negotiate unity with Jinnah but they also failed. And the strange thing was that one failure did not make the path easier for an eventual success; on the contrary it made the next negotiation a surer failure.

The fact has to be noted. The explanation of this fact was in a way given by Gandhi when speaking on his constructive programme he emphasised that a political unity by means of a pact was superficial effort. It was sought to be imposed from without. We had little compelling spirit within to feel united and keep us united. Gandhis idea of "heart unity" has also been expressed by Dr. Sultan Ahmed who has been quoted in Rajendra Prasads India Divided. Dr. Sultan Ahmed says :

"Our problem is no doubt vastly complex. Yet the heart of the problem is the problem of the heart. It is essentially a matter of relations and so a matter of the mind. No wonder that a mental machinery cannot be run by political engineering alone. Commenting on the failure of the minorities settlement in Europe Macartney offers his basic postulate : If once the mentality is correct the machinery will soon be found." It is the age long cry of Macbeth : Doctor can you cure the mind diseased. However, what was stranger still that the Rajendra formula had stirred little enthusiasm in Hindu circles too. That shows not the defect of the formula but the poisonous mental climate of the day. "Pandit Malaviyaji" Birla wrote Gandhi "tries to reason now with this group now with that but it is evident he cannot go beyond the scope of the Jinnah–Rajendra Babu formula." And even the Congress in Bengal did not sup port the formula. Birla wrote Mahadev Desai that it was useless to condemn Bengal on that account and that as the Congress central command had not "backed any one in Bengal" there was no one here who could be expected to be boldly or spontaneously forthcoming to back the formula.

There was no Bengal member on the Working Committee Rajendra Prasad regretted to note in his autobiography. As President Rajendra Prasad addressed himself to the duty of touring round the country despite of his failing health. His personal contacts appreciably stimulated in men the love of Congress. And it stimulated courage too. In 1932 33 people feared not a little to receive Congress guests and entertain leaders. But in 35 they gave him enthusiastic receptions. These signs of reviving courage and conviction greatly pleased him but he felt a great deal of delicacy to be taken round in large processions even though he loved so much the spirit of welcome. The shy gentleman realised embarrassed. But Gandhi asked him not to fight shy of the Swagat (welcome) functions because it provided popular enthusiasm and it was of first class significance to generate enthusiasm in view of the fact that for this dearth of life in national affairs Satyagraha had been stopped.

4

Rajendra Prasad and Cooperative Planning

In 1919 cooperation became a provincial subject. Since then in every province emphasis has been laid on the type of cooperation that suited the province. Up to 1929 the movement grew in strength, but on account of the depression which began in that year it received a severe set-back. Accordingly from 1929 up to the beginning of the war, emphasis in the cooperative movement was more on consolidation and rehabilitation rather than on expansion. It was but natural that on account of the need for reorganisation, official control on the movement increased during this period. When war began the agricultural prices started going up in-common with other prices. The cooperative movement received an impetus. The members repaid their debts, deposits with cooperative banks increased. In fact they increased so rapidly that, with the proportionately smaller demand for loans, the banks were faced with the problem of surplus funds.

The significant feature of the movement during the war was the growth of consumers cooperative societies and stores especially for the procurement of foodstuffs. Cooperative marketing also grew. In the post-war period which has just begun, we are now confronted with the problem of fitting the cooperative movement in the general plan for the economic development of the country. In the earlier years, the movement was confined to the provision of rural credit, based on the principle of unlimited liability. The development of cooperation was guided and controlled by the Government; Government control had both advantages and disadvantages. The advantage was that an experiment in social economics, largely dealing with the poor cultivators, was started with the authority of Government behind it and this helped to sustain the movement in its infancy in spite of failures here and there. We must accept that this foundation has been of immense value in making possible much rapid development in the later years. At the same time, with the development of a cooperative consciousness among the more intelligent public, several leading non-officials interested themselves in the development of cooperation. It would be true to say that, under the conditions of Government then existing, the cooperative movement offered about the only opportunity for the Government and the public to get together for improving the conditions of life of the people. Under the Reforms Act of 1919, cooperation became a provincial transferred subject, and was placed under the charge of a Minister. During this period, there was considerable development. Non-credit cooperation came to increase in importance. Provincial legislation, to suit the special conditions of each province, was introduced, Non-official institutions for propaganda and education were encouraged. Certain provinces appointed committees of enquiry to report on the progress of the movement. It was clear by then that the movement had taken root in the country and both official and non-official opinion came to be directed towards guiding its future along proper lines.

The depression during the last decade no doubt checked the rapid expansion of the movement but it helped to focus attention on defects that naturally assumed importance during a period of stress and strain, and, in this sense, had a beneficial effect on the movement. During the war, the elaborate controls instituted by the Government imparted a stimulus to consumers societies-a side aspect of the movement, which has long continued to be rather weak and marketing activities, by the cooperative method. The Cooperative Planning Committee have defined cooperation to be a form of organisation, in which persons voluntarily associate together on a basis of equality for the promotion of their economic interests. Those who come together have a common economic aim which they cannot achieve by individual isolated actions because of the weakness of the economic position of a large majority of them. This element of individual weakness is to be overcome by the pooling of their resources, by making self-help effective to their mutual aid and by strengthening the bond of moral solidarity between them." The essentials of the cooperative movement as distinguished from other forms of organisations are (a) the willing cooperation of the members, and (b) the recognition of the democratic principle as evidenced by the practice of one man having one vote and not more. It is those principles which make the cooperative movement so different. As has been said, "Economic security could conceivably exist with a high degree of material prosperity in the slave state, but at the price of slavery." That kind of economic security is however hardly worth having. In formulating policies of further development of the cooperative movement so as to suit the needs of this stormy Post-war world in which we find ourselves, it is well to remember how eminently suitable the cooperative method is to the peculiar problems of India. Two Committees set up by the Government of India, namely, the Agricultural Finance Sub-Committee presided over by Professor D.R. Gadgil, and the Cooperative Planning Committee of which R.G. Saraiya was the Chairman, agree that the cooperative movement will provide the best solution of many of our problems. Cooperation is primarily a poor man's organisation. It fits in with an economy in which the small cultivator is the central figure. As an individual the cultivator is weak and cannot hope to stood up against the gigantic forces that lead to his exploitation. Through cooperation he acquires strength. At the same time the cooperative method affords sufficient freedom to the individual, unlike extreme forms of planned state control in which the individual is perhaps better housed and better fed and clothed, but is drilled into a uniformity that cannot but ultimately stunt his stature as a human being. There is an element of democratic freedom inherent in cooperation and this freedom has to be prized above all things. The freedom of the individual, however, has to be used for the benefit of the community of which he is a part, and it is this healthy compromise between discipline and freedom that is embodied in the cooperative method-"all for each and each for all." One cannot think of a more wholesome philosophy for a country of self-reliant cultivators living in communities small enough for one person to know another, and willing to pool their resources and create social and economic, unity and strength. The various organisations in the cooperative movement have to be conceived and created in this combined spirit of advantage to one's self and benefit to others. Without the background of this ideology, individual institutions will lose much of their significance. In turn, this background of the cooperative movement points to the importance of looking at cooperation more as a way of lire than as a series of separate institutions for specific purposes. The various forms of cooperation are intended to subserve the varying needs of the cultivators, the labourers and the general public.

All these various institutions together help the individual to lead a better life. The cultivator should be made to feel that the cooperative movement can help him at all stages. It affords credit for redeeming past debts through land mortgage banks. For his cultivation expenses it extends facilities for securing good seed, manu-e and implements. It is a healthy sign that these facilities are increasingly being provided in kind rather than in cash. Societies for consolidation of holdings help to arrest the evil of fragmentation. He can improve his land by digging wells or raising bunds by loans of a medium dated character. The cooperative society purchases his produce, stores it and sells it for him, thereby helping him to secure fair prices for his produce which be has to sell. His daily needs are met by the consumers' society which secures to him what he needs to purchase at fair prices. Cottage industries to occupy the spare time of the cultivator and his family offer a fruitful field for cooperative effort. Thus, the movement contacts the cultivator at every point. This· is proper and healthy, and the tendency to bring together as many aspects as possible in one institution which has a "multi-purpose" character is to be welcomed. It is true that the movement originated with credit, and that original sin still sticks to it. Even today the primary credit society is the base of the movement, hut it has to be enlarged so-is to move one step higher up and provide those facilities for which credit is utilised. The cooperative circle will then start with the provision of seed and manure, and will be completed by the marketing of the produce. That credit should have played and should continue to play such an important part in the movement is but natural inasmuch as the want of it or the lack of the capacity to command it at reasonable rates is the greatest weakness of the small man.

The two Committees have accordingly recommended that the financial structure should be reconstructed so as to provide agricultural producers with an agency of credit alternative to the private money-lender. The village money-lender is and has been the target of much criticism. Whatever his sins may be, it must be admitted that in the absence of credit societies he played a most useful part in supplying credit. His terms may have been exorbitant and his methods not always and in all cases quite honest. But I cannot help saying that I have seen cooperative credit societies charging something like 15 per cent per annum as interest on the loans advanced by them, and that when they had not only the benefit of the unlimited liability of all the members of the society for the default of any member but also of the legal right to claim facilities for quick realisation of their dues. The village money-lender had none of these and if be charged more than 15% interest in some cases for the extra risk involved, I for one would not be prepared to blame him. Dishonest dealings of those who indulged in them are apart and of course deserve strongest condemnation. One great weakness of the cooperative movement proceeded from what we regarded as its strong point. Cooperative societies could not charge interest at lower rates from their borrowers, when to attract deposits they were themselves paying 7 or 8% to their depositors.

The unlimited-liability of their members and the facilities for enforcing their claim created a facile complacency and loans were advanced which did not fall strictly within the objects for which they could be advanced and further hardly any check was exercised on the utilisation of the loan by the debtor who very often used it for non-productive purposes.

The natural consequence was strict enforcement of the rules for realisation of the debt, taking over of lands in lieu of the debt not only of the debtor but in many cases of others who had unwittingly assumed unlimited liability and had been too lazy to see to it that the debtors did not abuse the trust and thus throw their own liability arising out of their impecuniousness on others. When debts could not be realised in spite of all this, societies were unable to fulfil their obligations to the cooperative bank, and the latter in their turn closed their doors in several cases and those who had deposited their savings and earnings in the hope of getting interest at a higher rate than was available from other banks lost heavily not only the interest but in some cases also their principal. Efforts were made to stop the rot and provincial Governments came to the rescue of the movement after this period of depression, and but for the events that followed the starting of the World War It the movement in many places would have collapsed. In any scheme of reorganisation the defects and weaknesses should not be lost sight of and should be provided against. The Gadgil Committee have recommended that the alternative agency should be an Agricultural Credit Corporation to which the State should provide a part of the working capital and take responsibility of administration. It is further recommended that each State or Province should prepare separately a scheme for such a Corporation for themselves.

The Saraiya Committee however feel that much time may be lost in preparing such a scheme and recommend that the existing number of cooperative banks and other central cooperative financing organisations should considerably be reconstituted. Whatever may be the form of the organisation. It is clear that our cooperative movement would have to be strengthened and reorganised so as to save our agriculturist from the clutches of the unscrupulous money-lender and to provide him with a more satisfactory and adequate form-of credit. Further, cooperative societies should be reformed and reorganised so as to serve as a centre for the general economic improvement of its members. It is considered that it should develop into a multi-purpose society. It should not only finance crop production, but also act as an agent for the sale of crop; supply the farmers with seed, cattlefeed, fertilisers and agricultural implements; serve as a milk collecting station for the nearest dairy and as a centre for animal first-aid; serve as a centre for maintaining agricultural machinery for joint use of members; and encourage subsidiary occupations for its members. The Cooperative Planning Committee has suggested that a target should cover 50% of the villages in British India and 30% of the rural Population within the ambit of the reorganised primary societies within a period of 10 years in two 5 year periods. The membership of a primary society should be at lea-It 50. To reach the target it will be necessary to increase the number of members in the existing societies and to start new societies and it has been calculated that 1.7 million members should be added to the existing 97,357 societies and 21,600 new societies should be established annually for 10 years. It has further been recommended that the Government should give a subsidy amounting to 50 per cent of the cost of management to all the societies-old and new-for the first five years. We have met in this Conference to consider these and other recommendations of the Cooperative Planning Committee which are of a very far-reaching character and involve heavy cost.

In doing so we shall have to bear in mind that cooperation is a provincial subject and the Government of India can only guide and suggest and offer such financial and technical assistance as it can afford; but the burden of giving effect to and implementing the recommendations will fall mainly on the provinces. It is possible that in the new set-up which will follow in train of the impending constitutional changes the scope of the functions of the Central Government may be still further circumscribed. Whatever the future may bring, we have to give our considered views on the recommendations and a detailed agenda has been prepared for the Conference. I now indicate only some of the points of principle which should receive the careful attention of the Conference. Of there the first and foremost is the suggestion to increase and widen the scope of cooperative activities from being very largely credit societies to multi-purpose societies. In this connection the question whether the liability of members should be limited or unlimited is one of fundamental significance Another question of importance is whether cooperation can at all have recourse to compulsion in any form, and, if so, the extent to which it can go in that direction. Cooperation is based primarily on voluntary association and should not be departed from. But there may be certain activities essential for economic progress, like consolidation of holdings, crop production or irrigation in which the desired object may not be attained without resort to compulsion and the question arises as to what may be regarded as essential schemes and what should be the proportion of the community which through cooperative societies could make its decisions binding on others. A third fundamental point requiring consideration is the extent of Governmental control, interference and assistance in the affairs of cooperative societies. Apart from these and such other questions, there are other recommendations dealing with details relating to each particular kind of activity that cooperative societies may undertake.

These relate to supply of agricultural credit, cooperative farming, milk production and supply, cooperative marketing of agricultural produce, small and subsidiary industries consumers, cooperatives, urban credit, cooperative housing societies-urban and rural; cooperative insurance including life insurance, fire insurance, cattle and crop insurance, general administration and training of workers, and propaganda etc. I would invite the Conference to take up the consideration of these according to the agenda. I am glad and grateful to have this opportunity of joining in your deliberations and hope the decision we shall be able to arrive at will result in expanding and strengthening the cooperative movement which holds out such a rich promise of progress for the great bulk of our vast population. We have to tackle the problem of the poverty of our masses and improvement of agriculture and animal husbandry and expansion and improvement of industries are essential for this purpose. We have to tackle the problem of illiteracy and insanitation and disease and in all these and many other spheres cooperation has a great part to play.

The prospects are vast and varied and it requires a correspondingly increasing interest on the part of the people at large to be evinced and taken in the work. That depends upon the numbers of workers available, and even more upon the qualities of head and heart and the equipment of those who will choose this line of public service. It requires an even-increasing number of enthusiastic public spirited workers imbued fully with the spirit of cooperation and in the difficult and interesting times ahead let us hope we shall get them.

5

Rajendra Prasad : A Suffering Servant

It is unequivocally recognised that Rajendra Prasad rose to great heights because of his own virtues. He was extremely gentle. He was 'Ajatshatru' and remained throughout his life an idol to many. To his colleagues and Satyagrahis, he was a great Source of inspiration and a tower of strength.

The words of wisdom which he gave to persons in distress proved to be much more than material assistance. His mental grasp, the power of will and the consistent habit of industry gave Rajendra Prasad the unmistakable character of a man fashioned in a large mould. Undoubtedly there was nothing small about him. His sacrifice for the cause of his motherland can easily match with the most prominent Indian patriot of the time. His anti-Raj stance was mingled with the Gandhian ideology of non-violence and truthfulness. He never permitted the satyagrahis to behave in a violent way rather perfect discipline was inculcated among them in all the movements launched under his supervision. Nehru opined at the time of unveiling a life-size portrait of Rajendra Prasad in the Kerala Assembly on 27 April 1958, 'Rajen Babu not only occupies the highest office in our country but is something more.

Perhaps more than anyone else he embodies in his life the Indian national movement through which we have passed. The great national movement had many facets and it had with it many types of leaders. Dr. Rajendra Prasad presents the basic Indian tradition and more especially, our rural India. He is not an ordinary peasant. He is highly intellectual, a great educationist and an able lawyer.... It is a good fortune for us that we should have him still with us, not only because of his wisdom, his quiet dignity, but also because of this link that he has with the leadership that launched many a great struggle in this country, a reminder to us of those days. Morarji Desai called him a symbol of the Gandhian philosophy who had left deep impression on him. He was a rare person who not only believed in high ideals of simple living but also practised them. "Even Bapu consulted Rajen Babu on various issues." He was often remembered as a Ptaunch Gandhite, a fearless patriot, a religious soul, an erudite scholar and an unassuming modest human being. He was also a great educationist. He had deep connection with several educational institutions which flourished under his benevolent patronage. He opined, 'The question of education is all embracing. Our first ideal should be to extend the surface of education, even though we cannot raise its height, to bring light to the door of the rich and the poor alike '3 He was an ardent advocate of basic education. He believed that the scheme of basic education would give a practical character to our education, instead of its being mere bookish or theoretical. He was unhappy to note that education was getting more and more divorced from actual life and its requirements. This, in return, was responsible for the ever increasing unemployment among the educated classes. He realised the fact that one of the greatest needs of our time was the spread of education among our women. He opined that women should assume their rule as the ministers of the mind and the spirit of man. As Chairman of the Municipal Committee, Patna, Rajendra Prasad took to civic work with enthusiasm. At that time, there was a complete lack of civic amenities. The drains were uncovered and bred mosquitoes. There was proper arrangement for disposal of sewage. There was difficulty in getting pure milk in the town. Graft and bribery were rampant in the municipality. 'The only achievement we could claim during our term of office was the installation of a power house. Efforts were made to improve the living conditions of municipal sweepers In fact they were paid a very small amount; Rs. 12/-to men sweepers, Rs. 10/-to women and Rs. 5/-to children per month. They were given several concessions and gifts. 'There was a tragic aspect of local bodies which left a trail of misunderstanding and disunity. Hindu-Muslim riots had been occurring here and there since 1922. The Khilafat movement had petered out and with it the basis for joint endeavour. In Bihar, in spite of our best efforts, communal trouble rared its head and cast its shadow on the social and political life of the province. Unanimity of opinion on any problem receded into the background and only differences were accentuated. A prolific writer as he was, Rajendra Prasad wrote several works during his long political career. Very often he built up the themes of his writings in jails. The History of the Champaran Satyagraha was published in 1917. His Autobiography (Atmakatha) was at first published in 1946 in English in 1957. The other monumental work is India

Divided in which he gave comprehensive details about the political, social and economic developments in our country. A true Gandhian as he was, he also wrote At the Feet of Mahatma Gandhi., In this work, he depicted the teachings and philosophy of life of Mahatma Gandhi. During his school and college days he was a brilliant student. He always showed keenness to learn Indian languages in order to have a better mass contact. He learnt Hindi, Sanskrit, Urdu, Persian and English. This enabled him to give vent to his feelings in a more comprehensive way. As the President of India, from 1950 to 1962, he lived a very simple life. Undoubtedly he discharged his official duties like a noble soul. His lofty 'idealism integrity and noble character were examples for his colleagues. He tried to avoid political controversies and thus maintained decorum of the highest office in our country. Officially, he could draw Rs. 10,0001/-per month, but he drew only Rs. 2,500/-and after retirement led again a very simple life in the Sadaqat Ashram, Patna. On account of his patriotic services, he was awarded Bharat Ratna in 1963. At the time of his election as the President of the Constituent Assembly in December 1946, several leaders paid him tributes for his high calibre and meritorious services for the nation.

Dr. S. Radhakrishnan stated, 'In Dr. Prasad, we have one who embodies the spirit of gentleness, the gospel of India. He has the soul of goodness; he has great patience and courage; he has suffered-Rajendra Prasad is the suffering servant of India, of the Congress, who incarnated the spirit for which the country stands', Mrs. Sarojini Naidu opined that Rajendra Prasad was descended spiritually from the Great Buddha, the embodiment of compassion, understanding, sacrifice and love. He would make a reliable guardian and father of the Constituent Assembly because, 'in him there is essential wisdom that is part of his experience, there is essential clarity of vision, creative imagination and creative faith that brings him very near the feet of Lord Buddha himself.' At this point of time, Rajendra Prasad observed, 'Whatever the Constitution may or may not provide, the welfare of the country will depend on the way in which the country is administered. That will depend upon the man who administer it. It is a trite saying that a country can have only the Government it deserves. Our Constitution has provisions in it which appear to some to be objectionable from one point or another. We must admit that the defects are inherent in the situation in the country and the people at large. If the people who are elected are capable and men of character and integrity, they would be able to make the best even of a defective constitution. If they are lacking in these, the Constitution cannot help the country.

After all, a Constitution like a machine, is a lifeless thing. It requires life because of the men who control it and operate it, and India needs today nothing more than a set of honest men who will have the interests of the country before them. There is fissiparous tendency arising out of various elements in our life. We have communal differences, caste differences, language differences, provincial differences and so forth. It requires men of strong character, men of vision who will not sacrifice the interests of the Country at large for the sake of smaller groups and areas and who will rise over the prejudices which are born of these differences. We can only hope that the country will throw up such men in abundance. 'Mahatma Gandhi laid great stress on the purity of methods which had to be pursued for attaining our means. Let us not forget that his teaching has eternal value and was not intended only for the period of struggle but has as much authority and value today as it ever had before.' Rajendra Prasad's survey of the long-drawn political struggle speaks of his mental make-up and his ideology. "Fifty years ago the Indian National Congress met for the first time in Bombay with a small number of delegates who could hardly be called elected representatives, but who were nevertheless true servants of the people. Ever since then it has been striving for winning freedom for the people of India. In the beginning its aim was indefinite but it has always insisted on a democratic form of Government responsible to the people of India and representative of all communities and classes inhabiting the vast country. It started with the hopes and confidence that British statesmanship and the British Government would rise equal to the occasion and establish truly representative institutions giving the right to the people of India to government India in the interest of India.

The early history of the Congress is full of resolutions and speeches giving expression to this faith and confidence. The very demands of the Congress took the form of resolutions suggesting reforms and removal of objectionable measures-all having as their basis a hope that, if the British public and Parliament could be fully informed of this position in India and of the desire of Indians, they would set things right and ultimately confer on them the inestimable boon of self-Government. That hope and confidence have been gradually but nonetheless completely shattered by the action of the British Government in India and in England. The attitude of the British Government has become more and more expressive. The initial confidence in the intentions of the British Rule received a shock during the administration of Lord Curzon who partitioned Bengal, and the great agitation that followed against that ill-fated measure was an index of the rising tide of popular national consciousness which had not a little been influenced by world events, such as the victory of Japan over Russia in the beginning of the 20th century. But India had not yet lost faith and during the great war, partly as a result of this faith resuscitated by the annulment of the partition of Bengal and partly on account of want of proper appreciation of the situation as a whole, the country responded to the call of the British Government to help the British Empire in its time of need. India's splendid help was acknowledged by all British statesmen and hope was engendered that the war, which was being ostensibly fought for the principle of self-determination of nations and for making democracy safe, would result in the establishment of Responsible Government in India. The announcement made by the Secretary of State for India on behalf of the British Government in 1917 promising Self Government by stages occasioned difference of opinion amongst Indians which became more and more acute as the result of investigations undertaken by the Secretary of State and the Viceroy became known and the Bill, which ultimately became the Government of India Act in 1920, took shape and form.

During this time of incubation of the Bill the war had ended in a victory for the British, and the feeling grew in India that as the pressure in Europe had relaxed on account of the successful termination of the war for Britain, the British attitude had changed for the worse towards India. This feeling was confirmed and strengthened by what was regarded as breach of faith with in spite of the unanimous protest of t he country at large, of what were known as the Rowlatt Bills, thereby the stringent provision of the Defence of India Act which had been tolerated during the war were sought to be perpetuated, depriving the people of the elementary rights of free citizenship. These naturally created an intensive agitation in the whole country, and Satyagraha, which had been tried in South Africa, and in a small way in Champaran and in Kaira in India, was out forward by Mahatma Gandhi for the first time as a method to be adopted by the country whereby to secure redress of these and other grievances. There were unfortunate popular disturbances in the Punjab and Ahmedabad resulting in loss of life and property which were followed by the Jallianwala-bagh massacre and the horrors of the Martial Law regime in the Punjab. There was naturally great indignation throughout the country which was not assuaged by the Report of the Hunter Committee appointed to investigate into these happenings and was considerably intensified by the debate on the Report in Parliament. This Non-cooperation movement was inaugurated with its programme of resignation of titles of honour granted by the Government, boycott of Legislative bodies, Government-recognized educational institutions and Law Courts and of foreign cloth on the one hand, and on the other the establishment of Congress Committees, enrolment of Congress members, collection of Tilak Swaraj Fund, opening of national educational institutions, establishment of Panchayats for decision of village disputes and the revival of hand-spinning and hand-weaving, all to culminate by stages in a campaign of Civil Disobedience and non-payment of taxes.

The Congress Constitution was changed and its object was defined as the attainment of Swaraj by peaceful and legitimate means. There was country-wide awakening followed by repression by Government, when thousands of men and women including some of the most reputed leaders were imprisoned towards the end of 1921. Efforts at bringing about a settlement with the Government did not fructify and the programme of non-payment of taxes at Bardoli had to be suspended on account of serious disturbances at Chauri Chaura in the United Provinces. Subsequently the other items of the Non-cooperation programme were one after another suspended or withdrawn, and Congress members entered the Legislatures. The appointment by the British Parliament of what is known as the Simon Commission, from which Indians were excluded, for the purpose of investigating the working of the Constitution of 1920, led to another serious upheaval in the country and the Congress in association with other public bodies framed a Constitution with Dominion Status as the objective for India for the acceptance of the Government. In the absence of any adequate response by the Government, the Congress at its session at Lahore in December, 1929, changed its objective as the attainment of Purna Swaraj (Complete Independence) by legitimate and peaceful means, and organised a campaign of Civil Disobedience of non-moral laws and non-payment of taxes, in the beginning of 1930.

The Government of England on the one hand called a Conference in London to which it nominated certain Indians to advise it about a Constitution for India, and on the other adopted repressive measures, including the promulgation of a number of most drastic Ordinances for suppressing the Civil Disobedience movement in India. In March, 1931, there was a Pact entered into by Lord Irwin the Viceroy representing the Government, and Mahatma Gandhi representing the Congress, as a result of which Civil Disobedience was suspended and Mahatma Gandhi attended the Round Table Conference in London towards the end of 1931. As was to be expected, nothing came out of the Conference and the Congress was forced to revive the movement early in 1932 and carried it on till 1934, when it was suspended again. In the two movements of 1930 and 1932 hundreds of thousands of men and women and even children courted imprisonment, received lathi blows and other kinds of torture and suffered loss of property. Many were killed as a result of firing by the Government forces on crowds. The Satyagrahis showed remarkable power of organisation and suffering and were on the whole, completely non-violent in the face of the greatest provocation. Congress organisation showed great vitality and powers of adaptability and survived the great attack made on it by the Government. The country has come out of the fiery ordeal with credit but without achieving its great objective of Purna Swaraj. By a resolution passed at Karachi the Congress has assured to all Indians certain fundamental rights and has drawn up an economic and social programme. It has made it clear that, in order to end the exploitation of the masses, political freedom must include real economic freedom of the starving millions and has laid down fundamental rights of citizenship, such as freedom of speech and-conscience. It has also laid down that the interests of industrial labour shall be safeguarded by securing for them healthy conditions of work, limited hours of labour, suitable machinery for settlement of disputes and protection against economic consequences of old age, sickness and unemployment and the fight to form unions. It has assured the peasants to secure equitable adjustments of the burden on agricultural land by reduction of rent and revenue and exemption from rent or revenue for uneconomic holdings with such relief as may be quit and necessary to holders of small estates affected, by such exemption or reduction in rent. It has also provided for a graded tax on net incomes from land above a reasonable minimum, death duties on a graduated scale on property above a fixed income, and drastic reduction of expenditure on military and defence and civil administration, fixing the salary of State servants at a maximum of Rs. 500 per month. It has also laid down an economic and social programme of excluding foreign cloth, protecting indigenous industries, prohibition of intoxicating 'drugs and drinks.

State control of key industries, relief to agricultural indebtedness, regulation of currency and exchange in the interest of the country and provision for the military training of citizens for national defence. The last session of the Congress at Bombay in October, 1934, endorsed the policy of entering the Legislatures and laid down a constructive programme including revival of an(encouragement to hand-spinning and hand-weaving, promotion of useful village and small industries, re-construction of village life in its economic, educational, social and hygienic aspects, removal of untouchability, promotion of inter-communal unity, total abstinence, national education, spread of useful knowledge among the adult population, organisation of industrial labour and peasants and strengthening of the Congress organisation. Under a revised Constitution it reduced the number of delegates and 'made it proportionate to the number of primary members on the Congress roll and insisted on manual labour and habitual wearing of Khadi on all elected members and office-bearers of Congress Committees. The Congress has thus marched on from stage to stage and covers practically every sphere of national activity. It is at present engaged in constructive work which is calculated not only to improve the economic condition of the masses but also to create that self-confidence among them which can be born of work accomplished and which can enable them to win Purna Swaraj. Starting as a small organisation it now covers the entire country with a network of branches and enjoys the confidence of the masses of the country. It has called forth sacrifice on an extensive scale for the attainment of Swaraj from people of all classes and has a remarkable record of work and achievement. The organisation itself is a great national asset which it should be the duty of every Indian to increase and preserve. It is bound to play an ever increasing part in the struggle for freedom that still lies ahead. This is no time for resting on our oars.

The work yet to be accomplished is great and needs much patient toil, endless sacrifice and unflinching determination. It is nothing less than the attainment of Purna Swaraj. Let us bow down our heads to all those men, women, and children, known and unknown, who have laid down their lives, who have suffered woes and privations, and who are still paying the penalty for loving their Motherland. Let us also in grateful reverence recall the services of those who sowed the seeds of this mighty organisation, who nurtured it with their unremitting labour and sacrifice. The small seedling that was planted fifty years ago has now grown into a mighty tree with branches spreading over this vast country and has now blossomed in the sacrifice of countless men and women. It is for those that are now left behind to nourish the tree by their further services and sacrifice, so that it may bear fruit and make India the free and prosperous country that Nature intended her to be. The pages that follow relate the story of the growth of the Indian National Congress. The author's knowledge and experience of the men and affairs of the Congress is wide. He himself has played the inconsiderable part in the later phases of its development. He is not a detached historian writing after the events and basing his conclusions on cold recorded facts. He has seen things with his own eyes and has himself acted and reacted on them. He is willing not only with knowledge but also with faith. His conclusions and opinions are therefore his own, and need not be treated a in every case representing the official view of the Working Committee of the Indian National Congress which publishes the book and sends it out to the world. It is hoped, however, that it contains a faithful record of facts and will be found helpful to students of contemporary history.

Resolution of Lahore

The following resolution of the Muslim League at Lahore had deep implications on the line of action taken by the Congress and its prominent leaders including Rajendra Prasad, The All-India Muslim League at its Lahore Session in March 1940 passed the following resolution :

(a) While approving and endorsing the action taken by the Council and the Working Committee of the All-India Muslim League, as indicated in their resolutions dated the 7th of August, 17th and 18th of September and 22nd of October, 1939, and 3rd of February 1940 on constitutional issue, this Session of the All-India Muslim League emphatically reiterates that the scheme of federation embodied in the Government of India Act, 1935, is totally unsuited to, and unworkable in the peculiar conditions of this country and is altogether unacceptable to Muslim India.

(b) It further records its emphatic view that while the declaration dated the 18th of October 1939, made by the Viceroy on behalf of His Majesty's Government is reassuring, in so far as it declares that the policy and plan on which the Government of India Act, 1935, is based will be reconsidered in consultation with the various parties, interests and communities in India, Muslim India will not be satisfied unless the whole constitutional plan is reconsidered de novo and that no revised plan would be acceptable to the Muslims unless it is framed with their approval and consent.

(c) Resolved that it is the considered view of this Session of the All-India Muslim League that no constitutional plan would be workable in this country or acceptable to Muslims unless it is designed on the following basic principle, viz. that geographically contiguous units are demarcated into regions which should be so constituted, with such territorial readjustments as may be necessary, that the areas in which the Muslims are numerically in a majority as in the North-Western and eastern zones of India should be grouped to constitute 'Independent States' in which the constituent units shall be autonomous and sovereign.

(d) That adequate, effective and mandatory safeguards should be specifically provided in the constitution for minorities in these units and in these regions for the protection of their religious, cultural, economic, political, administrative and other rights and interests in consultation with them; and in other parts of India where the Musalmans are in a minority. adequate, effective and mandatory safeguards shall be specially provided in the constitution for them and other minorities for the protection of their religious,

> cultural, economic, political, administrative and other rights and interests in consultation with them. This Session further authorizes the Working Committee to frame a scheme of constitution in accordance with these basic principles, providing for the assumption finally by the respective regions of all powers such as defence, external affairs, communications, customs, and such other matters as may be necessary. It appears from the resolution that it deals with the scheme of federation embodied in the Government of India Act, 1935, which it considers totally unsuited to, and unworkable in the peculiar conditions of this country and hence altogether unacceptable to Muslim India.

After recording its emphatic view that the Muslims of India will not be satisfied unless the whole constitutional plan is reconsidered de novo and that no revised plan would be acceptable to the Muslims unless it is framed with their approval and consent, it proceeds to lay down the basic principle on which any plan to be workable and acceptable to the Muslims should be based. That basic principle is that geographically contiguous units are demarcated into regions which should be so constituted with such territorial readjustments as may be necessary, that the areas in which the Muslims are numerically in a majority as in the North-Western and Eastern Zones of India should be grouped to constitute 'Independent States' in which the constituent units shall be autonomous and sovereign.

The resolution then proceeds to lay down that adequate, effective and mandatory safeguards should be specifically provided in the constitution for minorities in the regions for the protection of their religious, cultural, economic, political, administrative and other rights and interests in consultation with them and similar safeguards are to be provided for the protection of Musalmans and other minorities in other parts of India where the Musalmans are in a minority. The League authorized its Working Committee to frame a scheme of constitution in accordance with these principles providing for the assumption finally by the respective regions of all powers such as defence, external affairs, communications, customs, and such other matters as may be necessary. No scheme prepared by the Working Committee of the League as authorized by the Resolution has yet been published, even if it has been framed. Mr. M.A. Jinnah, the President of the Muslim League, declared at Madras as follows : 'Let me tell you as clearly as I can possibly do so that the goal of the All-India Muslim League is that we want to establish a completely independent state in the North-West and Eastern Zones of India with full control finally of defence, currency, exchange, etc. We do not want under any circumstances a constitution of an all-India character with one Government at the Centre.' When invited to elaborate the scheme and furnish details as regards the territories to be included in the Regions and other matters he has refused to do so, insisting that the principle should be first accepted and then and only then will he be prepared to work out or disclose details. So late as the last week of April 1944, during the course of discussions that were taking place between Mr. Jinnah and-Malik Khizir Hayat Khan, Premier of the Punjab, regarding Mr. Jinnah's proposal to establish a Muslim League or Muslim-League Coalition Ministry instead of the Unionist Party Ministry in the Punjab, the non-Muslim ministers desired that 'in order to enable all concerned to judge the merits of the scheme its precise political and constitutional implications (should be) fully explained, and the geographical boundaries of the Punjab under the scheme of Pakistan as well as the principles to be adopted for the fixation of such boundaries (should be) indicated as clearly as possible on which the comment of Mr. Jinnah was that it was 'an all-Indian question and irrelevant for the present purpose of forming the proposed coalition.' It is difficult to understand this reluctance on the part of the President of the League to disclose the scheme in its entirety, if there is a scheme ready. It would be unreasonable to suppose that a responsible body claiming to represent the Muslim Community of India would propound a theory and propose a scheme for the partition of the country without fully working out the implications of the former and the details of the latter. On the other hand one would naturally expect that if the League desires its scheme to be considered and adopted on its merits, it should be willing, if not anxious, to furnish such elucidation as may be desired by other in respect of mere details but are of a fundamental nature whose knowledge is essential for a fair consideration of it. For example, it is necessary to know what areas, according to the Resolution, will fall in Pakistan, and which areas will constitute the Hindustan of the League conception. Similarly it is essential to know what the size of the non-Muslim minority in Pakistan and of the Muslim minority in Hindustan will be and what the safeguards and guarantees are that the League considers sufficient for the protection of the non-Muslim minorities in Pakistan and what safeguards and guarantees it would assist upon for Muslim minorities in Hindustan. It is not enough for the League to say that it A ill vouchsafe the same safeguards to non-Muslim minorities that Hindustan will guarantee to the Muslim minorities. No other group has put forward any scheme of partition and claimed or proposed to guarantee Minority rights from or to others. It is, therefore, up to the

League to formulate its own proposals for the consideration Of others no less than of Muslims themselves. Again, any scheme Of reciprocity may prove unworkable on account of the size of the minority in the none part or the other.

For example, if the minority happens to be something between 40 and 50 per cent of the total population in one part and only about 10 per cent or so in the other part, it is obvious that a large minority of 40 or 45 per cent will be in a very much better position than a minority of say 10 per cent or thereabouts to enforce and implement the guarantee by its own inherent strength. It may also be that reciprocity may not be acceptable when what One may offer may prove of so little value to the other that it is no inducement.

The matter may be put in a concrete form. Suppose the Hindus of North-Western and Eastern Zones, and particularly of the Punjab and Bengal, say that although they are in a minority in their Provinces they do not want any concession or weightage in representation in the Legislature or in public services for themselves, that they are content if they get representation according to their proportion in the population and that such weightage as may be demanded by or conceded to other minorities like the Christians should be given by the majority community out of its own share; suppose further that they say that because they do not demand any concession or weightage for themselves, no concession or weightage should be given to the Muslims in the Provinces where they are in a minority and that the Hindu majority in those Provinces should give such concession or weightage as may be required to other minorities like the Christians.

The matter might be put in another way by the Hindus of Provinces in which they are in a majority. Suppose they say that they are not prepared to concede any weightage to the Muslim minority in their Provinces and that the Muslims of the Provinces in which they are in a majority need not give any weightage to the-Hindu minority in their Provinces. Let us also suppose that in both the above cases the Hindus all over the country whether they are in a minority or majority adopted this attitude, the position would be on a basis of perfect and complete reciprocity and no objection could be taken to it on that ground. There is no reason why the Hindus may not adopt this attitude. In Bengal the Hindus would stand to gain. In place of 32 per cent of the seats in the Legislature as given by the Act of 193 5, they will get 44 per cent. In the Punjab also their position will improve to a small extent. In services instead of 50 per cent given to them they would get about 44 per cent in Bengal and their position in the Punjab will remain more or less unaffected. The Hindus of the North-West Frontier Province, Sind and Baluchistan will stand to lose to an appreciable extent but their total population is only 14.50 lakhs and the total number of seats in the Legislatures and posts in services that they will lose will be negligible. Let us see what the Muslims of a single Province like Bihar will stand to lose against this. Their representation in the Legislature and in services will have to be reduced from 25 per cent to 12 per cent and the number of seats and posts they will lose in one Province will be considerable-more then all the seats and posts that the Hindus will lose in both the Muslim zones put together. The number of Muslims affected by this cut in one single Province will be 47 lakhs against 14 50 lakhs of Hindus affected in the North-Western Zone. The position of Muslims in regard to the rest of the Hindu zone can easily be imagined. Reciprocity thus will have no attraction for the Hindus and will not induce them to offer any concession or weightage to the Muslims. Again, each party should be made clearly to understand what sanction will be constituted to enforce the guarantee. I have indicated only some of the points amongst many with which the whole scheme bristles, that require elucidation and elaboration, for a fair and reasonable discussion and understanding acceptance of it. The two nations theory also has its implications which have to be understood. It appears that the protagonists of Pakistan base themselves on the religion of Islam and the social and political system which may be derived from it, for treating the Muslims as a separate nation. Other attributes which are generally supposed to attach to a nation do not apply to Muslims alone as such, and are shared in common by Muslims and non-Muslims of particular areas of India.

Thus, in the matter of language the Punjabi Hindu, the Punjabi Muslim and the Punjabi Sikh speak the same language irrespective of their religions. So do all the Pathans, whether Muslims or Hindus, of the N.W.F.P. speak Pushto alike. And so do all Bengalis whether Hindu or Muslim-speak the same language, Bengali. In all these areas they occupy the same land. In all these places they have lived under the same Government with the rest of British India during the British period for over one hundred years at least-even if we leave out the long period of Muslim rule. Religion being put forward as practically the sole criterion, it is well worth remembering that people agreeing with one another in many if not most other things that matter but differing in religion, inhabit this country from one end to the other. It is reported that commenting on this aspect of the question M r. Edward Thompson put it to Mr. Jinnah that it would imply two nations confronting each other in every village and in every street and that it was a terrible prospect to contemplate. Mr. Jinnah is said to have replied that it was a terrible prospect but there was no alternative. Mr. Jinnah has recently in a press statement contradicted that he ever gave a Press interview to Mr. Thompson or that he said the words attributed to him. But whether he said what is attributed to him to Mr. Thompson in a Press interview or otherwise or at all is beside the point and cannot alter the fact that the only result that can follow from a two nations theory on the basis of religion is the emergence and establishment of two nations in every village and every street of India. If a Muslim in any part of India by reason of his religion alone belongs to a nation comprising all Muslims in any and every other corner of India and separate from all non-Muslims including those adjacent to him, then the question naturally arises-to what state does the Muslim owe allegiance.

To the state within which he lives and moves and which may not be a Muslim state-not falling within 'Pakistan-or to a distant Muslim state with which he may have no connection except that a majority of people living in it follow the same religion as be does? The same question will arise in regard to a non-Muslim living in a Muslim state, unless it is postulated that whereas the Muslims can and do constitute a nation, all others are formless without the essential attribute of a nation-a single religion. Or will such a Muslim or non-Muslim have a double personality and divided allegiance How will such divided allegiance work in an emergency like a war? Another set of question arises in regard to the status of such a member of a separate nation. Ordinarily a man living within the territory of a particularly state, whatever his previous nationality may have been, becomes on fulfilling certain conditions a citizen of that state. That gives him a status, confers certain rights, and imposes certain responsibilities. If the Muslim in India is a member of the Muslim Nation by reason of his religion, irrespective of the fact whether the state in which he resides is a Muslim or non-Muslim state, then can he claim and can he in justice and fairness be given the status of a citizen of that state when it does not happen to be a Muslim state? Is he not more in the nature of an alien there, looking for protection and other advantages that citizenship confers, to his Muslim state which will be his national state? He can claim the rights and privileges, if any, of an alien. There is a difference which cannot be slurred over or ignored between aliens working and carrying on business within the territory of the state of another nation, and members of the same nation working and carrying on business within their own territory but being in a minority as compared with other groups of the same nation.

The minority consists of members of the same nation and has rights which are well recognized. Aliens cannot have the same rights as a minority in a nation. So Muslims in Provinces and States where non-Muslims will be in a minority will not be able to claim the rights of a minority, if at the same time they claim to be members of another nation. This will be true of non-Muslims also in Muslim States, if they claim to be members of another nation. If the Muslim League wants Muslim States in the North West and East of India for the purpose of running them according to the Muslim conception of a state, the question arises what will be the status of non-Muslims in those states? Are they to be treated as equal citizens of the state or are they to have an inferior status? The Muslim public law recognizes a distinction between Muslims and Zimmis. Are non-Muslim to get the status of Zimmis or of equal citizens as in a modern democratic state? Mr. A.S. Tritton of the Muslim University, Aligarh, has written a book, The Caliphs and their non-

Muslim Subjects, in which he has discussed at great length the position of non-Muslims in the Muslim states under the Caliphs. It is not possible to summarize the book here and content myself with quoting a few sentences from the concluding chapter of the book. Mr. Tritton says : The rule of Islam was often burdensome, the revolt in Egypt proved it. Umar II might order a governor to distribute the surplus cash in his treasury among the Dhimmis after the needs of the Muslims had been satisfied, but as a rule they had to provide the money which the state wanted and got nothing for it. Probably, at first, the subjects did not pay heavier taxes then they had paid to the previous Governments, but in one way and another the burden grew steadily heavier.

There can be no doubt that, at the end of the first century, the reign of Umar II saw the beginning of definite disabilities for the Dhimmis. Restrictions were placed on their dress, and the attempt to oust them from official posts began during the second century the Muslim spirit hardened... the laws about dress were made more stringent, and the idea took shape that churches might not be built... It is only fair to say that the conduct of the rulers was often better than the law demanded... On paper, many things were forbidden them [Dhimmis], the public celebration of weddings and funerals, feasts, and church ceremonies. It was a punishable offence to tread intentionally on the skirt of a Muslim's garment and they had to leave the centre of the road to the Muslims... 'Muttasim brought the monastery of Samara that stood where he wanted to build a palace. Other Caliphs destroyed churches to obtain materials for their buildings, and the mob was already ready to village churches and monasteries. They, Dhimmis, might enjoy great prosperity, yet always they lived on sufferance, exposed to the caprice of the ruler and the passions of the mob. The episode of Al Hakim must be regarded as the freak of a madman, and not typical of Islam. But in later times the position of the Dhimmis did change for the worse. They were much liable to suffer from the violence 0" the crowd, and the popular fanaticism was accompartied by an increasing strictness among the educated. The spiritual isolation of Islam was accomplished. The world was divided into two classes, Muslims and others, and only Islam counted. There were brilliant exceptions, but the general statement is true. If a Muslim gave any help to the religion of a Dhimmi, he was summoned thrice to repentance, and then, if obdurate, he was to be put to death. Indeed, the general feeling was that the leavings of the Muslims were good enough for the Dhimmis.' It has been expressly stated by some writers who have written in support of Pakistan that the state contemplated by them will be a Muslim state. They think that means justice to all. In view of what has been quoted above, non-Muslims may not accept that opinion and it is necessary to have a clear and well-defined scheme to enable a correct Judgement to be formed on it. It is thus clear that the demand for elucidation and elaboration of the bald Lahore Resolution is clearly justified. The League, before it propounded the theory of two nations and put forward the scheme of partition, must have considered those and many other questions of a similar nature, and if it wants others who are not within it-whether they are Muslims or non-Muslims-to accept its programme, it must be prepared to share with them its solutions of these and similar knotty problems that arise, unless it wants them to vote for partition blindfolded. It would be uncharitable to suggest that the League wants others to commit themselves to a vague general theory and to an undefined scheme; and then gradually to unfold the implications and details, to force them to accept the implications and details so unfolded, and in case of their inability to subscribe to the latter in spite of their acceptance of the former, to charge them with bad faith and with having gone back on their previous acceptance. But the way in which the matter is being exposed to public view lends support to this uncharitable suggestion. At first the League President insisted that the principle of partition should be accepted first and cited the instance of a joint Hindu family in which when a partition has to take place the principle has first to be accepted and then the details of partition are worked out. This position has since been changed. When Mr. C. Rajagopalachari, with the consent and approval of Gandhiji, put forward a concrete scheme which, he claimed, fulfilled the terms of the Lahore resolution of the League, Mr. Jinnah denounced it in unmeasured terms. It may be pointed out how the position has shifted. When Mr. Jinnah announced his decision to receive Mahatma Gandhi at his Bombay house, he after denouncing the C.R. formula stated : 'Mr. Gandhi has, at any rate in his personal capacity, accepted the principle of partition or division of India. What remains now is the question of bow and when this has got to be carried out.'

After the declaration one would have thought that the principle of partition or division-on which such emphasis was laid before the details could be released or worked out-having been accepted, the next step would be to tackle the details and Mr. Jinnah would put forward his scheme and show how and wherein it differed from the 'maimed, mutilated and moth-eaten Pakistan' of Mr. Rajagopalachari. But in the prolonged discussions which followed and the results of which are embodied in the letters exchanged between Gandhiji and Mr. Jinnah, fresh demands are made for acceptance of the two nations theory and of the Lahore

Resolution in its entirely before any further progress can be made with the elaboration of the details of the scheme. Once again the insistence is on acceptance of a bald general principle and bald general proposal for partition as distinguished from the mere principle of partition which in Mr. Jinnah's own words had been already accepted by Gandhiji.

The acceptance of the proposition that the principle of partition should be accepted before details can be discussed has led not to the discussion of the details, but to a further demand for the acceptance of the theory of two nations which is said to underlie the whole idea of partition and of the Lahore Resolution. One wonders what further demands will be made if these two are also accepted. This is a natural result of insistence on a piece-meal consideration of the scheme of partition and the principle underlying it.

Proposal for Framing of Constitution by the British

Since the Muslim League passed the Pakistan resolution at its Lahore session in March 1940, various schemes have been put forward with a view to meeting the legitimate desires of the Muslims of India. These may be treated as alternatives to Pakistan. The first and foremost place should be given to the Draft Declaration of the British War Cabinet which has become popularly known as the Cripps proposal on account of its being first known to India by Sir Stafford Cripps. We are concerned here only with that part of it which deals with the nature of the Indian Union and the agency for drawing up a constitution for it, and not with the ad interim arrangement proposed in it nor with the negotiations which Sir Stafford Cripps carried on and the ultimate outcome thereof. The Draft Declaration was intended to 'Jay down in precise and clear terms the steps which they [His Majesty's Government] propose shall be taken for the earliest possible realization of Self Government in India. The object is the creation of a new Indian Union which shall constitute a Dominion, associated with the United Kingdom and the other Dominions by a common allegiance to the Crown, but equal to them in every respect, in no way subordinate in any respect of its domestic or external affairs.' Immediately upon the cessation of hostilities steps shall be taken to set up in India, in the manner described hereafter, an elected body changed with the task of framing a new Constitution for India,' with provision 'for the participation of the Indian States in the Constitution Making Body', and 'His Majesty's Government undertake to accept and implement forthwith the Constitution so framed subject only to :

'(i) the right of any Province of British India that is not prepared to accept the new Constitution to retain its present constitutional position, provision being made for its subsequent accession if it so decides.

With such non-acceding Provinces, should they so desire, His Majesty's Government will be prepared to agree upon a new constitution, giving them the same full status as the Indian Union, and arrived at by a procedure analogous to that here laid down.

(ii) the signing of a Treaty which shall be negotiated between His Majesty's Government and the Constitution Making Body covering all necessary matters arising out of the complete transfer of responsibility from British to Indian hands and for the protection of racial and religions minorities : but, will not impose any restriction on the power of the Indian Union to decide in the future its relation to the other Member States of the British Commonwealth.

The Constitution Making Body shall be composed as follows unless the leaders of Indian opinion in the principal communities agree upon some other form before the end of hostilities. 'Immediately upon the result bring known of the provincial elections which will be necessary at the end of hostilities, there entire membership of the Lower Houses of the Provincial Legislatures shall, as a single, electoral college, proceed to the election of the Constitution Making Body by the system of proportional representation. This new body shall be number about one-tenth of the number of the electoral college. Indian States shall be invited to appoint representatives in the same proportion to their total population as in the case of the representatives of British India as a whole, and with the same powers as the British Indian members. It will appear from the summary given above that the British Government proposed that steps should be taken on the cessation of hostilities to create a new Indian Union which would have the full status of a Dominion with the power to secede, if it so chose, from the British Common weal t h. The new constitution was to be framed by a Constitution Making Body which was to be elected by the method of proportional representation by an electoral college consisting of all the members of the Lower Houses of the Provincial Legislatures for which fresh elections would have been held. It would also have representatives appointed by the Indian States would be in the same proportion to the province, representation as their population bears to the population of the Provinces.

The Constitution framed by the Constitution Making Body be accepted and implemented by the British Government subject to the proviso that any Province which was not prepared to accept the new Constitution would be free not to accede to the Union and would be entitled to frame a constitution of its own and to have the same status as the Indian Union. There would be a treaty negotiated between the British Government and the Constitution Making Body covering all matters arising out of a transfer of responsibility and the protection of racial and religious minorities. It did not start with separate independent States but with an Indian Union, leaving it to any Province which did not accept the Constitution not to accede to the Union and to have the same status vis-a-vis the British Government as the Indian Union. In the words of Professor Coupland, the British Government had already clearly stated its objective as a new Indian Union to form a Dominion under a new constitution for India. No one can read the Draft Declaration without recognising that the non-adherence provisions are intended only as a means of preventing in the last resort a breakdown of the whole scheme for setting India free. It was principally for this reason that the Muslim League rejected the Draft Declaration in that it did not contain a definite pronouncement in favour of partition, and while it recognized Pakistan b implication, it relegated the creation of more than one Union to the realm of remote possibility. In his Presidential address at the Allahabad session of the All-India Muslim League on April 4,1942, Mr. Jinnah was quite clear and rejected the scheme on the grounds (i) that its main objective was the creation of a new Indian Union; the alleged power of the minority the matter of secession suggested in the document was illusory; (ii) that the Constitution Making Body would be a sovereign body, elected from amongst the members of the eleven Assemblies meeting together as one college by means of proportional representation, no' separate electorates. Musalmans even by separate representation would not be more than 25 per cent in it but by the system of proportional representation they might be less in number; its decisions would be taken by a bare majority and so it was a dead certainty that from it would emerge a constitution for an All-India Union; (iii) that the most vital point was as to how a province or provinces would exercise their right not to accede-that if a Province in the Legislative Assembly of the Province was in favour of accession by sixty per cent votes, then that would be the end of it; but if they got fifty-nine per cent and the minority happened to forty-one per cent, then there would be a plebiscite of the people of the Province.

Thus, the entity and integrity of the Muslim nation had not been recognized; territorial entity of the provinces which are mere accidents of British policy was over-emphasized and the right of national self-determination of Muslims as distinguished from that of the two nations put together was not unequivocally recognized. In the Legislative Assemblies of the Punjab and Bengal-the two largest Muslim majority Provinces, the Muslims were not in a majority and the Muslims would be at the mercy of the Hindu minority; and in the N.W.F.P. and Sind the weightage given to non-Muslims would make it extremely difficult for Muslims to realize their goal. The scheme was thus not acceptable because Pakistan was not conceded unequivocally and the right of Muslim self-determination was denied, although the recognition given to the principle of partition was much appreciated. Statement issued on the political situation by the Congress Working Committee at its meeting held at Wardha from 17 to 21 June 1940. The Working Committee have been deeply moved by the tragic events that have taken place in Europe in startling succession and in particular by the misfortunes that have befallen the people of France. These events have already had far-reaching consequences and they are likely to be followed by other happenings which will lead to novel situations and complex problems. Ever since the commencement of the European War the Congress has followed a policy which was confirmed in the Ramgarh Resolution based on the principles of the Congress, and the attitude of the British Government towards the demand that India should function as a free and independent country. The manner of the application of this policy will necessarily depend on the situation which changes from day to day. Problems which were distant are now near at hand and may soon demand solution.

The problem of the defence of the country against possible external aggression and internal disorder has-attained urgency and importance. The war in Europe, resulting from a desire for imperialist domination over other peoples and countries and suicidal race in armaments has led to human sorrow and misery on a scale hitherto unknown. It has demonstrated the inefficacy or organised violence on however vast a scale for the defence of national freedom and the liberties of peoples. It has shown beyond a doubt that warfare cannot lead to peace and freedom, and the choice before the world is uttermost degradation and destruction through warfare or the way of peace and non-violence on a basis of freedom for all peoples. Mahatma Gandhi has presented to the peoples of the world, crying for relief from the crushing burden of war, a weapon in the shape of organised non-violence designed to take the place of war for the defence of a people's rights and freedom against armed aggression.

Mahatma Gandhi feels that at this critical phase in the history of the nations the Congress should enforce this ideal by itself declaring that it does not want that India should maintain armed forces to defend her freedom against external aggression or internal disorder. While the Working

Committee holds that the Congress must continue to adhere strictly to the principle of non-violence in its struggle for independence, the Committee cannot ignore the present imperfections and failings in this respect of the human elements they have to deal with and the possible dangers in a period of transition until the Congress has acquired nonviolent control over the people in adequate measure and the people have imbibed sufficiently the lesson of organised nonviolence. The Committee have deliberated over the problem that has thus arisen and have come to the settled policy of the Congress beyond assail. It must be admitted this success cannot be claimed for non-violent effort in the case of communal riots. The W.C. are of opinion that the fault must be laid at the door of volunteer organisations. The W.C. hope that at this critical hour in the history of India volunteer organisations would be able effectively to deal with riots and the like in a non-violent manner. The Working Committee never had occasion to determine whether India can be defended non-violently, nor is it even now called upon to do so, though the proved futility of violence to defend the nations of Europe is sufficient indication for the W.C. for coming to a decision. But till the hour for taking a final decision arrives, the W.C. must keep an open mind. But so far as the present is concerned, the W.C. are jointly of opinion that in pursuance of their non-violent policy Congressmen must not have anything to do with military training activities calculated to make India military-minded. Therefore the W.C. cannot but view with grave alarm the attempt made in an organised manner to prepare India for war. If India were free and independent without any army she would have no fear of external aggression. The best defence that free India can put up if the people accepted the Congress policy would be to cultivate friendliness with the whole world. To invest crores of rupees in armaments, fortresses and the like would be to invite foreign attack. The W.C. believe that India is too poor to invest money in costly defence forces and modern equipment. The W.C. therefore warn the British Government against the feverish preparations that they are making for the professed defence of India. They are of opinion that they are intended merely to help Britain. These preparations cannot help India in any real sense. The W.C. draw the attention of the British Government and people that although India is claimed by their to have Provincial Autonomy and every Province has elected assemblies, and there is also a partially popularly elected Centra" Legislative Assembly, the huge expense is being incurred without any reference to these legislatures. The W.C. believe that it is wrong and immoral to arm one man, however honest and distinguished with unlimited powers to utilise the resources of a great count like India and to impress her people in any manner he chooses without any control or check on the part of her people. It is a procedure in no way in keeping with the British Government's declarations, however unsatisfactory from the Congress standpoint, about the freedom of India. The W.C. wish to declare that the Congress claims to be wholly friendly to the British people. But the friendliness and goodwill can have no play and no meaning, so long as India remains in helpless bondage and her resources in men and money are utilised without ascertaining the wishes of the representatives of the people elected under a system established by Great Britain.

The W.C. ask the British Government to revise their suicidal policy and take the popular assemblies into their confidence. The W.C. associate themselves with the appeal recently made by Gandhiji to every Briton and hope that Great Britain will accept the policy of non-violence whose potency has been proved beyond doubt even though its application was admittedly imperfect. British Government may rely upon the fullest and friendliest cooperation of the Congress in the direction of peace effort in the non-violent way commended by Gandhiji. In spite of the repeated and firm declarations of the Congress to the contrary, there seems to be a belief among the public, including even some Congressmen, that the Congress will be satisfied with Dominion Status.

The W.C. warn to concerned that they will accept no status lower than complete independence and that declaration should be made now and given effect to immediately so far as may be. The legal formality may await a suitable future period. Only India free and independent in action can decide upon the part she should play in the present war. There is talk among some Congressmen that the Congress may countenance resumption of ministerial office.

The W.C. wish to make it clear that there is no prospect of the Congress countenancing such a step without a satisfactory settlement with the Government and in no case of promoting a war effort in which they have no faith. In view of the foregoing it is superfluous to say that the W.C. cannot associate themselves with any Government proposals to expand the Central Executive. In view of the recent development the W.C. decide to remove the ban upon Congress members of the Central Legislative Assembly attending its sessions. In as much as it is necessary still further to enforce strict discipline, the W.C. ask all those who do not strictly believe in non-violence to resign from the Congress. It is against the Congress constitution for anyone to become a four-anna member unless he, believing in it, signs the Congress pledge. Mahatma Gandhi wrote to

Lord Linlithgow on 30 July 1940. I think it will be mutually helpful if I reduce to writing the substance of the advice I tendered you yesterday as a personal friend and friend of the British. I had made it clear at the outset that I had no representative capacity and that, after the last resolution of the Working Committee, I could only speak as an individual in any case. Your first proposal was to advise H.M.G. to let you announce that a status similar to that of the self-governing Dominions would be granted to India within one year of the termination of the war, subject to an agreed understanding about British commercial interests, defence, external relations, rights of minorities and the position of the Princes-regard being had to treaty obligations with them.

Granted these reservations, a Constituent Assembly may draw up the Constitution which, unless there were unacceptable provisions, will be adopted by H.M.G. and placed before Parliament for acceptance. I said as to this that I personally could never accept it and that so far as I know, the Congress also would never approve of it. My strong advice was that it should not be put before the Secretary of State or before India. Any such announcement would further embitter the relations between H.M.G. and India. I stressed the point that nothing short of immediate, unequivocal declaration of independence, free of all control by the British Government, would be accepted by the Congress. (India free will no doubt have to negotiate a treaty, I hope, of partnership, with Great Britain, will have to make provision for protection of legitimate foreign interests, guarantee to the full the rights of the minorities and make adequate arrangements with the Princes consistently with due protection of the people living within their jurisdiction. All this is inherent in the non-violence policy of the Congress.

For, its predominant sanction will be, not the force of arms behind it, but its sense of fairness and absolute justice. In the absence of these two, independence will go as soon as obtained. The thought thus expressed parenthetically was not put before you as part of my advice. I see as I am writing this letter that it was incomplete without it.)

The question of drawing of the Constitution by a Constituent Assembly might be postponed to a future suitable date. I suggested too that it would be a catastrophe not to make the aforesaid unequivocal declaration of Independence, for whilst the Congress was openly pledged to it and had been fighting for it persistently and consistently for a long time, all parties, whether it be the Muslim League or the Hindu Mahasabha or even the Princes, could not but prize Independence, if it could be had. Therefore it passed [my] comprehension why there should be so much ado about making the overdue declaration that India was free of all external control. Your second proposal was that subject to the acceptance of the proposed declaration, and pending the war, you would increase the number of [members of] the Executive Council so as to include representatives of various parties. As to this I advised that without the vital declaration of Independence, the Congress was not likely to serve on the Council. I added that I adhered to the view expressed in a recent Harijan article of mine, entitled 'Two Parties'. Unless the parties had one mind on the question of fighting for immediate independence, and the method thereof, no joint effort was possible. You had also in mind a proposal to convene a miniature Round Table Conference composed of representatives of various parties, groups and interests. I strongly dissuaded you from entertaining any such proposal as being doomed to failure. I then enlarged upon my confirmed opinion that time had arrived for a revision of Britain's war policy. Frank recognition of German superiority in organisation and technique would be no derogation from British valour and would add to it because of conformity to truth. Even if it were otherwise, and Britain could show her superiority to Germans in every department and defeat them, given sufficient time, my proposition would still hold.

In order to prove its validity, admission of German superiority is unnecessary. As you know, I had made this suggestion before the fall of France. My proposition is based purely on humanitarian grounds. I have chosen the present time as being opportune for pressing it. Assuming that Nazis are as bad as they are said to be, victory must be unattainable without copying the Nazi methods. That would mean no deliverance from Nazism. Sufficient has happened to prove the utter futility of armament for the protection of small nations, no matter how brave they are. Britain's victory after the slaughter and ruthlessness which it must involve could never make the world safe for democracy nor bring it peace. Such a victory must mean another preparation for a war more inhuman than the present, as this one had proved more inhuman than the last. For this and similar reasons I urged with all the earnestness and force at my command that if Britain could accept the non-violent method, it would redound to her eternal glory and would count for much greater bravery than her proverbial bravery in war. I hoped too that it would not be retorted that I had no warrant for appealing to Britain suddenly to accept the nonviolent method when I had failed in persuading my colleagues and co-workers to accept it when the time had come for its enforcement in its fullness. I said in anticipation of the possibility of such a retort that my colleagues and I represent a weak and subject people wholly unarmed and untrained in the use of arms. The non-violence of my conception was essentially for those who were conscious of their ability to wield them with effect.

Therefore I suggested that if Britain could be convinced of the superiority of non-violence over violence, now was the psychological moment for the full adoption of the non-violent method. Britain with all her intentions could not protect Abyssinia, Czechoslovakia, Poland, Finland, Norway, Denmark, Holland, Belgium and France. If Britain could accept the method presented by me, it would point to all these countries the way of deliverance and ensure the peace of the world as no other method ever would or could. It would confound Nazi wisdom and put all the Nazi armaments out of use. Lastly, I said that my proposal was based on practical experience of non-violence extending over half a century of ceaseless striving, experiment, research and prayer. I therefore requested you to present my proposal to H.M.G. for acceptance as coming from a lifelong friend and well-wisher of the British people. You were good enough to tell me that I could give the purport of our conversation to the members of the Working Committee. This I propose to do by showing a copy of this letter to them. Unless you have any objection, I would like also to make a public appeal to the British people to accept the non-violent method at this supreme juncture in their life as also the life of mankind. "Quit India" Resolution adopted by the All-India Congress Committee on 8 August 1942 : Its elaboration—The All India Congress Committee has given the most careful consideration to the reference made to it by the Working Committee in their resolution dated July 14, 1942, and to subsequent events, including the development of the war situation, the utterances of responsible spokesmen of the British Government, and the comments and criticisms made in India and abroad. The Committee approves of and endorses that resolution, and is of opinion that events subsequent to it have given it further justification, and have made it clear that the immediate ending of British rule in India is an urgent necessity, both for the sake of India and for the success of the cause of the United Nations.

The continuation of that rule is degrading and enfeebling India and making her progressively less capable of defending herself and of contributing to the cause of world freedom. The Committee has viewed with dismay the deterioration of the situation on the Russian and Chinese [fronts and conveys to the Russian and Chinese] peoples its high appreciation of their heroism in defence of their freedom. This increasing peril makes it incumbent on all those who strive for freedom and who sympathise with the victims of aggression, to examine the foundations of the policy so fir pursued by the Allied Nations, which have led to repeated and disastrous failure. It is not by adhering to such aims and policies and methods that failure can be converted into success, for past experience has shown that failure is inherent in them. These policies have been based not on freedom so much as on the domination of subject and Colonial countries, and the continuation of the Imperialist tradition and method. The possession of Empire, instead of adding to the strength of the radical power, has become a burden and a curse India, the classic land of modern Imperialism, has become the crux of the question, for by the freedom of India will Britain and the United Nation be judged, and the peoples of Asia and Africa be filled with hope and enthusiasm. The ending of British rule in this country is thus a vital immediate issue on which depend the future of the war and the success of freedom and democracy. A free India will assure this success by throwing all her great resources in the struggle for freedom and against the aggression of Nazism, Fascism and Imperialism. This will not only affect materially the fortunes of the war, but will bring all subject and oppressed humanity on the side of the United Nations, and give these nations, whose ally India would be, the moral and spiritual leadership of the world. India in bondage will continue to be the symbol of British Imperialism and the taint of that imperialism will affect the fortunes of all the United Nations. The peril of today, therefore, necessitates the of India and the ending of British domination.

No future promises or guarantees can affect the present situation or meet that peril. They cannot produce the needed psychological effect on the mind of the masses. Only the glow of freedom now can release that energy and enthusiasm of millions of people which will immediately transform the nature of the war. The A.I.C.C., therefore, repeats with all emphasis the demand for the withdrawal of the British power from India. On the declaration of India's independence, a provisional Government will be formed and free India will become an ally of the United Nations, sharing with them in the trials and tribulations of the joint enterprise of the struggle for freedom. The provisional Government can only be formed by the cooperation of the principal parties and groups in the country. It will thus be a composite Government, representative of all important sections of the people of India. Its primary functions must be to defend India and resist aggression with all the armed as well as the non-violent forces at its command, together with its Allied Powers, and workers to promote the well being and progress of the essentially in the fields and factories and elsewhere to whom essentially all power and authority must belong. The provisional Government will evolve a scheme for a Constituent Assembly which will prepare a Constitution for the Government of India acceptable to all sections of the people.

This Constitution, according to the Congress view, should be a federal one, with the largest measure of autonomy for the federating units, and with the residuary powers vesting in these units. The future relations between India and the Allied Nations will be adjusted by representatives of all these free countries conferring together for their mutual advantage and for their cooperation in the common task of resisting aggression. Freedom will enable India to resist aggression effectively with the people's united will and strength behind it. The freedom of India must be the symbol of and prelude to this freedom of all other Asiatic nations under foreign domination. Burma, Malaya, Indo-China, the Dutch Indies, Iran and Iraq must also attain their complete freedom. It must be clearly understood that such of these countries as are under Japanese control now must not subsequently be placed under the rule or control of any other Colonial Power. While the A.I.C.C. must primarily be concerned with the independence and defence of India in this hour of danger, the Committee is of opinion that the future peace, security and ordered progress of the world demand a world federation of free nations, and on no other basis can the problems of the modern world be solved. Such a world federation would ensure the freedom of its constituent nations, the prevention of aggression and exploitation by one nation over another, the protection of national minorities, the advancement of all backward areas and peoples, and the pooling of the world's resources for the common good of all. On the establishment of such a world federation, disarmament would be practicable in all countries, national armies, navies and air forces would no longer be necessary, and a world federal defence force would keep the world peace and prevent aggression. An independent India would gladly join such world federation and cooperate on an equal basis with other countries in the solution of international problems. Such a federation should be open to all nations who agree with its fundamental principles.

In view of the war, however, the federation must inevitably, to begin with, be confined to the United Nations; such a step taken now will have a most powerful effect on the war, on the peoples of the Axis countries, and on the peace to come. The Committee regretfully realizes, however, that despite the tragic and overwhelming lessons of the was and the perils that overhang the world. The Governments of few countries are yet prepared to take this inevitable step towards world federation. The reactions of the British Government and the misguided criticism of the foreign Press also make it clear that even the obvious demand for India's independence is resisted, though this has been made essentially to meet the present peril and to enable India to defend herself and help China and Russia in their hour of need. The Committee is anxious not to embarrass in any way the defence of China or Russia, whose freedom is precious and must be preserved, or to jeopardise the defensive capacity of the United Nations. But the peril grows both to India and these nations, and inaction and submission to a foreign administration at this stage is not only degrading India and reducing her capacity to defend herself and resist aggression but is no answer to that growing peril and is no service to the peoples of the United Nations.

The earnest appeal of the Working Committee to Great Britain and the United Nations has so far met with no response and the criticisms made in many foreign quarters have shown an ignorance of India's and the world's need, and sometimes even hostility to India's freedom, which is significant of a mentality of domination and racial superiority which cannot be tolerated by a proud people conscious of their strength and of the justice of their cause. The A.I.C.C. would yet again, at this moment, in the interest of world freedom, renew this appeal to Britain and the United Nations. But the Committee feels that it is no longer justified in holding the nation back from endeavouring to assert its will against an imperialist and authoritarian Government which dominates over it and prevents it from functioning in its own interest and in the interest of humanity. The Committee resolves, therefore, to sanction, for the vindication of India's inalienable right to freedom and independence, the starting of a mass struggle on non-violent lines on the widest possible scale, so that the country might utilize all the non-violent strength it has gathered during the last 22 years of peaceful struggle. Such a struggle must inevitably be under the leadership of Gandhiji and the Committee requests him to take the lead and guide the nation in the steps to be taken. The Committee appeals to the people of India to face the dangers and hardships that will fall to their lot with courage and endurance, and to bold together under the leadership of Gandhiji and carry out his instructions as disciplined soldiers of Indian freedom. They must remember that non-violence is the basis of this movement. A time may come when it may not b-, possible to issue instructions or for instructions to reach our people, and when no Congress Committee can function. When this happens every man and woman who is participating in this movement must function for himself otherself within the four corners of the general instructions issued.

Every Indian who desires freedom and strives for it must be his own guide urging him on along the hard road where there is no resting place and which leads ultimately to the independence of India. Lastly, whilst the A.I.C.C. has stated is own view of the future governance under free India, the A.I.C.C. wishes to make it quite clear to all concerned that by embarking on a mass struggle, it has no intention of gaining power for the Congress. The power, when it comes, will belong to the whole people of India.

Resolution of CWC on War

I seek your permission to make my own position and that of some other members of the Working Committee clear regard ing the resolution. This resolution opens the door, however small the opening may be, for armed help in this war, particularly for the defence of the country and for the larger causes which are emerging out of it, provided that British Government accepts India's demands. Our belief is that arms have not settled any dispute in the world nor are they ever likely to do so in future. It is the universal experience of all countries that dependence on arms leads from one war to another. The defeated party start preparing for another war so that it may defeat the victor and in this way one war lays the foundation of another war. We therefore believe that war has not solved any problem and nothing can be finally settled so long as dependence on arms continues. What I am stating here is not a mere theoretical proposition. We are convinced that it is also politically necessary. The happenings in the world even in the course of the present war have shown the futility of armed resistance in the case of many countries which have had warlike traditions and had made tremendous preparations for war. It is politically wrong in our opinion to involve the country in war at this time. Having accepted the path of nonviolence the country has made tremendous progress during the last twenty or twenty-two years. The benefit which the country had derived from it is obvious. We do not like to give up this tried principle at this critical time even to a limited extent. We therefore consider that the opening that this resolution provides for armed assistance in this war is not in the best interests of the country and we wish that India should not in this war and on the present occasion also in the least relax its hold of the principle of Ahimsa. We realise at the same time that by merely passing the resolution we are not called upon to take up arms today. That can happen only if the British Government makes a declaration in favour of Independence of India and transfers the responsibility of administration to our people. There appears to be no chance of that happening today. We have not accordingly thought it necessary to resign from the Working Committee. When the British Government opens the way for armed assistance by the Congress, then will be the time for us to make our choice.

Reaction on Separation

The grounds on which separation is claimed are thus either unsubstantial or such as are not likely to be accepted as a just and fair basis for separation. On the other hand there are very substantial reasons against separation. We may shortly indicate some of them here.

(a) The national resources of the country as a whole can be much better utilized to the benefit of all, if there is mutual accommodation and agreed joint action, which will become impossible in case of independent states. The mere fact that two states are independent puts up a barrier against much mutual accommodation and joint action between them. Planning on a large scale becomes impossible in case of small states, all of which are not equally well endowed by nature and most of which have to be dependent on others for some very important article or other absolutely necessary for the welfare and protection of a modern state. The larger the area, the greater the variety, the wider the distribution of natural resources agricultural, mineral and power-producing-the better the chances of a planned economy. India will have lost this advantage as a result of division, and in this respect the Muslim states on the North-West and East will be the worst sufferers, as has been indicated elsewhere in this book. We have seen how the Muslim states will not have the resources to run the administration and meet the cost of defence.

(b) The days of small independent states are numbered if not gone already. Recent experience has shown that no small state can preserve its independence. Even large states are hard put to it to preserve it. The natural tendency is in favour of combinations of states. Something in the nature of a Super-State even above the bigger states is not beyond the range of practical politics today. It would therefore be flying in the face of world forces to reduce the size and strength of India and establish in its stead a number of small states. It may well be that the spirit of separation may not end with the partition of the Muslim zones and once it begins to operate it may lead to a situation in which India may have to be cut up not only into Muslim and non-Muslim states but even the Muslim And non-Muslim states may be cut up into several smaller states apart from the states of the Princes. This will make India, if it ever attains independence after being thus cut up into numerous small principalities, a house divided against itself and exposed to intrigues by foreign powers. As a result all its component independent states will be weak, unable to protect themselves against foreign aggression, and liable to played against one another."

(c) The modern tendency even in Muslim countries is to base politics and economics more and more on other considerations than religion. Whatever the Muslim League and the protagonists of Pakistan may say, there is no doubt that the Muslim states of the world today are becoming-if they have not become already-secular states, just like the Christian countries of Europe. The question is whether Indian Musalmans will be able to turn the tide of events and establish and maintain the state on any other basis in India.

(d) The crying need of India today is that the state should spend more and more on the nation-building departments. India has suffered immeasurably in the past under the British Government which has regarded itself more as a police state than anything else, neglecting and starving the nation-building departments. The whole country has a great way to make up and the Muslim states will be no exception to this. Division of the country will inevitably lead to reduction of resources and make it difficult for each of the Muslim and non-Muslim zones to meet this growing demand.

(e) It is well known that the proposal for partition has aroused strong opposition from all non-Muslims and also from Muslims. It is not for me to say whether the Muslim League or those other groups like the Jamiat-ul-Ulema, the Jamiat-ul-Mominin, the Ahrars, the Nationalist Muslim organizations, the All-India Shia Conference and others represent the majority of Muslims. The fact remains that these latter have expressed their opposition to separation. Whatever the position may be so far as Muslims are concerned, the Hindus and Sikhs have declared their unequivocal determination to resist partition. This is bound to become more pronounced and more bitter with the persistence with which the proposal for division is pressed. It is difficult to forecast what shape this conflict may take in the future.

One thing is certain : partition is not likely to be attained with the goodwill of those most concerned, and this ill-will is bound to persist on both sides, even if the proposal succeeds, even after the separation is effected. Distrust which is the basis of the proposal is bound to grow and any hope that after separation things will settle down and the independent states will soon become friendly will have been built on sand. The chances are that bitterness and distrust will make mutual accommodation more difficult and necessitate the maintenance of protection forces on both sides. Economic warfare is not beyond the range of possibility, even if nothing worse happens.

(f) All this is bound to make the position of minorities in the independent states infinitely worse. As a result of this conflict between the majorities in the Muslim and non-Muslim Zones they will have lost what sympathy and goodwill they should have and their position will have become far worse than what it is today. For the minorities it will veritably be a case of jumping from the frying pan into the fire.

The non-Muslim minorities will have the situation forced upon them, if the proposal succeeds. But the Muslim minority will have chosen it, worked for it and extorted it from the non-Muslims and could not blame any one else for it. Further, as explained elsewhere the minorities in the Muslim states will be better able, on account of their numbers and concentration, to protect themselves than the Muslim minorities in non-Muslim zones on account of their small size and because they are dispersed over a vast area. Nor will there be much chance of any reciprocity in regard to privileges and concessions for the simple reason that the Muslim states will not be in a position to reciprocate adequately and the non-Muslim state will have no adequate inducement for invoking reciprocity. Undoubtedly Rajendra Prasad identified himself with several causes having deep linkage with the political, and socio-economic life of the people. His direction to them was much valued and was carried out with a sense of devotion and responsibility. People followed him with an ardent hope that he and Mahatma Gandhi would get Swaraj from then by getting rid of the machinery of the Raj. With the passage of time, they began to show more faith and confide-nee in doing in the way to which they were directed. The task was difficult and the journey to be covered was fairly long, but people followed him with a smile on their faces. They suffered the pangs of jail life; they tolerated all kinds of repression, they even got their property and valuable assets confiscated. But they never flinched from their duty. Rajendra Prasad was a leader of the poor peasants, landless, labourer, Harijans and other weaker sections of our society. He always showed willingness to support their cause whenever the need arose.

He moved amidst then, listened to their woeful stories and solved their problems by generating a new spirit of awakening and patriotism among them. He always acted in accordance with the manifesto of the Congress party which sought solution of numerous socio-economic ills in our society. As a lawyer he achieved success in the profession at a young age. He would take up cases which had fair dealings with his clients and the opposite party. He never tried to put his clients in any kind of suspense. Undoubtedly he worked hard and prepared the cases well before going to the court. His arguments were fairly comprehensive and to the point It was therefore obvious that his fame and reputation as a lawyer soon spread all over Bihar and he began to receive legal cases from the far-flung areas. Indeed his fee was moderate and the, client showed much faith in his capability and legal acumen. At that point of time, the cult of swadeshi was much in rife. It was propagated by the Congress leadership and the satyagrahis functioning in several regions of our country. The spinning of khadi, its use by dedicated workers, and its sale were propagated by them. Indeed khadi was hawked by the workers from street to street and its national efficacy was propagated amongst the masses. In fact there was a propaganda in favour of swadeshi for the achievement of swaraj. Moreover it was argued that swadeshi would remove our socio-econo ills. With the promotion of swadeshi, the boycott of foreign cloth was also propagated. There was bonfire of foreign cloth all over India including Bihar. Undoubtedly Rajendra Prasad greatly encouraged this programme of the Congress. People of Bihar came out voluntarily to participate in the bonfire programme of the foreign cloth. Thus, a respect and new urge for the promotion of khadi was generated among the people.

Specially the womenfolk were advised to carry out the programme of spinning regularly for a few hours. They adhered to this programme with patriotic spirit and set an example for others who were yet to make up their minds for a new challenge. Rajendra Prasad was a protagonist of Hindi as our national language. He propagated its ideology among the people and apprised them to patronise it as their national language in comparison to the English language. He patronised several educational institutions and saw to it that the educational standard of boys and girls in schools and Colleges should improve. He encouraged the idea of opening vidyapiths where the education having deep linkage with Indian education nationalism be imparted to the students. The idea was to boycott the government and the government-aided institutions. He was always accessible to the common man and listened to his personal problems with interest. He sought solution to his problems by affording him every kind of help. He well understood the, woes of the poverty-stricken people living in the villages. He was unhappy to see the lack of basic facilities like food, housing, education, medical etc. He realised that any part of our country could not expect to develop economically so long as the Raj lasts. He discussed these problems with his people and advised them to organise themselves in a disciplined way so that they could fight against several ills in a better way. In fact a common man in Bihar needed a leader and in Rajendra. Prasad people-found sincerity and patriotism personified. On account of his simple living and true identification with the teeming millions he could represent his personality in a better way. So people showered their faith in him and he, on his part, guided, advised and organised them in a way which could enable then to see swaraj after a long drawn political struggle against the Raj. The constructive programme was vigorously preached and popularised by a deputation composed of Babu Rajendra Prasad, C. Rajagopalachari, Seth Jamnalal Bajaj and Devadas Gandhi, which toured the country widely and made a good collection for the Tilak Swaraj Fund. They submitted a report of their work to the Working Committee that met in Bombay on the 25th, 26th and 27th May, 1923. There took place an important meeting of the A.I.C.C. as well, at which it was decided that no propaganda be carried on amongst voters in furtherance of the resolution passed at the Gaya Congress relating to the Boycott of Councils. It was just a month previous to that, that the Deshbandhu has made a suggestion that the work of the Congress should be divided into various sections including the capture of the Councils, and that each section be entrusted to persons interested in it and that five to six crores of rupees be collected for the purpose. This proposal was explained to the Working Committee by Messrs. C. Rajagopalachari and Babu Rajendra Prasad, but was dropped as impracticable and applied to the Gaya Congress resolutions, so far as the Councils were concerned.

The moment the A.I.C.C. passed the aforesaid resolution, and on account of it, six members of the Working

Committee tendered their resignations of membership of the Committee. These were Messrs. C. Rajagopalachari, Vallabhbhai Patel, Rajendra Prasad, Brij Kishore Prasad, G.B. Deshpande, and Jamnalal Bajaj. After some parley for a reconsideration, at the instance of Jawaharlal-Nehru, the resignations were accepted and so was the President's resignation. The Committee was reconstituted and work was carried on under Dr. Ansari's chairmanship. There was nothing further of any importance done at this meeting. Only, we must pause at the Committee's congratulations offered to the volunteers of the Central Provinces carrying on their Flag Satyagraha and the call to the volunteers throughout India to be ready to join the struggle when required.'

The year 1923-24 marked the beginning of a critical period in the history of Indian nationalism due to the increase in communal tension and widening of cleavage among the different parties and sectional groups. But in spite of these unfortunate developments, Gandhiji's faith in Satyagraha remained unshaken and he tried his utmost to utilise the two wings of the Congress. The Swarajya Party and the country as a whole suffered a serious loss in the death of Deshbandhu C.R Das at Darjeeling on June 16, 1925. Pandit Motilal Nehru now piloted the Swarajya Party with much tact and it was invested by the entire machinery of the Congress with authority to deal with the political affairs of the country at a meeting of the All-India Congress Committee hell at Patna on September 22, 1925. It was now at Patna that the All-India Spinners Association was started "as an integral part of the Congress organization but with an independent existence and powers."

The liabilities, assets and investments of the All-India Khadi Board were transferred to the All-India Spinners'

Association with the consent of the Swarajists. Gandhiji drew up a constitution for it and became its Chairman. Rajendra Prasad was made one of its life trustees and member of its executive. There was to be an Agent as also a Secretary for each Province. Rajendra Prasad was the Agent for Bihar, Jawaharlal Nehru for U.P., Satish Chandra Das Gupta for Bengal and Rajagopalachari for Tamil Nad. Lakshmi Narayan became the Secretary of the Bihar Branch of the All-India Spinners' Association. Under Rajendra Prasad's 'guidance Khadi work was recognised there on new lines. It progressed both qualitatively and quantitatively and prices of Khadi were low. Owing to the greater importance of north Bihar for Khadi production, the office and chief depot of the Bihar Branch of the All-India Spinners' Association was shifted from Patna to Muzaffarpur and later to Madhubani where it constructed its own buildings.

Gandhiji and his devoted followers including Rajendra Prasad had already been engaged in pushing ahead the programme of constructive work particularly the spread of Khadi and national education, almost from the beginning of the year 1924. In recognition of his valuable services in regard to Swadeshi, Rajendra Prasad was given the honour of inaugurating the All-India Swadeshi Exhibition at the Belgaum Congress on December 23, 1924. On this occasion, he delivered a very interesting speech in Hindi. He said : "It is a well known fact that whenever a country or a nation falls on evil days, its decay is not confined to any one department of life but pervades its whole being and signs of a failing off are visible in everything that its culture connotes, and if this process lasts for any length of time many things which are involved in its own culture are forgotten and it begins to live on the initiation and mimicry of other nations and countries which are strong enough to impose their own culture and civilisation on it. The modern history of India shows how she had been conquered by the British and how this conquest has been becoming more and more complete. The flow of this current is now stopped and we are trying to find means to revive our past glory.

A proof of this national reawakening is furnished by an exhibition like this, which I hope to open today. You will see in it specimens of the art of this ancient land. I do not know anything about art and so say nothing about it. But there is one thing which we were going to forget but which is as necessary for our national life as the air or the food is for individual life and that is Khaddar. About Khaddar also Mahatmaji and other individuals like any old teacher, Sir P.C. Ray, have said and written a great deal and whatever I may say will only be a repetition. "But I think I may tell you something about my own Province which you may not possibly know and which will show the possibility of Khaddar. At one time I calculated on the basis of the population of my Province that it would be possible and with some effort it would be easy enough for the people of our Province to supply enough hand-woven cloth made of hand-spun yarn for the whole population. Leaving out Orissa and confining myself to Hindi-speaking Bihar only, our population is about three crores.

The average quantity off cloth per head used by our people is about eleven yards. We would, therefore, require about 33 crore yards of cloth for my Province. If you take to handloom work for only 300 days in the year leaving 65 days for festivals, ceremonies, illness, etc., we require 11 lakhs yards of yarn to be woven every day in the year to get 33 crores of yards of cloth and if one loom could weave 5-1/2 yards per day we would require about two lakhs of such looms to give us 33 crore yards of cloth. But it is a known fact that an experienced weaver can weave much more than 5-1/2 yards in a day, and if I take an average of 8 yards per day it would not be, I think, too much. Therefore, we will require 1,36,250 looms to weave at the rate of eight yards per head per day. I found later on that the Government took a census of the handlooms working in my Province and the Government report is that more than 68,000 looms are working there.

There are thousands of weavers who, having given up their profession, are working in Calcutta and other places in jute mills or have taken to other professions altogether. If these people could be assured of a settled income, they would gladly return to their ancestral profession of weaving. It will not be necessary for them to learn the art because they know it and have not yet forgotten it. It will not be very difficult for them to set up the looms because in most houses the looms or at any rate parts thereof are still kept hanging from the roofs. It is thus clear that if we wanted to have a complete boycott of mill-made cloth, whether foreign or country-made, we have even now enough weavers in my Province and we cap easily have the necessary looms set up. But if we want to exclude only foreign cloth, it is possible to do that even with looms which are already working with some addition. I think that what is true of my Province is true of other Provinces also and of the whole country and if a census were taken of the working looms, of al I such looms as may easily be set up, there will be no difficulty so far as weaving is concerned. The earnings of the weavers are also not small. They can earn Rs. 15 to 20 per month and I know from personal experience that weavers who have not given up their looms are quite happy. But it is said that spinning is not paying, and that the wages of spinners are so small that on one would consider it worth his or her while to spin. If the wages are enhanced the cloth will become so dear that no one would agree to purchase it. We have to consider this from two points of view.

The first is : Are there enough spinners in this country so that they can supply all the yarn that may be necessary and secondly, are their wages such as to make it worth their while to spin without making the cloth very dear? I will again take my own Province. We require nearly three pounds of yarn for about eight yards of cloth and if the yarn is fine we shall require less. But I will take the coarser kind of yarn because the coarser cloth is dearer. If we assume that a spinner can spin 320 yards of yarn of 10 counts in an hour he can spin in six hours about 10 tolas and to make up three pounds of yarn we require about 12 Charkhas working for six hours a day. We thus require about 12 Charkhas to feed one loom. Reducing the number of hours to a certain extent and also assuming that the spinner spins less than 320 yards in an hour, it may rightly be said that 20 Charkhas can easily feed one loom. I may add, however, that experiments have shown that a speed of six or seven hundred yards per hour has been reached by our spinners and the fineness has reached much over 300 counts. So I think the average I have taken will not be considered very high. We would, therefore, require about 27 or 28 lakhs of Charkhas to supply us sufficient yarn to cloths all our people. Now 27 lakhs out of a population of three crores is not large. Therefore, there is no difficulty so far as mere numbers are concerned and it will be remembered that we require 27 lakhs of Charkhas for effecting a complete boycott of all kinds of mill cloth, whether foreign or Indian. If we leave out of account for the present the Indian mill cloth, the work becomes very much easier." Regarding the question whether the wages of the spinners were enough, Rajendra Prasad observed from his personal experience of the Province of Bihar that there were many women who had never given up spinning and who were earning a living with the help of Charkha alone, and also that many families purchased their salt, grains, vegetables, oil clothing, etc., with the income of their women from spinning. He further noted that if one could earn Rs. 4 a month by spinning he did not "earn a negligible amount considering that the average income of our people" did not "exceed two rupees four annas a month." He emphasised that if people devoted themselves to proper organisation and propaganda for Charkha and Khaddar, it would not be "impossible to effect a complete boycott of foreign cloth" in Bihar and also in the country as a whole. Under Rajendra Prasad's guidance, a Khadi Exhibition was organised at Patna on December 13 and 14, 1924. It was a nonpolitical function and was attended by Judges of the High Court including the Chief Justice, the Hon'ble Sir Dawson Miller, and high officers of the Government, most of whom purchased Khadi. Lady Miller gave away the prizes to the prize winners in a spinning competition held on the occasion.

Rajendra Prasad and some others tried this year to revive the Bihari Students' Conference on its old model. At a preliminary meeting held at Patna in this connection in April 1924, Rajendra Prasad delivered an inspiring speech appealing to the people to push on constructive activities with greater zeal and sense of dedication. It was also at his invitation that in this year an eminent servant and scientist, Sir J.C. Bose, one of his old teachers at the Presidency College, Calcutta, who still remembered him with affection, and who had then come to deliver the Convocation Address of the Patna University, made a highly instructive speech at the Bihar Vidyapith. The Bihar Provincial Hindu Conference was held at Muzaffarpur on April 4, 1925. Rajendra Prasad proposed Lala Lajpat Rai to the chair and this motion was seconded by Ram Dayalu Singh. Lala Lajpat Rai delivered his Presidential Address extempore in Hindi. In conclusion he congratulated Bihar on having a personality like Rajendra Prasad and wished that every district in the other Provinces should produce a Rajendra Prasad. Gandhiji's Bihar tours gave considerable impetus to the production of Khadi. To popularise it further, more exhibitions were held at different places in Bihar in 1926 and 1927 under the guidance of Rajendra Prasad. The first one was inaugurated on the grounds of the Bihar Vidyapith by Satish Chandra Das Gupta of the Khadi Pratisthan, Calcutta. The second one was opened in the Bihar Young Men's institute, Patna, by Sadhu Vaswani of Sind. The third one was organised at Arrah, the fourth one at Muzaffarpur (opened by Maulavi Muhammad Shafi) and the fifth one at Chapra (opened by Mazharul Haque), the sixth one at Mairwa, a small village in the district of Chapra, the seventh one at Gaya (June 11, 1926) and the eighth one at Girdih on August 16, 1926, opened by Rajendra Prasad. "Congressmen, non-Congressmen, Government officials, zamindars, lawyers, big and small merchants and in some cases even Europeans" visited these exhibitions.

Khadi exhibitions were opened at several places, such as Motihari, Jamshedpur, Laheriasarai (opened by Rajendra Prasad), Deoghar, Hazaribagh and Ranchi. On the last day of his Bihar trip in 1927, Gandhiji met the khadi workers of Bihar and a special Khadi exhibition was organised on the occasion by Rajendra Prasad in the Sinha Institute at Patna.

There was a tremendous rush at the function on the opening day. So, the Ministers, high Government officials, and some barristers whom Rajendra Prasad had invited to the exhibition, visited it the next day and Rs. 2,000 worth of Khaddar was sold in a day. Rajendra Prasad's activities for promotion of Khadi were not confined to Bihar only. These were extended to other places when he visited them. On hearing that Gandhiji was suffering from high blood pressure and had gone to the Nandi Hills in Mysore State for rest, Rajendra Prasad went there and stayed with him for a few days. Later, he accompanied Gandhiji to Bangalore where a Khadi exhibition had been organised and in which the Tamil Nadu and the Andhra branches participated. He went to Tiruppur, where the chief depot of the Tamil Nad Charkha Sangh was located, and then to Thiruchengode in Salem District, the site of an Ashram started by Rajagopalachari, where good work was being done in regard to Khadi. He studied Khadi production and organisational methods at these centres and tried to introduce them in Bihar. He visited several Khadi centres in Andhra at the request of Sita Ram Shastri, Secretary of the Andhra Charkha Sangh, and delivered speeches relating to the utility and economics of Khadi. Realising the importance of these speeches, Congressmen in Andhra requested him to publish them in book form. These were published in English under the title, Economics of Khadi, and a Hindi translation of it came out later. As regards elections to the Legislatures, Rajendra Prasad retained his conviction as a no-changer. Still keeping in view the decision of the Congress for fighting elections, he rendered all possible assistance to it. In the elections of 1926 in Bihar, the general result was return of the Congress candidates to both the Central Assembly and the Provincial Council in good numbers. To the Council of State, out of the four candidates nominated by the Congress in Bihar, three were elected. Rajendra Prasad did not believe in the efficacy of Council Entry. But considering that his "personal views had to be submerged before party considerations", he devoted his "energies and time to working in the Congress election campaign", by undertaking extensive tours which affected his health. He regretted that various caste groups among the Hindus were guided by mutual jealousies and tried to outmanoeuvre one another. He expressed his views about it in an article in the Desh. Tension between the Hindus and the Muslims had increased and communal riots broke out at several places. There were minor clashes in Bihar also. Deeply mortified at this, Mazharul Haque organised on June 10, 1926, a conference of the leading Congressmen of Bihar, some members of the Khilafat Committee and several others not belonging to those organisations. They decided to take proper steps to restrain the pernicious effects of communal frenzy. Some of them including Rajendra Prasad toured the Province for this. This produced some soothing effect, but excitement did not completely disappear. The assassination of Swami Shraddhanand by a Muslim fanatic on December 23, 1926 aggravated it. The canker of communalism, entering into the vitals of our national solidarity, presented a grave problem before the country. The Indian National Congress meeting at Gauhati in Assam on December 26, 1926, with S. Srinivasa Iyengar as President, deplored the tragic death of Swami Shraddhanand and passed a resolution for removing the growing differences between the Hindus and the Mussalmans. Resolutions for restoring cordiality between the two communities were passed also at the Unity Conference hold in Calcutta in October 1927, and at the meeting of the All India Congress Committee held in Calcutta at the same time. Besides being a good writer in

Hindi, Dr. Rajendra Prasad was closely associated with many poets and authors and special mention may be made of Pandeya Jagannath Prasad, M.A., B.L., Kavyatirtha, Darshankesari, an erudite scholar of Sanskrit and Hindi and a born literature, at whose sad demise he made touching observations at the Bihar Hindi Sahitya Sammelan held at Laheriasarai in 1925. The Conference of 1925 was of special significance since the-question of the controversy regarding Hindi and Urdu and Devanagri script and Persian script Was one of the subjects discussed in it. In his Presidential Address, Dr. Rajendra Prasad expressed his regret at the growing feeling of distrust amongst those who held opposite views.

He said : "Some Mussalman brethren of the Province have been of late developing ideas of doubt and mistrust regarding Hindi language, Hindi literature and the Devanagri script. When I hear that insinuations are made against Hindus and those fostering the cause of Hindi literature that they intend to abolish Islamic culture from this country and that the basis of Islamic culture is imbedded in Urdu literature and the Persian script, I feel not only astonished but greatly worried. As a Hindu I do know and can assert that all this is nothing but a figment of the mind-a hallucination... Although today the gap between Hindi and Urdu vocabulary has been widening, yet I am not prepared to accept that Urdu belongs to Islamic culture or is the property of the Mussalmans and the Hindus have nothing to do with it. Similarly, I am not ready to admit that Hindi is the property of the Hindus alone and the Mussalmans have no right over it. Both in Hindi and Urdu literatures there are instances to prove that though politicians may create differences as they like, yet those devoted to literature have never accepted the bondages of religion or community and, if we reasonably consider the matter, there can be no question of controversy between Hindi and Urdu."

Another important point discussed at this Conference was the question of the medium of instruction. About it Dr. Rajendra Prasad said : "I believe that so long as our children are not educated through the medium of their own language they will neither be good or talented scholars nor shall they be able to assimilate knowledge and contribute to literature or bring about any improvement in the literary field... This is why the well-wishers of our country and sincere teachers have all along been pressing that in our elementary schools and institutions for higher education the medium of instruction should be the mother-tongue." Dr. Rajendra Prasad considered Hindi to be quite suitable for being the Indian national language, as it was "the most common and most widely understood" of all the Indian languages.

So, the Constituent Assembly adopted Hindi as the State language for all-India purposes. As perhaps the switch over from English to Hindi in matters of all-India importance was to be slow and gradual, the Constituent Assembly stipulated that within fifteen years of the promulgation of our Constitution, Hindi would replace English in the "agreed spheres". Dr. Prasad, however, did not like any attempt to impose Hindi on the people of any area and again and again assured the people of the South to this effect. He duly recognised the value of scientific research and the application of their results for amelioration of the conditions of life of the masses. "Science", as he pointed out, "has succeeded in working wonders in many spheres of life", and he advised our people to improve their agriculture and industries by proper utilisation of the discoveries of science. While inaugurating the 17th Annual Meeting of the Indian Academy of Sciences at New Delhi on December 27, 1951, he said : "Today, no country can afford to lag behind in scientific study, if it desires to keep out of the current set in motion by science and scientific work done in other countries, even if we wish to do so. We must, therefore, keep ourselves abreast of progress in the world at large. For that purpose, two aspects, which to a layman like me appear to be rather distinct from each other in their practical application, have to be kept in view.

One is research of a theoretical or fundamental character, and the other is the application of the results of such fundamental research to the solution of the problems of everyday life and further the spread of practical scientific knowledge in our daily life in the field, factory, or home, by every man and woman-young or old, rich or poor." Two most significant social changes in modern India are the uplift of the Harijans and the removal of untouchability. Recalling the noble traditions of our country for the service of humanity and inspired by the most liberal attitude of his great master in such social matters, Dr. Rajendra Prasad did much to facilitate these changes.

While inaugurating the Mahatma Gandhi Community Centre at the Harijan Colony, New Delhi, on the April 5, 1954, he observed that "the Father of the Nation has lived here for many a week. This place has been sanctified by his sermons, which, delivered after the prayer meetings held in this Colony before and after India's independence, still echo in our ears." Referring to the provisions in our Constitution regarding equal opportunities for all, he observed "I have an unswerving faith that the silvery rays of the sun, which has arisen on the Indian horizon after centuries of slavery, will brighten up every nook and corner of this land and that every citizen, irrespective of any distinction of colour, caste or creed will feel the life-giving warmth of these rays." Dr. Prasad was anxious for improvement in the social and economic conditions of the Adivasis, with whose problems in different parts of India he was familiar, particularly because of his close connection with the Bharatiya Adamjati Sevak Sangh. It was certainly an uphill task but it was laid down in our Constitution and it was "very essential and urgent." He attached special sanctity. He felt that it involved "the clearing of centuries-old cobweb and improving the lot of a long-suppressed section of the Indian population." He gave the following advice to the office-bearers and workers of the Adamjati Sevak Sangh. "They should go to the Adivasis in a spirit of modesty and equality. If, for any reason, these people get the impression that we are helping them out of pity or because we consider ourselves more advanced than they, you can be sure that your efforts will hardly bear fruit. It is after all a fact that it is not in the feeling of pity that the spirit of our action lies. If the Adivasis have remained backward for ages, it is none of their fault. Let us tell them that India is now a free country in which every citizen, including the Adivasis, has equal rights.

This is possible only if we develop a sympathetic attitude towards them, an attitude which does not smack of superiority. We should also be sympathetic towards the customs and traditions of these people. Then alone will the prospect of economic and social improvement attract these people." Dr. Prasad had sympathies also with the tribal people. In his anxiety to meet them and to get first-hand knowledge about their condition, he visited their area in 1954. In his reply to the address of welcome presented to him at Tura (Garo Hills, Assam), he observed : "I am not one of those who look upon the tribal people as backward. I know you have your own customs, your own culture, your own way of life. We are anxious that you should progress and do so in your own special way." He was the first Head of the State to visit those parts and he assured the people there that their interest would be the interest of the country as a whole.

"Eminent persons, in and outside India, paid high tributes to Dr. Rajendra Prasad for his manifold qualities of head and heart before and after he became President of India. For whole-hearted and ungrudging service to Mahatma Gandhi during his Champaran Mission in 1917-18, the latter wrote : Rajen Babu and Braj Kishore Babu were a matchless paid. Their devotion made it impossible for me to take a single step without their help." Mahatma Gandhi considered the village of Zeradei as "a place of pilgrimage for us being the place where Rajendra Babu was born." The Editor of The Searchlight, a nationalist daily of Patna, wrote on April 11, 1931 : "Babu Rajendra Prasad has not only the spiritual fervour but has got intellectual keenness of a very high order, and be is a man of action too like Sardar Patel. He was incessantly moving about, and perhaps no leader in his own province worked as hard and moved so much during the last revolutionary upheaval as Babu Rajendra Prasad did in his own province. He has, what Newman describes, the chief characteristic of a gentleman-the talent of not offending and perhaps that is the reason why no leader in his own province enjoys in the same measure the popularity and respect among non-Congressmen or political opponents that Babu Rajendra Prasad enjoys in his own Province. He is an untiring worker.... For good or ill, be has merged himself in Gandhi. It is not merely hero-worship. It is devotion to an ideal."

"A peasant in his garments but a prince among workers," thus Nariman described the frail figure of Rajendra Prasad when he stood up at Bombay as President of the forty-eighth session of the Indian National Congress in 1934. Referring to his address on this occasion the Amrita Bazar Patrika, of October 27, 1934, observed : "The most noticeable thing about the Presidential Address is that the speech is like the man.

It is quite in keeping with his character. Simple, unassuming, immensely patriotic and extremely self-sacrificing, Rajendra Prasad of Bihar has been one of the most apt pupils of Mahatma Gandhi. His whole life has been dedicated to the cause of truth, non-violence and the service of the motherland. He is one of our few public leaders who has made silent and selfless work the mission of his life." Another Calcutta daily, The Forward, wrote on October 25, 193 4 : "But fortunately in Rajendra Prasad we have a leader who is well able to shoulder the heavy responsibility that has fallen on him by his transparent sincerity and integrity, and by his silent sacrifices, patient services and all-embracing sympathies, he has won universal respect and admiration in India." Referring to Rajendra Prasad in his article on the earthquake in Bihar, Jawaharlal Nehru said, "Truth looks at You through those eyes.

There may be controversies about the nature and content of truth; there will be none about the utter frankness and truth that looks at one through the eyes of Rajendra Prasad." Again Nehru spoke about him at the Ramgarh session of the Congress in 1940, "We often commit mistakes. Our steps falter. Our tongues falter and slip. But here is a man who never makes a mistake, whose steps do not falter, whose tongue does not falter or slip, and who had no occasion to withdraw what he once said or was undone what he once did." While unveiling a portrait of Rajendra Prasad in the Kerala Assembly Chamber on April 27, 1958, Nehru remarked : "Rajen Babu not only occupies the highest office in our country but is something much more. Perhaps more than anyone else he embodies in his life the Indian national movement through which we have passed. The great national movement had many facets and it had with many types of leaders. Dr. Rajendra Prasad represents the basic Indian tradition and more especially, of rural India, though he is not an ordinary peasant. He is highly intellectual, a great educationist and an able lawyer. On the occasion of Rajendra Prasad's birthday, Sri Prakasa (the then Governor of Maharashtra) said in December 1955 : "Today, I express the earnest hope that he might be spared to us for many years to come so that he might keep us, by precept and by example, on the strict path of righteousness, for to my mind, he is truly the embodiment of the spirit of Gandhiji.

Today, I also recall his many virtues of simplicity of personal life; of nobility of nature; of helpfulness to all; of sympathy with and understanding of persons in every grade of life; of devotion to the Master; of fulfilling in his own person the many things he undertook to do in times and circumstances that were very different from what they are at present. Today I would also like my countrymen not only to be satisfied by felicitations and good wishes but also to try to live in their own lives as he has lived his...... Sri Prakasa added : "Shri Rajendra Prasad is very keen in the fulfillment of the vows that he had taken in the past in very different circumstances, regardless of the difficulties that his present sphere of activity may entail in this regard. Few of us are so scrupulous and meticulous in this matter. We take vows because peculiar circumstances lead us to take them; but there is always the implied reservation in our minds that they are only meant to be fulfilled if and only so far as circumstances continue as they were at the time and if they permit fulfillment of these. Not so he. Guests at Rashtrapati Bhavan can still see through the windows overlooking the gardens the Rashtrapati himself sitting quietly, unconcernedly in some quiet carper plying his Charkha because thirty five years or so ago, he had said that he would ply it every day. The same applies in the matter of the use of Khadi which so many of us are non discarding because Swaraj having been won, we feel that the purpose of Khadi has been fulfilled." Comparing Rajaji and Rajendra Prasad, Michael Brecher wrote : "By contrast Prasad is a kindly, gentle-looking man. He is sturdy and tall, heavy, slow-moving with a muddy complexion and an impressive bushy moustache. Simple in dress and manners, never without his Gandhi cap, he looks very much like the father-figure he is to many Indians today.

An orthodox Hindu and a devout believer in pure non-violence. Prasad was among all Gandhi's political disciples, the most spiritually akin to the Mahatma... Prasad has been loyal to his mentor throughout his public life." Louis Fischer described him as "a gentle, modest, compliant, retiring, well-intentioned, high-minded person more inclined to serve them to lead." On the eve of his retirement, the citizens of Delhi presented an address to Dr. Prasad at a meeting held on May 10, 1962 on the Ramlila Ground, Delhi. Overwhelmed by the police and affection shown by him by the citizens of Delhi on the occasion, he said in a highly graceful, elegant and appealing speech : "I bow my head in gratitude to you." He noted that with hi, retirement within a few was a chapter of his life was coming to a close. "From Rashtrapati Bhavan", he said. "I will now go back to my small Ashram in Patna. Some people say it speaks of my humility and greatness. But I have no such claims to make. I have served the people in whatever capacity I have been called upon to serve from time to time. My entry into Sadaqat Ashram only means that from now onwards I will do my duty from new premises," Dr. Prasad stated that his health permitting, he would devote the rest of his life to the country's service. He mentioned how Mahatma Gandhi had taught the nation to be fearless and to attain objectives through non-violent means. This approach "represented the best in Indian traditions". "We shall advance", he observed, "materially but our roots must remain in our past." After his retirement on May 12, Dr. Prasad went to stay from May 14 at the Sadaqat Ashram, his old hermitage where he had practised for several years his yoga of selfless love for the country. One day when I met him here he, in his insatiable thirst for knowledge, expressed his desire to get books for his study from the libraries at Patna. In a message sent by Prasad to the All-India Writers' Conference held at Allahabad for two days from January 31, 1963, be observed : "Had my health permitted me, I would have tried to participate in this Conference, assembled at Prayag. Still my best wishes and those of others who love their country are with you. Our country faces today the greatest peril after freedom. In a moment like this, the nation naturally looks up to you for light and guidance. I am confident that your deliberations will greatly fulfil this hope. "The writer is not only a seer but also a creator. In spite of the ups and downs of history, the successful maintenance of the unbroken cultural unity of the country is largely due to the creative efforts of writers.

Today, this united voice or our culture is the basis of our nation-wide anger and indignation against Chinese aggression. This is the foundation of our national integrity whose roots cannot be shaken by any foreign invasion, howsoever huge it may be. To face the present challenge successfully, however, it is incumbent upon us to strengthen the cultural unity of the country along with political unity. This would not be possible without emotional integration.

Poets and artists, writers and intellectuals have today also to lead the way as their predecessors did in the past. We have, however, to bear it in mind that the path for free development of our various languages, religion and philosophies should be kept open. We never want to wage war against any nation. Peaceful co-existence has not only been our ideal, it has been our practice, too. But the present aggression has been forced upon by a treacherous neighbouring country in spite of the Panch Sheel agreement it had signed with its. "It is our sacred duty to resist unflinchingly this unprovoked, long-planned and wilful foreign attack on our motherland and such is our responsibility, too. "Even today our goal is the re-establishment of peaceful co-existence and maintenance of world peace. But we must defend the sovereignty and freedom of our nation with all possible means. "A flame burns in our hearts today to defend this freedom of our nation. It is our duty to keep it alive. It is in this direction that the country eagerly wants your fearless views." At 10.10. p.m. on February 28, 1963, Dr. Prasad breathed his last with the words "Ram, Ram" on his lips. He was 79. The Convocation Address, which he was to have delivered at Patna University that day, was read out by L.N. Sodhanshu, Speaker of the Bihar Legislative Assembly. Dr. Prasad's conviction was that the objectives of education were three, two of which "relate more or less to the life of the individual as such, while the third is concerned with his collective life." Its first objective was "to enhance the power and capacity of reason of the individual given to him by God". The second objective was "so to train the senses of every individual human being as will enable him to embody them for fulfilling successfully all his physical and other needs." The third purpose of education was that "it should evoke in the individual the qualities necessary to enable him to live and work with his fellow beings." He emphasised that education should aim at the development of the complete personality of an individual, as there were serious risks in what be termed "a split personality", particularly in a country having several historical traditions, cultures and social systems. The system of education which developed under British rule had, as he held rightly, some serious defects.

Though it helped the intellectual growth of some of our countrymen, it widened the gulf between the intelligentsia and the common people, the city and the village, and between modern men and our old healthy traditions. He pleaded a revolutionary change in the character of the Indian universities if they were to exist for the Indian people." He also felt that in the system of education the nation inherited from British rule there was "little provision for character-building and moral training of students", and this has been responsible for some of our "moral shortcomings", though otherwise the country had produced some highly talented men. With a feeling that quantitative expansion of education and growth in the number of educational institutions had become matter for serious consideration, he strongly urged fundamental changes in the prevailing system of education, particularly because, as he said, "the outlook and mental make-up of students have not improved in the same proportion in which their numbers have increased", He pointed out that instead of a more university degree, proper emphasis should be laid on practice and practical experience." He emphasised once and again that "in the present system of education there is no place for character-building; nor is any importance attached to it.

These days, on the other hand, so often hear of students going on strike against teachers and also of teachers organising themselves into groups and their students dividing themselves into groups likewise... If someone opposes them or criticises their activities, the students do not refrain from challenging him as well. If a stray student indulges in such a thing casually, it might be understandable. But when students of a school or college do such a thing in an organised manner, it becomes very distressing. As far as I can see, its basic reason is neglect of character-building and the lack of teachers' moral influence on students." He also regretted that the salutary influence of family and social life was "fading day by day". Dr. Prasad held that among other reforms in university education, there should be a change in the medium of instruction, that is, it should be imparted through "the language of the people". Like Mahatma Gandhi, be had an honest conviction that for free India there should be one common Indian language for the whole country in place of a foreign language like English.

As regards English language, he said : "We can neither boycott it nor ignore it. On the other band, we must continue to cultivate it so that we remain in touch with modern trends and thoughts and are able to take part in international affairs and other international activities to our advantage." He was in favour of encouraging our students to learn these languages-one regional language, Hindi and English-without much strain on them. Pointing out that human relationships in our educational institutions had become formal and mechanical, and that students' indiscipline was very much due to the absence of a close and intimate relationship between the teacher and the taught, he observed : "I have a feeling that much of what you bear about indiscipline among students is but a natural consequence of the present state of things. Discipline, after all, is not always enforced but has to grow from within and for that purpose it requires the existence of certain natural conditions. Thee conditions are wanting and we cannot expect any better results." He was opposed to uncontrolled cinema-mongering by the students in public cinema houses in the cities "where stories of crime, passion and gangsterism, lacking any moral purpose, are screened." Cinema as a recreation, he advised, could be arranged in educational institutions by careful selection of films, which did not produce bad effects on the minds of students. Rajendra Prasad's book, entitled Satyagraha in Champaran, in which he has given a detailed account of Mahatma Gandhi's successful crusade in Champaran on behalf of the peasants of the place against the tyranny of the European indigo-planters, was written in Hindi in 1919 and first published in 1922.

An English version of it came out in March 1928. A revised English edition of it was published in 1949 by the Navajivan Press, Ahmedabad, and a revised Hindi edition has been published recently by the Bihar Rashtrabhasha Parishad. Another book written by Dr. Prasad under the title Mahatma Gandhi and Bihar : Some Reminiscences was published in December 1949. The first fifteen chapters of this book were written in 1931 and came out in The Searchlight of Patna as a series of articles. Subsequently the narrative was continued up to the time of Gandhiji's cruel murder on January 30, 1948. Dr. Rajendra Prasad writes in the preface to this work : "He (Mahatma Gandhi) transformed the Province by his short stay of a few months in 1917-18 and the occasional tours he undertook in later year... We should feel satisfied that Bihar was privileged to earn his confidence. Let us strive to deserve it by fashioning the present and the future after the image of what he wanted Bharat to be". Dr. Piasad wrote in Hindi a valuable book entitled Bapu Ke Kadamon Men, which was published in 1950. The first edition Of Dr. Prasad's authoritative work on the Hindu-Muslim problem bearing the title of India Divided was published in January 1946. Its third revised edition, which came out in July 1947, was dedicated to the memory of Mazhar-ul Haque, "a devout Muslim, a staunch nationalist and a passionate patriot." In this work be had collected plenty of information and material on the question of the partition of India which had assumed importance since the All-India Muslim League passed a resolution in favour of it at its Lahore session in March 1940. The book is written in six parts. "Part I deals with the theory of Hindus and Muslims being two nations. While showing that the theory is as unsupported by history and facts of everyday life, as by the opinion of distinguished and representative Musalmans, it points out that even if it be assumed that the Musalmans are a separate nation, the solution of the Hindu-Muslim problem in India should, on the basis of experience of other countries and on the strength of the latest and most authoritative writers of international repute on the subject, be sought in the formation of a multi-national State in which a powerful political union guarantees cultural autonomy to different national groups and not in the creation of national States which will not only leave the problem of national minorities unsolved but will also create more new problems relating to questions-financial, economic, industrial and political and strategy-than it will solve." Our leaders agreed to the partition of India under the pressure of circumstances. But later events have justified the observations of Dr. Prasad. The most important book written by Dr. Prasad is his autobiography.

The major portion of this book was written by him in prison between 1942 and 1945 and its narrative was brought down to the year 1946. It was originally written in Hindi and it had two editions in that language. Its English version was published in December 1957. This work presents a highly fascinating story of the career and achievements of one of the greatest personalities of modern India, who records here his varied experiences of life particularly in connection with our national movement. It is in a sense an authentic and valuable source book for the history of this movement. Regarding the functioning of the Bihar Vidyapith and the efforts to promote khadi, Rajendra Prasad depicted a vivid picture in his Autobiography. The Vidyapith was moved to the Sadaqat Ashram.

A few more tenements were added in order to accommodate teachers and students comfortably. He mentioned the various kinds of hardships through which the Vidyapith had to pass. Rajendra Prasad tried to attract scholars of repute to the Vidyapith. They were the dedicated lot who came there from U.P., Bengal and other regions. So the Vidyapith began to show better results and created an academic atmosphere. Similarly the promotion of khadi was taken in hand. The dedicated and disciplined Congress workers like Ram Binod Singh and J.B. Kripalani started the khadi production centre at Madhubani. The Khadi

Board granted a huge financial grant to this centre so that it might progress for the welfare of the people. My principal preoccupation during this time was to collect funds for the Bihar Vidyapith and to look after the khadi organisational work. From the very beginning, people were generally indifferent to the Vidyapith and the tendency was accentuated later. It was surprising that some of the very people who had helped in its establishment were now antagonistic to it. The Vidyapith had been originally housed in a building on a monthly rental of Rs. 200. In order to cut down our expenditure, we moved the Vidyapith to the Sadaqat Ashram started by Mazharul Haq. To the buildings that were already there, we added a few more tenements in which all the teachers and students were accommodated. I liked the new location immensely. But the strength of the institution began to decline as popular enthusiasm for this type of education was on the wane. On account of lack of finance, several of the affiliated schools had to close down. Even then in 1926 there were affiliated to the Vidyapith 9 high schools, 16 middle schools and 30 primary schools with 797, 1,285 and 1,019 students respectively on their rolls.

The number of teachers was 79, 70 and 34 and the monthly expense incurred on these schools was respectively Rs. 1,950, Rs. 1,260 and Rs. 424. Some of these schools have managed to survive the hard times and exist even today. We considered the continuance of the Vidyapith very essential and tried to collect the necessary funds. I had seen in Maharashtra several institutions being run on public subscription, though no single individual's subscription amounted to any large sum. Subscriptions were recovered by sending the annual reports of these institutions to a large number of people by V.P.P. We felt like trying a similar experiment in Bihar. After some effort, we enrolled members willing to pay an annual subscription of Rs. 5. People paying larger amounts were enrolled as life-members or trustees. Unfortunately, people in our province were not in the habit of paying subscription regularly. Forms were filled, promises of payment were made but payments ceased after a year. It was very difficult to personally approach everyone every year for collecting subscriptions. Our plant thus failed and we had to collect money from different places. Only in Patna were there some 'regular payments. A gentleman, Bhagwan Das by name, donated some land to the Vidyapith and it fetched a regular income. Some time later, Gajadhar Prasad Sahu diverted some funds from his own trust to the Vidyapith. Thus, the institution carried on inspite of financial difficulties. We tried to attract scholars of repute to the Vidyapith. Ramdas Gaur, a famous scholar, came from Banaras. Highly qualified academicians came from Bengal. A reputed scholar of ancient Indian history, Jaichander Vidyalankar, joined the staff of the Vidyapith as a teacher in history. My acquaintance with him matured into intimacy and this association later on became one of the reasons for the founding of the Bharatiya Itihas Parishad. We tried to change the curriculum now and then with the object of turning our graduates who would now be mere scholars but genuine patriots and public workers.

All this did not take us very far; the number of students continued to fall and the scope of national education remained necessarily confined to very narrow limits. Nevertheless, our students and teachers gave a good account of themselves in public life, particularly whenever the call of Satyagraha came. The other thing which claimed my attention at that time was the organisation of khadi work. I had my heart set on it from the very beginning. The work was started in Bihar in 1921 with the allocation of a handsome amount to the Bihar Provincial Committee from the Swaraj Fund. The Committee appointed organisers in districts but neither the organisers nor the Committee members had any experience and the outcome was not very creditable. Ram Binod Singh, a Congress worker, started work on his own, and be was given assistance by Acharya Kripalani. At a production centre at Madhubani they started producing good khadi. It was exported to other provinces where it began to acquire a name for itself. On Acharya Kripalani's recommendation and my approval, Ram Binod Singh was granted a big loan by the Khadi Board. On the other hand, the Provincial Committee could not show satisfactory results. They had merely expanded the work but there was neither technical knowledge nor commercial talent to draw upon. Therefore they always recorded losses. The whole thing was reorganised after the establishment of the All-India Charkha Sangh, of which I was the agent in Bihar. We closed down several depots, keeping open only such of them as were self-supporting.

Those who joined the Sangh came under its strict discipline and this resulted in all-round improvement and an increase in the production and sale of Khadi. I visited these production centres generally once a year to supervise their work. I stayed for a day or two, sat in the depot, bought yarn and sold cotton, weighing them myself, supervised the weaving and assisted in the rixation of the price of the finished product. My own knowledge of khadi work grew and with it grew the realisation that the losses were entirely due to paucity of knowledge of the work. Our estimates of income and expenditure were subject to close scrutiny by the Secretary of the Charkha Sangh, Shanker Lal Banker and his office. Despite these precautions we sometimes suffered losses. The policy of the Sangh was to make cheap khadi available to the people. We, therefore, tried to buy yarn at the cheapest rates, to pay the minimum wages to weavers and to spend as little as possible on the sale depots. Compared to the production of all the provincial branches, the khadi produced in Bihar was considered cheap and of good quality. The handspun Kokti variety was popular in other provinces and it made Bihar famous. We also started printing and dyeing but because of the inexperience of our sales-depot workers, the sale of khadi could not be placed on a proper footing, the accounts were always in a mess and, in spite of improvements in other directions, arrangements regarding distribution seldom worked satisfactorily.

When we started the work we had our office and the principal depot in Patna. This created difficulties but as most of the lived in Patna we were reluctant to move the office. When Lakshmi Narain Sinha, Secretary of the Charkha Sangh, and I decided to expand the work and thought of moving the office to Muzaffarpur, we were opposed by our Patna friends. In view of the advantages, I stuck to the decision. We set up a number of huts at Akhara Ghat on the banks of the Gandaki to accommodate our workers and the workshop. It was a nice place and I often went to live there. Our godown and sales depot were located in rented buildings in the town. Our output increased a great deal. After some time we felt that even this arrangement was not satisfactory since the principal production centres were in Darbhanga district. Transport from Darbhanga to Muzaffarpur involved unnecessary expense. We decided to shift the main sales depot to Madhubani in Darbhanga district. But Ram Binod Singh already had a depot there.

To avoid unhealthy competition, therefore, we chose Pandaul as the field of our activities. Soon after, differences arose between Ram Binod Singh and his workers and his depot's output became less than that of the Charkha Sangh. Then we saw no harm in moving to Madbubani. It provided better scope for expansion and had better communications with other production centres. Our office and the principal sales depot were shifted to Madhubani. In his hour of the province in 1925, Gandhiji collected funds for Khadi work and the Deshbandhu Memorial Fund. He had collected about Rs. 50,000. This was handed over to us and added to our capital it helped us in extending our activities. One of the principal methods adopted by me to popularise Khadi was the organising of exhibitions at various places. The Patna exhibition of which I have written earlier was one of the most successful of the series. The Bettiah exhibition was inaugurated by the manager of the Estate, H.C. Prior, I.C.S., successor to Rutherford. The exhibition at Motihari was opened by the Rev. J.Z. Hodge, a reputed missionary. The one I organised in Jamshedpur was a daring venture and was very successful. It called for courage to hold an exhibition of the spinning wheel and its products in an industrial town like Jamshedpur where the chimneys ever emitted smoke, where molen iron flowed like a running river, and where giant slabs were rolled easily and quickly into rails. For the tiny Takli and the spinning wheel to demonstrate their pro i wess to the giant machines-it gave a strange sensation. But we did it and it went off quite well. Temple, a senior officer of the Tata firm and an engineer and the Town Administrator of Jamshedpur, opened the exhibition. The General Manager of the company, Keynen, and Mrs. Keynen, Americans, visited the exhibition and bought Khadi. Many officers of the company flocked to the exhibition and the sale of goods was brisk. The exhibition was such a success that we had to open another in another part of the town. Many more exhibitions were organised in Bihar towns that year, opened by prominent citizens and sometimes by me. These helped not only to further our propaganda but also to clear our accumulated stocks. I learnt that Gandhiji was suffering from high blood pressure and had gone to the Nandi Hills in Mysore State for rest. I went there and stayed with him for a few days. It was a fascinating place, though climbing the hills was rather tiring despite the fact that my asthma was not then quite so acute.

Later, I accompanied Gandhiji to Bangalore where a big Khadi exhibition, the first of its kind in Mysore State, had been organised, with the Tamil Nad and the Andhra branches of the Charkha Sangh participating in it. An interesting development was taking place in the south the progress of Hindi. A special conference was called in Bangalore where certificates were awarded-to candidates successful in the examinations held by the Hindi Prachar Sabha. For the first time I saw the great enthusiasm for Hindi in a non-Hindi-speaking area. We found husband and wife, mother and daughter and father and son learning and taking the examinations together. Then I went to Tiruppur, where the Tamil Nad Charkha Sangh had its principal depot, and Thiruchengode in Salem district, where Rajagopalachari had started an ashram and where valuable khadi work was being done. I studied the production and organisational methods at these centres and tried to introduce them in our province. I particularly liked their accounting system. Among khadi producers, Tamil Nad topped the lift, whereas in respect of fine cloth (excepting kakti) Andhra was ahead of other provinces. On the request of Sita Ram Shastri, Secretary of the Andhra Charkha Sangh, I visited several Andhra centres and made speeches there, trying as best as I could to explain the economy and utility of khadi. These speeches appeared to have made some impression on the educated people who were generally sceptical about khadi. When I later returned to Patna, Andhra Congressmen informed me that they thought that my speeches would prove helpful in their work and requested me to publish them in a book form. I followed their advice and published a Khadi collection of my Andhra speeches under the title, Economics of in English. A Hindi translation was also published later. During the earthquake in Bihar, Rajendra. Prasad did yeoman's services. His conscious pricked to see thousands of people being homeless, besides several thousands being killed under debris. He organised a dedicated band of workers who toured with him, raised funds, arranged food, clothes, drinking water and other basic amenities.

He thus made them feel that they had some helpers and sympathisers who listened to their false of woes and sorrows. He appointed the Bank of Bihar as the treasurer. On an average, three hundred money orders were received a day. Hundreds of parcels were received and they were distributed among the victims. On the day I received the news that I was soon to be released, I lay in my bed thinking of the changeableness of the authorities. During my second term in hospital they had tightened the restrictions and allowed my brother to visit me only once a week. When my brother's wife was away my daughter-in-law came to look after me but the police objected to her keeping her four-year-old child with he and she had to go away.

But now officialdom had suddenly softened and indicated their readiness to release me. I was thinking in this strain, wondering if I should agree to the release and was in a state of drowsiness when I suddenly felt that the bed was shaking. Then 1 heard the doors and windows rattling. I wondered if I had become so week that the little strain caused by some concentrated thinking had given me such a dizzy and reeling head, when I heard my brother's wife shouting that the earth was shaking. I realised at once it was an earthquake. Along with others in the ward I ran out and stood on the lawn opposite. The tremors were so terrific that I found it difficult to keep erect. The tremors were accompanied with gurgling and loud noises, as if a hundred railway trains had started moving together. There were a number of cows grazing nearby. They herded together and ran in panic towards us, their tails up. We became apprehensive. It looked they were determined to charge us. Suddenly, they stopped short, just near us, and calmed, as if under the feeling that particular spot was a safe place for them. The next instant, we saw the double storeyed residential quarters of the nurses collapse. Because of the din all round we did not bear the noise of its crash but merely saw a column of dust rising as the masonary came tumbling down. Parts of the hospital building also gave way, but fortunately none was killed or injured.

After a few moments everything was still. I thought the tremor must have lasted for about five minutes. Later, the newspaper reports from different parts of the province said that the tremors lasted from four to seven minutes. It was the first time I had come out of my room since my admission to hospital and had talked to any outsider. Friends from the city came rushing to me to see if I was well. I was told that many houses had collapsed in the city. We saw a number of injured people being brought to the hospital. Till the evening we all stayed on the lawn where the beds had been removed. It was the month of January and as night approached it was becoming extremely cold. I did not want to aggravate my malady by remaining in the open and I went in despite the fact that the walls of our ward had cracked and many people who had gone in had come out again on the lawn. On seeing me go in, some others followed.

Adjacent to our ward, was a children's ward, part of which had collapsed. The occupants were evacuated to the lawn and they all slept in the open. At one in the night, there was another tremor which sent us scampering out to the lawn again, but it was a short-lived one and we went in after some time. The next day, Dr. Banerji came to see me and while we were conversing in the verandah, we experienced a third tremor. For the first time, I learnt from him that while Patna had suffered considerably, the districts had been worse hit, particularly Monghyr. Faller news about the extent of the damage was awaited. Monghyr being his home town, he was very worried. He told me that the Government had asked for all available doctors to be kept in readiness to be rushed to the worst affected areas and for arrangements to be made in hospitals for the admission of the injured. I was also told that part of the Civil Secretariat had collapsed and that the resulting confusion was responsible for the delay in my release order. It was two days later that I got the order.

The Civil Surgeon told me that I was free to leave the hospital or stay there till I recovered. As the news of large scale destruction caused by the earthquake in North Bihar poured in, the Government released political prisoners hailing from that area. As I was thinking of how best to organise relief for the afflicted, the released friends came to me to discuss the matter. As, having been arrested in the summer, they had no warm clothes with them. I arranged for blankets and some funds and sent them to various places in the Tirhut division to find out the extent of damage and decide on the nature or relief to be organised there. As means of communications had been completely disrupted, my friends left for North Bihar by country boats. Several days after the earthquake information about the magnitude of the tragedy was still scanty. Whatever little we came to know was too terrible to contemplate. I was still very weak and the doctors detained me in the hospital. But I would move out and insisted on doing relief work which they allowed me to do. I felt better and better every day; my weakness left me and I began to devote myself whole heartedly to relief work. After their release from Hazaribagh Jail, Mathura Prasad and Satyanarain Sinha joined me. We decided to form a relief committee with members from all parties and groups.

Whenever an emergency arose in the past we had always organised relief work but the problem confronting us just then was tremendous and unprecedented. The Bihar Governor was also thinking of convening a meeting to discuss matters relating to the organisation of relief. Syed Abdul Aziz, one of the Ministers, met me in hospital and pleaded that we should not start a separate relief organisation but should co-operate with the Government. Shaffi Daudi also came and spoke in a similar strain. They said that while the Government would set apart some funds for relief in addition to what was collected, there was little hope of a large amount of money being collected from the public by the Congress as the organisation was not in proper trim and as many Congressmen were still in jail. I told both Aziz and Daudi that the Government was welcome to organise relief, and as both the efforts were bound to be in the same direction there was no room for conflict. There would be need, moreover, for a relief committee of the kind we contemplated because many people would like to donate money to a non-official organisation rather than to a Government agency. We would make the best possible use of our funds and we would be always willing to co-operate with the Government. There was no question of competing with the Government, I assured them. My friends approved of my stand. A few days later, a public meeting was called in Patna and the constitution of the Bihar Central Relief Committee was announced. I was made chairman of the committee. We immediately issued an appeal for funds. Then the Government also convened a public meeting which I attended and they also issued an appeal for funds. As details of the devastation caused by the earthquake appeared in newspapers, there was spontaneous sympathy in India and even abroad for the victims and money began pouring in. Jawaharlal Nehru came to Patna and from there he went to Monghyr and Tirhut areas to see the scenes of devastation himself. He set an example to others by helping in clearing the debris and digging out dead bodies 'himself. Satish Chandra Das Gupta came from Bengal with money and material. I apprised Gandhiji of the situation. He was in South India doing anti-untouchability propaganda and he immediately issued an appeal and started collecting money himself. We set up branches of the relief committee in all the districts. We began receiving contributions in the shape of money, rice, utensils, clothes, blankets and medicines from all parts of the country. We stored them in Patna and distributed them to the districts according to their requirements. Very soon the work became incredibly heavy.

Many of our workers who were still in jail were released by the Government and they all joined us in the relief work. Jawaharlal stayed in Patna and gave us many useful suggestions about the organisation of the central office. He visited Bihar twice during this period and he was preparing to devote himself to the work fully when he was arrested. Vallabhbbai Patel was in jail and we were therefore deprived of the advantage of the experience gained by him in organising relief at the time of the devastating floods in Gujarat. Gandhiji and Jamnalal Bajaj visited us. From the U.P. came Acharya Narendra Deo and Sri Prakasa. It is impossible to give the names of all the friends who came to our rescue but I cannot forget the help rendered by J.C. Kumarappa. He was a chartered accountant from the U.K. and boore Gandhiji took him to the Gujarat Vidyapith he had a very fine practice in Bombay having as his clientele many big companies. So Gandhiji sent him to us to take charge of our accounts. It would be no exaggeration to say that but for him we would have been in a terrible mess. We had more than 2,000 workers spread over twelve districts. Few of them knew accounting and the nature of our work was multifarious and separate accounts had to be kept for each kind of work. Our task was assuming formidable proportions but, thanks to Kumarappa, we were able to manage it. We appointed the Bank of Bihar as our treasurer. All the money we received was sent direct to the bank. We received, on an average, 300 money orders a day and hundreds of parcels containing various articles of daily use. Every item received was entered in our registers as were also the despatches to needy places.

After some time we brought out first report, the list of donors covering 400 pages. I requested the public to draw our attention to any omission. It is indeed gratifying to note that I received only a dozen complaints. When we looked into the matter it was discovered that even these were not cases of omission. The names had been printed in the list by overnight had been placed under the wrong district or province and this was pointed out to the donors concerned. I was very punctilious in this matter, because one his to be careful in handling public money, otherwise it creates unpleasant consequences. When funds and parcels poured into our office beyond our expectation, I was worried a great deal, but thanks to Kamarappa and his organisation, we can say that every penny and every article that we received was put to the best possible use. The state of my health compelled my stay in hospital for ten days after my release from jail. As my condition gradually improved, I began stirring out. The pressure of work was so great that I had to begin my day at four in the morning I had to read reports of damage and relief work. I had to attend to correspondence and issue fresh appeals for help. Abdul Aziz placed his house at our disposal, but the sudden increase of work rendered it inadequate and we had to shift our offices to more spacious premises. We set up many departments, each under a senior workers. Jayaprakash Narayan was in control of the whole office. He was later joined by Anugrah Narain Sinha who took over charge after his release from jail. On the Relief Committee were included representatives of all the groups and provinces which had sent us relief. After a few days, Gandhiji visited us, but before his arrival I wanted to visit the worst affected areas. So far, partly because of my weakness and partly because of pressure of work, I was tied down to the office in Patna. But as more and more helpers came in and division of work was possible, I was relieved to a certain extent. So a month after the earthquake I was able to undertake a tour. I used to send reports back to my office about the places I visited. These reports were later compiled in a pamphlet.

To keep all the donors, sympathisers and workers informed of the developments, we started publishing a bulletin. In addition to sending help in the shape of money and materials, certain social service organisations opened offices in Bihar and began doing relief work on their own. But they cooperated with the Central Relief Committee and we, while not hindering anyone, saw to it that duplication was avoided. We were thus able to ensure the best use of public money donated either to us or to other organisations. Such organisations were numerous, and while expressing my gratitude to all of them, I might mention the more prominent of them here : the Marwari Relief Society, the Memon Relief Society, Sri Ramakrishna Mission, the party of Baba Gurdit Singh, the Red Cross, the Indian Medical Association and the Sankat Tran Samiti of Bengal under Satish Chandra Das Gupta. Popular enthusiasm for helping the victims of the earthquake was so great that for some time money continued to pour into both the Government and our Funds more or less in equal volume. The Central Relief Committee and the Government published their daily receipts. With the coming of Mahatma Gandhi and the more or less permanent stay in Bihar of Seth Jamnalal Bajaj for relief work, I felt much relieved. The difficulties in the distribution of relief were many. All communications by rail and road had been disrupted. Houses were not available at most of the places to accommodate our workers. Drinking water was scarce in many places. By and by, roads were repaired and although bridges and culverts could not be rebuilt, diversions were made for traffic. All means of communication, from bullock-carts to boats, were pressed into service. The Relief Committee brought motor trucks for its use. Hundreds of cycles were provided for relief workers, for organising and training whom the Committee had to thank Acharya Kripalani, Dr. Hardikar and Miss

Sophia Somji. The Committee set up straw huts in many places to house the workers. It might surprise people to know that we never had to spend more than two annas a day per worker for meals. We had to provide for the immediate needs of those who had lost their houses and had nothing to eat and nothing to wear. Even if we provided them with cereals, they had no utensils to cook their food in and in many cases they had no drinking water at all. Therefore, as a measure of immediate relief, we arranged for the distribution of food and cloth and other necessities, after all that was possible had been done to clear the debris and remove the dead.

By the time Gandhiji arrived on the scene, we had almost completed the work of immediate relief Now we had to take in band the work of long term rehabilitation and as we had before us certain plans we had to decide the order of priority to be given to them. It was not possible for Gandhiji to visit all the places but he went to most of the worst-affected areas and saw the unprecedented and widespread destruction caused by the earthquake. We considered his visit necessary because first, we wanted him to see things for himself and advise us how best to provide relief for the victims; secondly, the sufferers also needed a word of solace and encouragement which his presence readily gave them. Hundreds of houses had been destroyed. To help people rebuild them was a Herculean undertaking. Then there was the problem of the supply of drinking water. Tanks and wells had gone dry or mysteriously disappeared.

Many streams, tanks and lakes had become flat land or mounds of sand. To tackle this problem seemed a super-human task. The presence of sand in cultivable fields posed another big problem. Large fields where rich, green crops stood where turned into sandy wastes. It seemed as if whole areas had turned desert overnight. We feared the land might become useless for cultivation if we allowed the sand to remain. We tried to remove it in one or two places, but it proved too expensive and ineffective and we gave it up as impossible. In North Bihar, sugarcane is grown in a large area and there are many sugar factories there.

The earthquake had damaged the machinery in many factories. But the sugarcane crop, worth millions of rupees, was still standing. To help the villagers, therefore, we somehow arranged the harvesting and crushing of the crop in indigenous crushers. With some difficulty, we collected a few thousand crushes and distributed them among the villagers. The Government liked the idea and cooperated in this work. Thus, we were able to save a major part of the crop. Luckily, some of the sugar mills also started working after some repairs had been effected, and quite a part of the rest of the crop could be sent there for crushing. There were many other questions like these to be considered. A general meeting of the Central Relief Committee was, therefore, called at Patna. All the prominent members from the different provinces were invited to attend it, The Committee expressed its readiness to offer the fullest co-operation to the Government. As the Committee was too large and cumber some, a compact Working Committee was set up. Rules were formulated for the conduct of business.

The Working Committee met often to discuss the problems before it and take decisions. Gandhiji advised us to tackle first the water problem instead of attempting the impossible task of removing the mountains of sand from land or helping to build houses. Accepting this advice, our workers devoted their energies towards constructing new wells and tanks and repair of old ones where possible to ensure an adequate supply of water. We found this undertaking too big for our resources but we did not flinch from our purpose. We got some tube wells bored with the help of some contractors but we found that they would not serve our purpose. First, it was a waste of time as only one person could draw water from a masonry well. Secondly, the upkeep of a tube well was complicated and the villagers could not understand it. As the masonly well only cost as much as a tube well we decided in favour of masonry wells. We wanted to build as many well as possible before the rains. Our workers started construction with cooperation of the villagers. We got many thousands of new wells built and perhaps an equal number of old ones repaired by July. Many old tanks were renovated for use by cattle. When we had completed this task we were faced with another problem. While the victims of the earthquake were on the way to being put on their feet again, another calamity struck Bihar. Swollen streams and rivers brought floods in the wake of the earthquake. We had feared that the beds of the Ganga, the Sarju, the Gandak and other rivers might have been lifted by sand deposits and had, therefore, anticipated to some extent the new calamity. We got boats and rafts made and kept them ready for an emergency at places usually affected by floods.

The Government too had prepared likewise. The poor villagers of the earthquake-affected areas had enough work to keep themselves gainfully occupied. One can distribute gratuitous relief to people for a few days in case of an emergency, but it is positively injurious to keep them on doles for a long time. Therefore, from the very beginning we had followed a policy of giving relief in the shape of work. Labourers for all kinds of work like clearing debris, repairing and constructing houses and sinkings wells were needed. The Central Relief Committee had also an elaborate programme of constructing new wells and tanks and repairing old ones. Besides, we had several hundreds of miles of roads repaired and built throughout the province. The villagers thus found employment readily available, but it was feared that during the floods they would be left without any occupation. Bhartua, a large tract of hollow land, situated on the way to Seetamarhi from Muzaffarpur, was once a fertile area. It was now water-logged and had been rendered unfit for cultivation even before the earthquake. The cause of this unhappy state of affairs in Bhartua was that the only outlet for draining the water from the low lying areas had been obstructed by the river Bagmati having changed its course.

The only way to bring life and fertility back to the soil was to clear the obstruction in order to provide an outlet for Bhartua's stagnant pools. The water, like the Kosi flood waters, caused even big trees to wither away and die. Gandhiji saw the scene of desolation and was greatly pained. The Central Relief Committee decided to undertake this task even if the Government were unwilling to help. We therefore, estimated the cost and then wrote to the Government and a the same time started the work of digging a canal to drain the stagnant water. Our endeavours paid ample dividends. Life returned to Bhartua as its soil once again became productive. We had several other small canals dug. Employment was also provided to village women through spinning. We thus combined relief work with the work or propagation of khadi. The Bihar Charkha Sangh took over the areas thus developed. Houses were being constructed in large numbers, and this resulted in an acute shortage of building materials. We had stores opened at several places on behalf of the Relief Committee for the sale of bricks, lime, bamboo, timber and steel at fair prices. During the monsoon months, we began feeling the effects, of the shortage of rice, and prices started rising. We purchased stocks of rice from Burma and distributed them to the Relief Committee's sale depots.

To meet and check any possible outbreak of malaria and cholera, the Committee set up a number of dispensaries all over the affected areas. Our work was rendered more difficult during the rainy season, but somehow we managed to maintain our services with the help of our fleet of rafts. In addition to this, we gave cash grants to many people for repairing their houses. Because of its limited resources which could be better spent in helping the poor, the Committee decided against helping the well-to-do and those who owned big houses before the earthquake. The maximum sum given was Rs. 250. The work of helping the rich was left to the Government. Two Englishmen accompanied Gandhiji to several places during his tour of the affected areas. One of them was Miss Muriel Lester, Gandhiji's host in London at the time of the Round Table Conference, and the other was Miss Agatha Horrison, a public worker and a sympathiser of India. Besides these women, many other Europeans visited Bihar to see the devastation and wrote about it to their friends overseas. C.F. Andrews too toured the province and wrote a booklet for circulation in England and America. The result of these efforts was a surge of great sympathy in those countries for Bihar's miseries and substantial contributions to the Relief Fund. There is an organisation in Europe which is opposed to war. The members, while rating very high the great qualities of selflessness and courage which a war brings out in men, thought it would be much better if those qualities were diverted for the service of humanity rather than be used for slaughter. The organisation had imposed on its members the discipline of an army.

Irrespective of any considerations of religion or nationality, they hastened to do social service and offer relief wherever it was needed. They had experience of organising relief at several places destroyed during the First World War. The leader of the organisation was Pierre Ceresole, a Swiss. An engineer by profession, he was highly connected and its ancestors had held high positions in his country's administration. Since his joining the anti-war organisation, Ceresole had given up everything else in order to devote himself entirely to it. He had also been punished for refusing to take military training. Bihar had the good fortune to have the services of Ceresole who came to the province with a band of workers on his mission of service. Some places had suffered such damage by the earthquake that we asked the people to settle elsewhere. We prevailed unon some landlords to place lands at the disposal of the uprooted persons and tried our best to persuade the villagers to move to the new areas, but no one was prepared to quit the site of his ancestral home. We then modified our settlement plans on large scale resettlements. Some villages of Muzaffarpur district were fed up with the yearly visitation of floods and its people agreed to settle down in the places we suggested. We decided to build new villages for them. The Government agreed to help in this project with funds. The building of houses was entrusted to as local committee and the Central Relief Committee nominated Dr. Ceresole to serve on the committee with one of our workers, Maninder Mohan Dutt, as his assistant. New villages were brought into being on the new sites within the period of a year or two. Dr. Ceresole remained on the job throughout except for a few months when he returned to Europe. He and his companions did not hesitate to do heavy manual labour, although Dr. Ceresole, a well-built man, was more than 60 years of age.

Bihar's heat was too much for them sometimes, but they gladly put up with it and continued to stay in the villages without any of the comfort and amenities of life to which they were accustomed in Europe. The manner in which these men kept themselves busy the whole day put heart in our people. One of the new village was named Shantipur (abode of peace). This beautiful village still stands today as a model settlement. On account of the earthquake and the floods, malaria broke out in epidemic form and the Relief Committee provided medical aid in the area, particularly in the districts of Muzaffarpur, Darbhanga and Bhagalpur. We were able to do all this primarily because of the enthusiasm of the workers and their devotion to service. Paid workers could not have accomplished as much. From the very beginning, the Central Relief Committee knew that the least amount must be spent on the organisation and machinery of relief and most of it on actual relief. The Committee was fortunate in having a large band of voluntary workers to do the job. But because the work continued for over 18 months, we had to employ some paid workers to look after the office work. On every other item like accommodation and transport we were able to economise to the utmost.

Our periodical reports showed the relief and organisational expenses separately so that the people might know how little we were spending on those who carried out relief operations. Transport cost us a good deal in the beginning, but gradually the Committee concentrated on digging wells and tanks and distributing cash grants for building houses, we were able to reduce this expenditure considerably. The Government had appointed an experienced civilian, Brett, as Relief Commissioner. He compiled a report of the relief operations, in which he preferred to the work of the Central Relief Committee and observed that the establishment expenses of the Committee were high. By the time, the report was published, Brett had gone on leave to England.

Finding that all the facts about the Relief Committee expenses in the report were wrong, we wrote to the Government, inquiring from what source they had got their figures. They Government could not give an answer, the reply said, in the absence of Brett, and they new confessed their error. When the relief operations were wound up, the Relief Committee entrusted to the balance of the funds to a Trust which maintained it as a reserve fund to be used in an emergency in Bihar. It was used occasionally for the relief of flood victims. Later, as the money was lying idle, the trustees, in consultation with Gandhiji, advanced it as a loan to the Charkha Sangh. Sardar Patel, Seth Jamnalal Bajaj and I were the three trustees.

6

Rajendra Prasad and Political Activities After Second World War

The announcement of World War Second by Britain against Germany was seriously viewed by various political parties, including the Provincial Governments. The non-Congress ministries in Punjab, Sind and Bengal pledged their full support to the Government. The Indian States, as usual, offered their full support in men and money. The Hindu Mahasabha and the National Liberal Federation offered unconditional support to the Government. The Congress Working Committee protested against the exploitation of our resources for imperialist ends and openly declared that "India cannot associate herself with a War said to be for democratic freedom, when that very freedom is denied to her.... (It) 'therefore invites the British Government to declare in unequivocal terms what their war aims are in regard to democracy and imperialism, and the new order that is envisaged in particular how those aims are going to apply to India and to be given effect to in the present'. The AICC endorsed this resolution on 10 October, 1939 and demanded that "India must be declared an independent nation". The attitude of the Muslim League, however, hardened and its conditions for support in war were laid down in a resolution passed by the Working Committee of the Muslim League. It was critical of the plight of Muslim minority in the Congress governed provinces, condemned the scheme of all-India federation and appealed to the Raj for greater protection for Muslims against 'Congress oppression'. It also stated that no declaration regarding constitutional advance for India should be made, nor any constitution farmed without the consent and approval of the Muslim League. This, in fact, amounted to a Veto on future constitutional advance by the minority, irrespective of the interests of the majority. The resolutions of Congress were not taken seriously by the Viceroy and soon after the declaration of war on 3 September, 1939, he strengthened the position of his Government by promulgating the Defence of India Ordinances. This step of the Government was met with criticism by the administration of popular ministries operating in eleven provinces of India. At this point of time, the Congress too tried to seek the support of Jinnah, but he refused to come forward in any more proposal sponsored by the leadership of the Congress. In August 1940, Jawaharlal Nehru gave vent to his feelings thus : 'The situation in Europe in August 1939 was threatening and I did not want to leave India at a moment of crisis. For years past we had thought about this and proclaimed our policy. Yet in spite of all this, the British Government declared India to be a belligerent country without any reference to our people, to the Central Assembly, or to the Provincial Governments. The Congress

Working Committee issued a long statement in the middle of September 1939, in which our past and present policy was defined and the British Government was invited to explain their war aims, more particularly in regard to British Imperialism. We had frequently condemned Fascism and Nazism but we were more intimately concerned with the imperialism that dominated over us.' The British Government's answer was clear. It felt no doubt that they were not prepared to clarify their war 'aims or to hand over control of the Government to the people's representatives.

The Congress Ministries resigned as they were not prepared to cooperate on these terms in the prosecution of war. The developments in the War situation posed new questions before the Congress Working Committee. Gandhiji wanted the Committee to extend the principle of non-violence to which we had adhered in our struggle for freedom to the functioning of a free State. 'A free India Must rely on this principle to guard itself against external aggression or internal disorder.... Every one of us was convinced that we must adhere to our policy of non-violence, as we had so far done, in our own struggle. The War in Europe had strengthened this conviction. But to commit the future State was another and a more difficult matter, and it was not easy to see how anyone moving on the plane of politics could do it'. Undoubtedly, Congress had to wait and assess the mood of the Raj for three years, from 1939 to 1942.

The Cripps Mission met with failure as it put certain conditions, to be taken up after the expiry of the war. To wait for a longer time was thought to be inexpedient and politically unsound. The demonstration of dissatisfaction and resentment, therefore, became a glaring phenomenon under the banner of the Congress. The Viceroy gauged the political atmosphere with a sense of seriousness and had consultation with as many as fifty-two eminent leaders. The main' purpose of interviewing these leaders was to apprise them fully of the plan and policy of the Government in connection with the war. He shrewdly put forward the sentiments of the Prime Minister to the effect that the Home Government had no inclination of any kind to reap material advantage from the Second World War. He further explained that his Government had the supreme aim of softening and smoothening the international system seriously perturbed by the onslaughts of Fascism and Nazism. He also, made it clear that his Government was committed to the principle of Dominion Status. The constitutional problem was, however, to be taken up soon after the end of the war.' The Congress Working Committee passed a resolution and handed it over to Stafford Cripps on 2 April, 1942. It clearly spelt out the reaction of the leadership of the Congress to the proposals made by the Raj : 'The Working Committee have given their full and earnest consideration to the proposals made by the British War Cabinet in regard to India and the elucidation thereof by Sir Stafford Cripps.

These proposals, which have been made at the very last hour because of the compulsion of events, have to be considered not only in relation to India's demand for independence, but more especially in the present grave war crisis with a view to meeting effectively the perils and dangers that confront India and envelop the world. On 14 July, 1942, the Congress Working Committee passed a resolution, generally referred to as the 'Quit India' resolution. It renewed the demand that the 'British rule in India must end immediately', and reiterated the view that the freedom of India was 'necessary not only in the interest of India but also for the safety of the world and for the ending of Nazism, Fascism, Militarism and other forms of imperialism, and the aggression of one nation over another'. It was resolved that on the withdrawal of British Rule in India, responsible men and women of the country would come together to form a provincial Government, representatives of all important sections of the people of India which would later evolve a scheme whereby a Constituent Assembly could be convened in order to prepare a Constitution for the government of India acceptable to all sections of the people. Representatives of Free India and representatives of Great Britain were to confer together for the adjustment of future relations and for the cooperation of the two countries as allies in the common task of meeting aggression. It was the earnest desire of the Congress to enable India to resist aggression effectively with the people's united will and strength behind it. In making the proposal for the withdrawal of British Rule from India, the Congress had no desire whatsoever to embarrass Great Britain or the Allied powers in their prosecution of the war, or in any way to encourage aggression on India or increased pressure on China by the Japanese or any other power associated with the Axis group. Not did the Congress intend to jeopardise the defensive capacity of the Allied powers. 'The Congress would plead with the British power to accept the very reasonable and just proposal herein made, not only in the interest of India, but also that of Britain and of the cause of freedom to which the United Nations proclaim their adherence.' Among Mahatma Gandhi's staunch disciple was Miss Slade, popularly known as Mira Ben, the daughter of a British Naval Admiral. She was sent to Delhi to apprise the Viceroy of the purport of the Congress Working

Committee's resolution and the nature of the movement proposed by it. But the Viceroy refused to interview her as he thought that Gandhi was going to launch a rebellion during the war.

Nor was the Government prepared to meet or discuss with any representative of an organisation which spoke in such terms. Having lost all hopes of settlement with the Government, the All India Congress Committee met at Bombay on 7 August, 1942. It took into consideration the resolution passed on 14 July, and also adopted a long resolution which spelt out justification for asking the British to quit India and explained its implications.

The operative part of the resolution was : 'The Committee resolves, therefore, to sanction for the vindication of India's inalienable right to freedom and independence, the starting of a mass struggle on non-violent lines on the widest possible scale, so that the country might utilize all non-violent strength it has gathered during the last twenty two years of peaceful struggle'. The Committee placed Mahatma Gandhi in command of the movement, but warned that a time might come when the Congress would be unable to issue instructions for people's guidance. It was decided that 'When this happens every man and woman, who is participating in this movement must function for himself or herself within the four corners of general instructions issued.' It solemnly declared that the transfer of power which the Congress was seeking 'will bring to the whole of India' as it had no intention of gaining power for the Congress. Mahatma Gandhi laid stress on the following fundamental points and stated :

(a) Forget the differences between the Hindus and Muslims and think of yourselves as Indians only.

(b) Our quarrel is not with the British people, we fight their imperialism, we must purge ourselves of hatred.

(c) In Satyagraha there 13 no place for fraud, or any kind of untruth.

(d) Feel that from today you are a free man and not a dependent.

(e) Do or Die. Either free India or die in the attempt.

Besides he gave advice to government servants, soldiers, students, princes and journalists regarding their duty towards the movement. He declared what the voice of his conscience was impelling him to do so. It told him : 'You have to stand against the whole world, although you may have to stand alone.... Do not fear. On the question of who should join, it was suggested that all Indians whether in the Congress organisation or not who desired freedom for the whole of India and fully believed in the weapon of truth and non-violence for the purpose of the struggle, would be expected to join. No one should undertake Satyagraha who barboured hatred or ill-will in his heart against any Indian or Englishman. It is indeed a remarkable aspect of Gandhi's working of mind that be told the Government that the passing of the resolution did not mean-that the actual struggle was going to commence immediately. He proposed to meet the Viceroy and plead with him for the acceptance of the Congress demand. Only after that he was to formulate his line of action for the movement. In war, surprise offence and first strike are the keys to success. In the early hours of 9 August, 1942, Gandhiji, Kasturba Gandhi, Sarojini Naidu and Mahadev Desai were arrested and were taken to the Aga Khan Palace at Poona.

Simultaneously all the members of the Working Committee in Bombay were taken into custody and were lodged in the old fort at Ahmednagar. Thereafter, arrests took place all over India and a large number of regional leaders were thrown into prison. The responses in the urban and rural areas was spontaneous. People came out in large numbers on hearing Gandhi's arrest, and their retaliation resulted into attacks on courts, burning of Government records and to bring police stations under popular control. In a few weeks, the machinery of the Government was paralysed and dislocated, and the worst effect was glaringly visible in U.P., C.P. and Berar, Bengal, Assam, Bihar, Gujarat, Andhra and Karnataka. At places railway engines were decorated with national flags. The people of Bombay Presidency showed much enthusiasm, organised capability and high sense of patriotism on the eve of the arrest of the front-rank leadership in the country.

The Shivaji Park and the Gowalia Tank were the main centres of activities of Satyagrahis in Bombay. In spite of warnings by the police, meetings were held at these two places and numerous other places. The Government, however, took prompt action soon issued an order bannings public meeting Picketing was made unlawful and the flogging was revived by the Whipping Act. The fire-arms were taken under police control and people were ruthlessly suppressed. The textile-mill hands struck work and this process continued for sometime. The mass demonstrations, of Course, an irregular feature, continued up to September in spite of the imposition of curfew by the Government. The popular demonstration in various parts of the presidency had deep linkage with the celebration of Independence-Day, Gandhi Jayanti, Tilak anniversary and other days of national importance. Elsewhere, students in

Maharashtra were fairly active in taking out processions, holding meetings and distributing Congress bulletins. The police lathi-charged them severely, but this kind of repression did not deter their enthusiasm and patriotic fervour. Their excitement for the movement proved a great asset as the message of Mahatma Gandhi reached the youths and the masses through their consistent efforts.

Both urban and rural regions of Maharashtra participated wholeheartedly in the movement. Strikes, processions and demonstrations were the glaring phenomenon. Students, both of schools and colleges, in prominent towns, i.e., Poona, Nasik, Ahmednagar, Sholapur and Satara showed much excitement, fervour and patriotic activities. Students hoisted national flags on their institutions. Besides police posts were attacked, railway lines were damaged and other means of communications were paralysed. The people of Satara organised numerous mass meetings not caring for the ban on such gatherings by the Government. Picketing of courts, post offices and other Government offices was the main programme of Satyagrahis in this district.

The strike of thousands of workers in Iron and Steel Factory at Kirloskar Wadi for fifteen-days was a glaring phenomenon in this region. This factory supplied material of the war-efforts of the Raj and the workers felt annoyed about it. This strike by thousands of workers brought about a huge loss in the manufactures of the biggest steel factory in this region. In Gujarat, much enthusiasm and excitement-was visible at various levels amongst the people. A protest meeting was held in Ahmedabad on 10 August which was attended by thousands of people. Besides, processions attended by men and women were organised in different localities of the town. The students also organised separate processions in which they raised anti Raj slogans. The local bureaucracy acted swiftly and sought the help of police which used lathi-charge and other means to disperse the crowd. This, however, did not diminish the spirit of defiance amongst the people and the students. Mills and commercial markets were closed. The Government did not hesitate to display even tanks and machine-guns in order to generate fear amongst the people. The mob even burnt numerous Government buildings including railway stations and post offices.

Telephone and telegraph connections were destroyed and consistent propaganda about the Congress programme was made amongst the people. In Ahmedabad, about one hundred textile mills were closed and the strike in numerous Tata establishments was a glaring phenomenon. The trade union movement, thus, showed its strength, unity, solidarity and better organization at many places. The Government showed much concern over the steps taken by the trade union movement as the loss accrued to it during the war was phenomenal. The demonstration of repression by the Government to bring back the worker to the factory proved effective but to much cost. In U.P. the movement spread like wild fire and people from every walk Of life answered to the call of Mahatma Gandhi. In Banaras, Allahabad, Lucknow, Kanpur, Agra, Gorakhpur, Moradabad, Ballia, Meerut and other towns the movement gained momentum at various levels. Complete hartals, meetings, processions, and courting arrests were the major planks on which the programme of the movement was based-Besides much damage was caused to Government property to paralyse the functioning of the administrative machinery. In Allahabad, a call for general strike was given on 9 August. Schools and Colleges were closed and there was a huge demonstration by the students. The procession of students in spite of obstacles by the police force on the way, rounded its way towards the district courts, and at last succeeded in hoisting the tri-colour flag on the courts building. The police lathi charged and later on firing on students proved fatal for one student. In another procession, when police resorted to firing, a fourteen year old boy was killed. Kanpur, a major industrial town of the United Provinces, the industrial labour took a prominent part.

The local leader and the students showed their sense of patriotism by participating in processions and meetings. The mill workers struck work during August. Damage was done to Government property including a few post offices and telegraph office. In brutal lathi charge by the police, people suffered much. Agra did not lag behind in showing its sense of patriotism. Like other towns of U.P., students came out Of schools and Colleges and brought about extensive damage to Government Property, mainly Government buildings, and railway stations. As usual, there were indiscriminate arrests and convictions. In Gorakhpur district, thousands of anti-Government slogans were raised. This kind of agitation took birth in some of the prominent villages like Debaria and Palli.

The District Magistrate took stern measures against the precisionists, by seeking support of the army which was commissioned for firing on the mob. About fourteen persons were reported dead on the spot on account of firing by the army personnel. Besides more than a hundred persons were severely injured. In Ballia, there was much excitement amongst the people, and when the call for hartal was given all observed it in an organised and disciplined manner. Like other towns of U.P., all the schools and colleges were closed, and the students organised themselves in a procession raising slogans against the Raj.

The Satyagrahis of the district damaged the Government property including railway lines, means of communications, post offices, district jail, police stations and other buildings. So far so Chittoo Pandey declared independence for Ballia. The bureaucracy, however, acted very severely and ordered the police to fire on the mob. As a result thereof two died on the spot and several persons were injured. The repression by police and army reached its highest degree. In Banaras, people got much excited at the arrest of Mahatma Gandhi and other members of the Congress Working Committee. A huge procession which culminated into a meeting, also attended by a large number of students, was taken out in the city.

When the students marched towards the court to press the Government servants to tender their resignations, they were severely lathi-charged. In spite of severe injuries, their enthusiasm was not mitigated and so far so one of the students was able to enter the court-premises, pulled down the Union Jack and in its place hoisted the national flag. The students also divided themselves into batches and traversed the suburban villages in order to make the movement broad-based by giving publicity to the message of Mahatma Gandhi amongst the village-folk. The Banaras Hindu University showed the spirit of patriotism when the students disobeyed the orders of the Vice-Chancellor, The army was called in and the students were beaten and made to vacate the campus. The Congress flag flying on the main gate of the university was pulled down, torn to pieces and trampled under foot by British tummies. The damage caused to the Government property was immense. The railway track from Banaras to Lucknow and Allahabad and Patna to Gaya was damaged at numerous places. Telegraph wires and the electric poles connecting them met the same fate. A few railway stations were burnt and the cash accumulated there for the sale of tickets and booking of goods was looted. National flags were hoisted at numerous places. Grain godowns were looted and burnt. Similar style of Satyagrahis was witnessed in several towns of U.P., i.e., in Meerut, Khurja, Moradabad, Faizabad, Ghazipur, Gonda, Bahraich, Azamgarh, Chanda, Sikandra, Fatehpur Sikri, Mathura and Bulandshahr. A large number of processions were organized and Government property worth lakhs of rupees was damaged. Lathi charges and firings by the police were the common phenomenon. Many student-picketers were severely beaten. Khadi Bhandars were burnt to ashes at many places. Central Provinces also responded well to the general call for processions strikes and meetings of common people, given by the leadership of the Indian National Congress.

The resentment of the people against the Raj reached its highest pitch, mainly on account-of the co-operation of the people and the student-community. In the major city like Nagpur, the capital of the province, whereas mills and factories struck work, the students boycotted their schools and colleges and participated in various kinds of demonstrations. On the following day, the mob of people damaged Government property worth lakhs of rupees. The damage was done, as usual, to post offices, railway tracks and police stations. Their records were burnt. Police resorted to firing on the mob and scores of people were killed and hundreds of them were wounded. The movement was not confined to the urban areas only. It also touched upon the rural areas. In the tahsil of Umerer, people showed much excitement and anger by bringing about a huge damage to railway station and its records, railway lines and telegraph wires. They also captured two police stations of Kuhi and Monda. Other prominent towns of Central Provinces which struck work and actively participated in the movement were Jabalpur, Betul, Sagar, Bilaspur, Narsinghpur, Damoh, Mandla, Katni. Hoshangabad, Chhindwara, Itarsi and Patheria.

At some places, currency notes worth lakhs of rupees were looted. Telegraph and telephone wires were damaged. The Government reacted with much sternness and used methods like lathi-charges, firings, arrests and convictions. As in other provinces, Orissa too was fully awakened to the call of the Quit India Movement. Specially in Cuttack. Balasore and Koraput the activities of Congress Satyagrahis were remarkable. In Koraput, four police stations were captured, a few bridges were destroyed and also excited the rural masses against the Raj. Similarly, at Balasore where people were agitated, they burnt the Government records in some departments. So far so, they caught hold of a few policemen and made a bonfire of their uniforms. Besides Maran Sena, i.e., Suicide Squads were formed in some regions of the province.

The volunteers of this Send defied the police, and although a few were killed on account of police firing, they carried on their activities without any kind of fear in their hearts. Telephone and telegraph lines were damaged; railway lines were dislocated and a few Government buildings in Cuttack were burnt. The Government, as a measure of punishment, collected thousands of rupees from villages which damaged the Government property. Besides, many persons were arrested. In some of the princely States, the movement was regenerated by the Congress

Satyagrahis, students of schools and colleges, labourers and mill-workers, women and children. These States were Mysore, Bhopal, Indore, Travancore, Udaipur, Rewa, Kotah, Porbundar and a few others. Like British India regions, meetings and processions were organised, students came out of their schools and colleges and mill-hands struck work for sometime in these States. The authorities suppressed the movement ruthlessly by lathi charges, shootings and killings and convictions. In Central India, the Praja Mandal of Indore and Bhopal State People's Conference carried on their Satyagraha as a mark of sympathy for the movement. They gave the ultimatum to the State Governments to disown the British Raj in their State and instead establish responsible Governments. Besides processions and meetings, hartals were observed by commercial centres, schools and colleges. Extensive damage to Government property was done in Indore. In both the States, repressive measures were the orders of the day. Lathi charges and firings by the police were very common and numerous Satyagrahis were put behind the bars. In the Baroda State, the response of the people for the movement was spontaneous. The Praja Mandal took initiative in mobilising the people, and they included numerous textile and mill-workers of the State.

The novel feature of the anti-Raj activity was to tender resignations by members of the Baroda Legislative Council, teachers and Patels, prabhat pheris were taken out to impress upon the people about the implications of the movement. People's Day was organised to protest-against the excessive repression by the police and army. The damage done to Government property including railway lines in the Baroda State was immense. As a result of damaged tracks, railway trains were delayed and there was much difficulty in travelling in the State. The resignations of numerous officials greatly paralysed the functioning of the State machinery. Similarly in Travancore much excitement was witnessed by persons representing different professions. In Travancore mainly students spearheaded the movement and gave a call for general strike in the university college at Trivandrum. There was so much excitement and fervour amongst the students that they hoisted national flags on their institutions. Specially at Nagarcoil, they showed much political activity by distributing leaflets and fixing national placards at numerous places. The State administration used all repressive measures against the students and threatened them, through a notification, of dire consequence if they continued the agitation in the State. Their hostels were searched by the police and many of them were put behind the bars. The police also used coercion in making some students to attend their classes. In the premier princely State of Mysore, people showed a united stand in taking out largely attended processions and organising meetings. Some of the mill-hands observed hartal as a mark of respect for Mahatma Gandhi and other Congress leaders.

Students of schools and colleges did not attend their classes for a few days. Women also came out to participate in the national movement. In spite of the ban promulgated by the Government of Mysore, people carried on these activities with full vigour and excitement. The mob burnt the city post office, damaged numerous electric poles and railway lines., To suppress the movement, the State Government used all repressive means. They made use of severe lathi-charge. So far so, the tanks and armoured cars were used against precisionists. About two hundred persons were killed and many more in number were lodged in the State jail." The national upsurge amongst the students was a unique phenomenon during the Quit India Movement. In their firm determination to 'Do or Die', they came out of their institutions in a large number in various regions of India. They took out processions, raised slogans and made use of handbill to put obstructions in the smooth functioning of the Government. To curb their activities, the Government used repressive measures which were phenomenal in magnitude. The Government sent a warning note to the principals of various institutions asking them to warn their students not to participate in the national struggle. And if the students disobeyed their orders, they were to be rusticated. The arrests of leaders of the Congress was a clear indication for the outbreak of an 'open rebellion' against the Raj almost in every nook and corner of the country. The arrests of their leaders like Gandhi and Jawaharlal Nehru greatly agitated their minds, and the retaliation in various forms erupted spontaneously. As soon as the news reached cities and towns, there were strikes and bandhs, and these strikes varied from place to, place. At prominent commercial towns like Ahmedabad, Bombay, Madras, Delhi, Kanpur and Amritsar, the strikes were observed from one week to two weeks. There was thus an expression of so much excitement and sympathy that it appeared a complete and unflinching identification of the common people with the cause Congress had taken up. This type of identification was to be shown at any kind of sacrifice—both physical and financial suffering. Another prominent feature of showing resentment, anger and dissatisfaction against the Raj was holding large scale demonstrations and taking out processions with placards inscribed in patriotic language.

The response of the people in terms of their attendance of mass meetings was immense. People of all professions thronged in thousands to join the mass rallies and meetings. The participation by students in these processions and meetings was a remarkable phenomenon in this regard. Schools and Colleges were closed and students organised mass demonstrations with patriotic zeal. As a result of these activities, numerous students suffered immensely in terms of loss in their educational career. The zeal and enthusiasm shown by the industrial workers was unparalleled in the annals of our country. They struck work and came out of their mills and factories en masse in Bombay, Ahmedabad, Madras, Delhi, Jamshedpur, Kanpur, Nagpur and other towns. They organised mass meetings, arranged demonstrations and educated their brethren about that fundamentals of independence. The crowds of people carried national flags and shouted national slogans in cities and towns.

Their purpose was to hoist these flags at numerous public places and Government buildings. Many of them succeeded in hoisting national flags on the buildings of schools, colleges, municipal boards, district courts and Government secretariats. The task indeed was risky, but the challenge the Satyagrahis posed to the Raj was full of complexities which created difficulties for the police to control and maintain law and order. The Quit India Movement clearly reflected the mood of the nation and clarified the fact that the awakening amongst them for a common cause, i e., to free India from the bondage of the Raj was a reality and its practicability was to be realized with a deep sense of patriotism tinged with mass action in all the regions of the country. It indeed was a serious challenge to the Raj which had deep repercussions on the functioning of the administration. Although well-entrenched on the soil of India, it gave it the realisation of the fact that it was, at this point of time was somewhat difficult to ignore a great spontaneous national upsurge which was found to be uncontrolled on account of a huge mass support. This kind of mass support to a common political aim, i.e., to attain independence had night-marish effect on the day-to-day functioning of the machinery of the Government in India and this fact was seriously realised by the Viceroy and the Home Government in England. Under these circumstances. 'The British, moreover, were moved by the challenge to strengthen their rule, responding with renewed determination to remove the conditions which made the rising possible'. The damage to Government property was immense. The Government buildings, police stations, municipal schools, hospitals and private buildings were severely damaged. The cases of bomb explosions were also noticeable in various regions. Special courts were set up to deal with criminal cases. Some cases were dealt with by military courts. The Government records stated that 23,358 persons were convicted by ordinary courts, 313 by military courts and 41 death sentences were confirmed out of 67 persons who were sentenced to death. The reception of the people accorded to the Congress Satyagrahis was unprecedented.

They were considered heroes of all sections of people. Besides the trials of Indian officers and the naval mutiny of February, 1946 had greatly engendered sympathy in the hearts of the people regarding the unchallenged and unquestionable patriotic zeal of young personnel of the army and the navy. In press and public meetings, they were greeted with affection thus creating an example for others to emulate. The Congress propaganda with the media of cyclostyled literature was a potent device among the masses of India. These machines operated by small and big shopkeepers proved instrumental in disseminating hand-bills and sheets which came secretly in hands of numerous Satyagrahis. This kind of style was a glaring phenomenon in cities like Bombay, Calcutta, Ahmedabad, Lahore, Patna, Allahabad and elsewhere. Such presses were actively hunted by the police and put under lock and key. The continuous searches of houses led to the arrests and convictions of numerous inmates.

Thus, official efforts were made to stop all possible sources of publicity and propaganda. The nationalist press was an eye-sore for the Raj. It was brought under strict Government regulations. The prominent newspapers which stopped publications as a result of Government's restrictions on them were the Amria Bazar Patrika, Hindustan Standard, Hindustan Times, Basumati, Jugantar, Matrubhoomi, Telegraph, Lokmanya, Jagriti, Daily Krishik, Bharat, Andhra Times, Dinamani, Hindustan and others. Devadas Gandhi, editor of the Hindustan Times was arrested for breach of the order of the Government that not more than three columns be devoted to news about the national movement. The part played by the Praja Mandal in States like Hyderabad, Mysore, Baroda, Gwalior, Indore, Travancore and Udaipur afforded much support to the movement.

They informed the rulers to realise the fact that the time was fast changing and they must value the sentiments and political demands of the people of their States. In some smaller States, people were in total rebellion. In some states, the rulers were reluctant to adopt repressive measures against Satyagrahis but the British Residents stationed in their States did not approve of their policy, and they recommended repressive measures against the Satyagrahis. As result of this policy, there were numerous arrests, convictions, beating, flogging, firing, suspension and dismissals from services. Prominent leaders along with numerous volunteers and Satyagrahis were put behind the bars under inhuman conditions.

This kind of repression, however, did not exhaust their zeal and enthusiasm. They moved from village to village to spread the message of Congress by issuing hand-bills, posters and news bulletins for wider circulation in towns and villages. This mode of publicity was a counter-move to the censor on news imposed by the order of the Government. The part played by the industrial labourers is no less in this movement. They did not demand any kind of increase in their emoluments, but their strikes were totally political in contents. So far so, at some places, the machinery halted causing a great loss to its productive capacity and affecting the war-efforts of the Government. The cooperation of the industrial labour was thus on a large scale compared to the Civil Disobedience Movement. In fact, the industrial labour showed a high sense of suffering and sacrifice for the cause of country's freedom. The retaliatory action by the police, army and bureaucracy in all the regions of India was proverbial in content.

In the name of the maintenance of law and order, every canon of morality, decency and law was violated. The dispersal of mobs were at the point of rifle, pistol and machine-guns. The beating and flogging to political prisoners were combined with all types of insults unheard of. Even women were not spared. 'Women were stripped, assaulted, raped : even children were not spared. In the villages numerous houses were razed to the ground, many actually burnt. People were tied to trees and beaten, sometimes undressed and whipped. Lathis, short staves, fists and even shoes were used.... One of the most effective form of punitive measures was the imposition of collective fines which were realized with the utmost rigour. The whole object obviously was to terrorize people, teach them a lesson and efface from their minds all thoughts of defiance. The role of the I.N.A. under the stewardship of Subhas Chandra Bose for the freedom movement of our country is unique in the annals of history. After his resignation from the I.C.S., he devoted his life and energy for the causes having linkage with anti-Raj stance. He became the Congress President in 1938 and 1939.

On account of differences with the Congress High Command, he formed a new party known as the Forward Bloc. In July 1940, Bose was arrested under the Defence of India Rules. But after a few months, the Government released him on account of his ill-health. He was, however, interned in his house under police surveillance. His disappearance from his residence on 26 January 1941 and reaching Berlin and later on Japan were events which enabled him to raise the Indian National Army with the help of Rash Behari Bose, who was made President of the Council of Action and Mohan Singh as the Commander-in-Chief. The Japanese authorities promised all support to Netaji in order to fight against the British and expel them from India. When he visited Singapore he was handed over the Presidentship of the Indian Independence League by Rash Behari Bose. Assuming full command of the Azad Hind Fauj, Bose was also instrumental in the formation of the Provisional Government of Free India. His famous battle cry was 'Chalo Delhi'. Many officers and soldiers of 'the Indian army joined under the command of Bose in order to liberate India. Assisted by the Japanese army, the I.N.A. forces marched towards India and reached Kohima where they hoisted their flag. But with the commencement of winter in 1944-45, the counter-offensive by the British led to the defeat of the Japanese. With this defeat, the plans made by the I.N.A. collapsed. Soon after, it was reported that Bose lost his life in an air crash. The selfless devotion to the cause of independence of India shown by Bose and his associates created much stir when some of the officers of the I.N.A., i.e., Sehgal, Dhillon and Shah Nawaz were tried by the court-martial in the Red Fort.

The Congress leaders took up their cause and Jawaharlal Nehru, Bhulabhai Desai and others pleaded their case. They were ultimately set free, and "Were accorded welcome befitting national heroes. The general elections in England were held on 25 July, 1946. The electorate gave to the Labour Party a landslide victory, 393 Labour candidates won against 213 of the Conservative Party and their allies, 19 of the other parties and 14 Independents, Attlee was elected as the Prime Minister. Soon after the Labour Party's assumption of office, the Americans dropped atomic bombs in Hiroshima and Nagasaki on 6th and 9th August and all Japanese resistance ceased. On 15 August the Victory Day was celebrated by the Allies. On 20 February, 1946, Attlee made a statement in the House of Commons. 'His Majesty's Government desire to hand over their responsibility to authorities established by a constitution approved by all parties in India... His Majesty's Government wish to make it clear that it is their definite intention to take the necessary steps to effect the transference of power to responsible Indian hands by a date not later than June 1948... His Majesty's Government will have to consider to whom the powers of the Central Government in British India should be handed over on the due date... The reaction of Gandhiji to the statement of Attlee was favourable. He observed in unequivocal terms, that whatever might have been the history of British rule in the past, there was not a shadow of doubt that the British were going to quit India in the near future. Nehru at once wrote to Mahatma Gandhi, '... I am convinced that it is in the final analysis a brave and definite statement. It meets our off-repeated demand for quitting India'. The elections had cleared the way for the subsequent steps towards the formulation of the new constitution.

On 1st January, 1946, Pethic-Lawrence conveyed the desire of the British Government 'to see India rise quickly to the full and free status of an equal partner in the British Commonwealth'. He also announced in the Parliament on 19 January, 1946, the steps which Government intended to take in conjunction with the leaders of Indian opinion for the early realisation of full self-Government in India. These steps were : (1) to hold preparatory discussions with elected representatives of British India and with Indian States in order to secure the widest measure of agreement as to the method of framing a constitution; (2) to set up a constitution making body; and (3) to establish full self-Government in India.

He also announced that a special Mission of Cabinet Ministers consisting of the Secretary of State, the President of the Board of Trade, (Stafford Cripps) and the First Lord of Admiralty (A.V. Alexander) would go to India to act in association with the Viceroy in this matter. On 23 March, the Cabinet Mission arrived in India. Pethick-Lawrence stated at a press interview that their primary object was to set up machinery whereby full independent status of India would be determined by Indians, and secondly, to make interim arrangements. The Mission spent nearly five weeks in discussion with the members of 'the Viceroy's Executive

Council, provincial Governors, party leaders, representatives of princely States and prominent individuals. The Congress point of view was presented by its President, Abul Kalam Azad. Its basic demand was for independence to be embodied in a constitution comprehending the whole of India and made by a Constituent Assembly.

But for the intervening period it was necessary to set up a provincial Government which would be responsible for arranging the various stages from the formation of the constituent assembly onwards. During his interview with the members of the Mission, Gandhiji considered the two-nation theory a falsehood which he was not prepared to accept. Regarding the interim Government, his suggestion was that Jinnah should be asked to form the Government of his own choice, but if he refused then the Congress should be given the chance to form the Government. On the other hand, M.A. Jinnah took a different stand and repeated his theory before the Mission that Hindus and Muslims could not be considered one nation. Only the British had imposed unity on India, but that unity was purely external, in reality India was many, not one. He further opined that after the withdrawal of the British there would be no power which could maintain this unity. He forcefully pleaded that it was essential to divide India and transfer power to two sovereign and independent States. The liberal leaders were against the division of India. The Sikh leaders were in favour of a united India. The Hindu Mahasabha insisted upon immediate transfer of power and the integrity and individuality of the country.

The two factions of the Scheduled Castes asked for guarantees of human rights and safeguards for their interests. The main proposals of the Mission were as follows : (a) There should be a Union of India dealing with three subjects, i.e., Foreign Affairs, Defence and Communications, having the necessary powers to raise the finances required for these subjects. (b) The Union should have an Executive and a Legislature of representatives chosen from British India and the States. (c) Provinces should be free to form groups (sub-federation with Executives and Legislatures, and each group could determine the provincial subjects to be taken in common. (d) The Constitution of the Union of the groups should provide for a reconsideration of the terms of the Constitution after an initial period of ten years. The Congress was unhappy about the scheme of the Mission and it rejected the idea of sub-federation. The Muslim League was also dissatisfied with the findings of the Mission. Jinnah regretted that the demand of Muslim League for Pakistan was rejected by the members of the Mission. The 16th of August was declared as the 'Direct Action Day' by the Muslim League. In fact it was the day of protests and meetings to propagate the Muslim demand, to explain the Muslim attitude towards the Cabinet Mission's offer and to condemn the conduct of the Congress. In Calcutta the day began with public demonstrations, closing of shops and hoisting of Muslim League flags, Soon resistance led to clashes and rioting spread over the city.

The mad fury continued for four days and then on 20th August the city began to return to normal life. The Government of Suhrawardy was criticised for its failure to take precautionary measures to avert conflicts, to protect life and property of the citizens and to maintain law and order. The number of persons killed was estimated at 5,000 killed and 15,000 injured. Besides there was huge loss of property." On 22 August, 1946, Jawaharlal Nehru informed the Viceroy that although he was anxious to form a coalition with the Muslim League, he wished to mike it clear that coalition did not mean a submission to the demands of the Muslim League. He, in fact, wanted a strong Government united in the pursuit of policies on which there was fundamental agreement. After two days, the new cabinet, with the following members, was formed. They were Jawaharlal Nehru, Vallabhbhai Patel, Rajendra Prasad, Asaf Ali, C. Rajagopalachari, Sarat Chander a Bose, John Mathai, Baldev Singh, Shafaat Ahmad Khan, Jagjivan Ram, Ali Zaheer and C.H. Bhaba. At this point of time, the Viceroy premised to give the new Government the maximum freedom of the day-to-day functioning of the administrative machinery. He however, regretted that though five seats had been offered to the Muslim League, it showed no interest to join the coalition. Jinnah showed anger over the Viceroy's statement but Nehru declared, 'We are perfectly prepared to, and have accepted, the position of sitting in sections, which will consider the question of formation of groups.... We seek agreed and integrated solutions with the largest measure of goodwill behind them'. The Muslim League, however, declared the 2nd of September as a day of mourning and Jinnah advised his followers to display black flags. Violence broke out at many places in Bengal, Bihar, Punjab and Bombay. The worried Mahatma remarked, 'We are not yet in the midst of civil war, but we are nearing it.' Meanwhile mutual meetings and exchange of letters amongst prominent leaders and the Viceroy, resulted into a temporary compromise, by which Jinnah agreed to nominate five persons to the interim Government. These were Liaqat Ali Khan, I. I. Chundrigar, Abdur Rab Nishtar, Ghaznafar Ali Khan and Jogendra Nath Mandal. Thus, the Muslim League entered the Government without commitment to join the Constituent Assembly. As a sequel to these political developments, violent communal riots broke out in some districts of the Punjab, forcing the

Governor to take over the administration of the province in his own hands. Mob frenzy of stabbing, killing and Hooting spread in Lahore, Rawalpindi, Amritsar, Multan, NWFP and other areas. Jawaharlal Nehru who visited Rawalpindi reported, 'I have seen ghastly sights and I have heard of behaviour by human beings which would degrade brutes. According to official account 2,049 persons were killed and over 1,000 seriously injured in course of a fortnight. The Congress Working Committee met on 8 March, 1947 and passed the following resolution foreshadowing the Partition of India. During the past seven months India has witnessed many horrors and tragedies which have been enacted in the attempt to gain political ends by brutal violence, murder and coercion.....

Therefore, it is necessary to find a way which amounts to the least compulsion. This would necessitate division of the Punjab into two Provinces so that the predominantly Muslim part may be separated from the predominantly non-Muslim part'. When a section of the Congress leaders showed a sense of disagreement to this proposal, the President explained that the Congress had only suggested a division of the Punjab as a means of putting an end to violence, and that the same remedy would hold good for Bengal if the circumstances in that province were similar. Lord Mountbatten assumed the office of Governor-General on 24 March, 1947. He had discussions with prominent leaders like Mahatma Gandhi, Jawaharlal Nehru and M.A. Jinnah and assessed the political situation in India in its proper perspective. A practical man with realistic approach as he was, he soon realized that in the present circumstances, the Cabinet Mission plan was unworkable and a partition of India inevitable. In fact he was deeply moved by the rapid deterioration in communal relations that he was eager to effect the transfer of power without any delay. The general principles of partition having been agreed upon, the question arose of the fate of minorities of the Punjab and Bengal. At first Jinnah was adamant that these two provinces should be transferred to Pakistan. The Congress leaders, were, however, agreeable to the creation of Pakistan but opined that the non-Muslims in the Punjab and Bengal living in districts contiguous to India and forming a majority of population in these areas, must be given the option to choose between Pakistan and India. This meant the creation of two separate Provinces of East Punjab and West Bengal. At this point of time, Jinnah protested but he was reminded of the Lahore resolution of the Muslim League passed in March 1940. On 18 May, Mountbatten proceeded to London to seek the advice of the British cabinet, and when he came back to New Delhi on 31 May, he announced the British Government's acceptance of the principles of partition, which would be effected probably on 15 August 1947.

The points of procedure were as follows. If the members of the Legislative Assemblies of the Punjab and Bengal were to decide in favour of partition by a simple majority, a boundary commission, set up by the Viceroy, would demarcate the appropriate boundaries. Sind and Baluchistan would decide which constituent Assembly to join. Regarding the Frontier Province there was to be a referendum to ascertain whether it would opt for Pakistan or not. Besides the Muslim majority district of Sylhet was to decide by means of referendum as to whether it would join East Bengal or remain in Assam. Both the major political parties of the country-Congress and the Muslim League-were agreeable to this plan. The Sikhs were dissatisfied with this plan as their population was divided in half by the probable line of partition in the undivided Punjab. The Red Shirts led by Khan Abdul Ghaffar Khan put forward the demand for an independent Pakhtoonistan. This was not acceptable and as a protest, they did not participate in the plebiscite which went in favour of joining Pakistan. Meanwhile the Boundary Commission under the chairmanship of Sir Cyril Radcliffe gave a verdict for the division of Bengal and Punjab.

Thus, West Bengal and East Punjab opted for India, and East Bengal, West Punjab, Sind and Baluchistan became parts of Pakistan. The district of Sylhet joined Pakistan. Vallabhbhai Patel was also agreeable to the plan of Mountbatten. His experience of working with the League members in the Executive Council convinced him that a stage had come when Hindus and Muslims could not be united into one nation. He 'came to the fateful decision that unless the country was partitioned, chaos and anarchy would spread throughout the land.' With the passage of Independence of India Act by the British Parliament in July 1947, the preliminaries for the relinquishment of authority were completed; administrative arrangements consequent upon the partition of India were largely accomplished and the preparation for the future relations of the Indian States and their accession to the Union of India were concluded with the signing of the Standstill Agreement and the Instrument of Accession by all the States, excepting three, i.e., Kashmir, Hyderabad and Junagadh. At this, Muslim League felt much satisfied and Jinnah was much jubilant at the achievement of the highest aim of his life. He got a part of Punjab, NWFP, Sind, a part of Bengal and Baluchistan as provinces of Pakistan. When be took over as the first Governor-General of Pakistan, he told his A.D.C. on arrival at Karachi, I never thought it would happen. I never expected to see Pakistan in my lifetime.' In fact, Jinnah had made up his mind as early as 1937 that the solution of the communal problem lay in the separation of the Muslims in the majority areas from India, and since then he played his cards well and never intended to compromise or surrender on his main demand. 'His attitude towards the Government was ambivalent-a combination of compliance and swagger. He cleverly exploited the British animosity towards the Congress and won the power of veto over all plans of Constitutional advance or administrative reform. The leaders of the Congress were yearning for power as Mahatma Gandhi commented. Jawaharlal Nehru confessed, 'Well, I suppose it was the compulsion of events.... A large India would have constant troubles, Constant disintegrating pulls.... And so we accepted and said, let us build up a strong India.... The truth is that we were tired men.... Few of us could stand the prospect of going to prison again and if we had stood out for a united India as we wished it, prison obviously awaited us. We saw the fires burning in the Punjab and heard every day of the killings. The plan for partition offered a way out and we took it'. At last the historic day of August 15 arrived and it indeed was the last day of the one hundred and fifty years of British rule in India. Exactly at the stroke of the midnight hour, Earl Mountbatten of Burma, the last British Governor-General and Viceroy of India entered the Assembly Chamber to address the Legislature and give a message of greeting and goodwill from the King, who ceased from this moment to be the Emperor of India.

Pandit Jawaharlal Nehru, the first Prime Minister of independent India, rose to move the adoption of the pledge of dedication to the new Dominion of India in an atmosphere surcharged with emotion. He said, 'Long years ago we made I tryst with destiny, and now the time comes we shall redeem our pledge, not wholly, or in full measure, but very substantially.... A moment comes, which comes but rarely in history, when we step out from the old to the new, when an age ends, and when the soul of a nation, long suppressed, finds utterance. That future is not one of ease or resting but of incessant striving so that we may fulfil the pledges we have so often taken and the one we shall take today.

The service of India means the service of the millions who suffer.... And so we have to labour and to work and work hard to give reality to our dreams.... Peace has been said to be indivisible, so is freedom, so is prosperity now, and so also is disaster in this. 'To the people of India, whose representatives we are, we make an appeal to join us with faith and confidence in this great adventure. This is no time for petty and destructive criticism, no time for ill-will or blaming others. We have to build the noble mansion of free India where her children may dwell'. These sentiments were expressed by a person, born with a silver spoon in his mouth, educated in the academic nurseries of Harrow and Cambridge, consistently guided and advised by a person than his own father, Pandit Motilal Nehru and later on by Mahatma Gandhi. He suffered in British-India jails, at intervals, for a long period of nine years, wrote about India, the Indian people and the world, travelled a lot to understand well the social and economic light of his people. In fact, during the long drawn struggle in which he participated along with members of his family, he had completely identified himself with the Indian masses.

At times, his differences with Gandhiji brought forth tangible results, because both loved and respected each other and it became difficult for them to function in isolation.

It in fact goes to the credit of the two leaders that they maintained perfect discipline in the cadre of Satyagrahis in various movements and launched a well-organised onslaught on the functioning of bureaucracy in our country. It would be pertinent to say that the activities of these two leaders had nightmarish effect on the successive Viceroys in India. The ceremony began with the swearing in of the new Governor-General, Earl Mountbatten. Then Rajendra Prasad read out the congratulatory messages from all over the world. This was followed by the address of Earl Mountbatten to the Assembly. He related briefly the events leading up to this great day. At the end he observed, 'From today I am your constitutional Governor-General and I would ask you to regard me as one of yourselves, devoted wholly to the furtherance of India's interests'. Rajendra Prasad reminisced thus in his Autobiography. At the Working Committee discussions, the proposal to launch a Satyagraha movement in 1942, was opposed by some. Dr. Syed Mahmud was one of them.

The discussions were prolonged but the Committee could not arrive at any decision. I was worried over this indecision and requested Gandhiji to advise us about the programme we should follow. He flatly refused to do anything till we had definitely resolved to launch Satyagraha, when alone he would be able to work out a plan. At the moment, the Working Committee was not of one view and how the Government would react to its decision could not be anticipated. In such a state of uncertainty, he said he would not be able to help the Congress. The Satyagraha, he said, was going to be extremely vigorous. It would not merely consist in courting imprisonment but would involve greater sacrifices. Possibly, all our personal belongings and household effects would have to be staked. It was very likely that the Charkha Sangh's entire property, of the value of about Rs. 40 lakhs, and all its workers would have to be sacrificed, though we had only a few days earlier decided to expand the Sangh's activities. It was thus necessary to get a clear picture of the situation before drawing up a plan for the movement. We all felt that this uncertainty was a great weakness, but we had to accept it because after all the programme had to be drawn up by Gandhiji and he was not able to do so at that stage. Eventually, it was decided that the Working Committee should meet in Bombay early in August to take the final decision in the matter. Before leaving Wardha I called on Gandhiji to take his leave. I found him surrounded by some friends who put to him the question whether cutting telegraph wires and dismantling railway lines could be considered compatible with nonviolence. I knew that this question had been uppermost in the minds of a few Congressmen ever since the talk of Satyagraha began. I immediately told Gandhiji that during the 1930 agitation when Gandhiji and many other leaders had been jailed and Pandit Motilal Nehru was acting as President and I had gone to Allahabad to attend a meeting of the Congress Working Committee, people had raised the same question and, in fact, had actually cut telephone and telegraph wires in a few places, but it was stopped as we discouraged the practice. I was not, therefore, surprised that the same question should be raised again and suggested that Gandhiji : should give us clear instructions about it while formulating his programme. Gandhiji replied that the question of non-violence or violence did not arise in respect of cutting steel or wood, which we did so often in our daily lives. But it was a different thing altogether to cut telegraph and telephone wires and to remove rails or fishplates. Whether a particular act was violent or non-violent depended on the motives behind, that act, the manner in which it was executed and the results flowing from it. If as a result of it people died and the innocent were made to suffer, it would constitute violence, but we could also imagine a situation in which the act would be non-violent. We interpreted his views to mean that the violence or nonviolence of an act would be determined by the fact whether it endangered anyone's life and the doer acknowledged full responsibility for his act so that others did not suffer for it. But all this was casual talk. The programme had not been decided nor was it likely to be decided till the A.I.C.C met in Bombay in August. Despite this, the Government later accused the Congress of disrupting communications as a part of the Satyagraha programme. Gandhiji replied that the Government had mistaken a theoretical discussion of a programme for the programme itself, and Gandhiji was perfectly correct. Then I left for Tarapur, in Monghyr district, where was held a kisan conference, which had been put off several times before because of my inability to attend it. Acharya Kripalani inaugurated the conference and Krishna Ballabh Sahay presided over it. Dr. S.K. Sinha, Anugrah Narain Sinha and other prominent Bihar leaders were present. On my arrival at the place I had an attack of asthma. However, I attended the conference. When I was asked to speak and I rose to do so, down came the rain and the conference was washed out just like the Ramgarh session of the Congress. After spending the night there, I left for Patna the next morning. My asthma grew more serious and I also developed temperature. Ever, during the Working Committee meetings at Wardha I had an attack, but somehow I had managed to be present throughout !he deliberations. Now the crucial session of the A.I.C.C. was only two weeks off and I was anxious that I should recover by then." I convened a meeting of the Bihar Provincial

Congress Committee at Sadaqat Ashram on July 31 to sound Congress men on the proposed Satyagraha to be discussed in Bombay. Despite my illness and consequent weakness, I addressed the meeting and made a forceful speech. I apprised the meeting of the discussions in Wardha and made the people realise what to expect from the forthcoming struggle and how it was of the utmost importance to the country. A day or two after the meeting, Bihar members of the A.I.C.C. left for Bombay, but my ill health kept me back in Patna. The newspapers of the times talked of the Government's determination and preparation to arrest all the leaders at the time of the A.I.C.C. meeting in Bombay with a view to suppressing the agitation at the very start.

Rumours were also afloat in Bihar of a move to arrest the leaders in the province and it was said that the Camp Jail, which was out of use just then, was being hurriedly got ready for our reception. If these reports turned out to be correct, I was afraid that the people would be left without a programme and so I thought that I should formulate some programme at least for my province. I was reminded of what Gandhiji had told us earlier that in case all leaders were arrested and no programme had been imparted to the people, every Congressman should look upon himself as a leader and, consistent with the principles of Ahimsa, decide on his own plan of Satyagraha and carry it to its final consummation as this was to be the last phase of our freedom struggle. Not being strong enough to sit down and write, I called Deepnarain Sinha and Mathura Prasad, detailed my proposals and asked them to prepare a draft on those aims. When they had completed it, along with Anugrah Narain Sinha, who had not gone to Bombay, I vent over it and made some amendments. Then the amended draft was sent for printing. I told my friends that should all the proeminent Congressmen be arrested and the A.I.C.C. programme not reach the people, the programme outlined in my draft should be followed in the province.

The programme of action, based on non-violence, which I laid down in my plan was not very different from the programme of earlier campaigns but it was now more intense. At the crucial meeting of the A.I.C.C. in Bombay, Gandhiji made a long speech in which he gave his message of "Do or Die" to the people. He also said that he would try to meet the Viceroy once again and make an effort at compromise. Sardar Patel made a fighting speech which roused the admiration of all. On the night of August 8, 1942, the A.I.C.C. passed the famous "Quit India" resolution. It called upon the British to withdraw from India forthwith. The next morning I heard the announcement over the radio of the arrest of Mahatma Gandhi and members of the Working Committee." On the morning of August 9, Mathura Prasad, my secretary, had gone to the city, and I was lying in bed at Sadaqat Ashram, reading the newspaper reports of the proceedings of the Working Committee, when Archer, District Magistrate, followed by the Civil Surgeon, Major Murdoch, put in his appearance.

Archer inquired of my health and programme. I at once understood the object of his visit. When I asked him to what I might attribute the honour of his visit, he told me that, in view of my illness, he had asked the Government for instructions and that the Government had referred the question to the Civil Surgeon who had been asked to report whether in his opinion it was safe to take me to a far-off place. That was why he had brought the Civil Surgeon with him. The Civil Surgeon examined me and decided that I was not fit to undertake a journey. Meanwhile, my wife and sister, who had been informed of the possibility of my arrest, came to see me. At mid-day I was taken to Bankipur jail. Mathura Prasad and Chakradhar Saran accompanied me to the jail and made all the necessary arrangements for my comfort and returned. Within a few minutes Phulan Prasad Varma was brought in. Towards nightfall, Mathura Prasad, who had a talk earlier with Archer, also entered jail. The rate of arrival of prisoners increased the next day. On their return from Bombay, Sri Krishna Sinha, Satyanarain Sinha and Mahamaya Prasad were arrested and, along with Anugrah Narain, they were brought to Bankipur Jail. I heard that the courts had been closed and that a huge procession had gone up to the gates of Government House, raising slogans. There was no ban on newspapers in the jail, but they did not tell us much. The only source or news was the newcomers. The jail was packed to capacity as, owing to the increase in dacoity and other crimes since the outbreak of the war, there were a great number of criminals in the jail. Many of them were under-trial prisoners. As they faced accommodation shortage with the influx of political prisoners, the authorities decided to keep the upper class prisoners in Bankipur Jail and transfer the others to the Camp Jail.

The forty young men who had been arrested that day were to be taken to the Camp Jail the next day. These young men who were lodged in a double-storeyed building were able to carry on a conversation with the crowd waiting outside the jail. The young men told the people of the plan to transfer them to the Camp Jail the next day. The crowd, therefore, waited patiently till 3 the next morning when lorries were brought in for the transfer of the young prisoners. As the first lorry moved out of the premises, the mob stopped the lorry, released the boys and set the lorry on fire. The other lorries, therefore, did not move out. The prisoners were brought back to the barracks. The military came on the scene and cleared the area. The boys were transferred to the Camp Jail thereafter under military escort. The "A" division prisoners increased every day so that there was no room left for them except in the jail hospital. There was talk of transferring them to Hazaribagh Jail, but by that time railway traffic had been completely dislocated and the trains had stopped running. For about a month the A division prisoners were kept in the hospital or somewhere else till they could be taken to Hazaribagh. But I remained in Bankipur since I was not in a fit condition to travel and since the climate of Hazaribagh would not suit me. A few days after my entering jail, it was rumoured that I would be taken to some place outside Bihar, where the other members of the Working Committee were kept. But the only mode of transport would have been the aeroplane and as I was not fit enough to stand an air journey the idea was dropped. After ten months in Bankipur, Major Murdoch, Civil Surgeon, came to see me. It was summer and my health had improved and I was, therefore, intrigued by the arrival of a doctor to see me. I guessed that there was another move to transfer me elsewhere. When I questioned Major Murdoch, he said, he had no official information and even if he had he would not give it out. Nevertheless, he told me confidentially that my conjecture was correct. I learnt further that the proposed transfer was not to Hazaribagh but to some place in the south, near Poona. But nothing came of it. It was after I was released that I learnt that they had intended to take me to Ahmednagar Fort, where the Working Committee members had been kept, and that, in fact, a room had been got ready for my stay there. But why the idea was given up I do not know. Patna newspapers suspended publication a few days after our arrest. The Bihar Government started publishing a daily newspaper called The Patna News. We were allowed to read it and one thing we learnt from it was about the imposition of punitive taxes or collective fines in the province and the exact sums levied in each area. We computed that within a few months the amount of the fines rose to nearly Rs. 20 lakhs! Prison life is bound to be irksome in so far as it deprives one of freedom, but I should say that I did not, after all, have a bad time in Bankipur Jail. I adjusted myself to nay surroundings soon and to the routine I had been accustomed to bile I was in Hazaribagh Jail years earlier. The arrival of new prisoners was always a cause of excitement since they brought fresh news.

Some time later we began getting newspapers but we were not carried away by the reports of what was happening in the country. When the flow of fresh prisoners ceased. I began devoting my time to spinning, reading and writing. My health, of course, was not good, though I was not always confined to bed. Members of my family used to visit me often, almost always accompanied by my grandchildren. They were joyous moments when I used to spend a half-hour playing with the children. Arun, my two-and-a-half year old grandson, became so used to the place that as soon as he arrived he would run from the jail gates to the hospital ward where I was kept. I used to give him and my grand-daughters the sweets they usually demanded but he would go away disappointed when I said I could not go back with him as he desired. Meanwhile, reports of the repressive acts committed by the army, the police and the magistrates trickled to us.

The new ordinances, veritable instruments of repression, were being pressed into service not only in matters political but also in ordinary cases. Two examples will illustrate this fact. During a fraca in a village in Patna district over some land a few days after our arrest, a man died. The police gave a political colour to the brawl and arrested eight men and alleged that the murdered man was killed by Congressmen because the deceased had joined the army against their wishes. A special judge who tried the accused found that the man had never been in the army, but as the fact of murder could not be disputed, sentenced the eight persons to death. According to the Ordinance under which the accused men were tried, the sentence had to be confirmed by a judge of the High Court. The High Court judge acquitted seven of the accused and confirmed the sentence of death on the eighth.

An appeal to the Privy Council was rejected. The jail authorities seemed to show some interest in mercy petitions being sent on behalf of people sentenced to death. I was asked to draft a petition for this man and when it was sent, the Governor accepted it and commuted the sentence. Because the police had classified him as a political prisoner, this man was released along with other political prisoners when the Congress Ministry was formed in 1946. As soon as he was released he came to Sadaqat Ashram to pay me his respects. During the previous Congress movement political workers never used to offer any defence in court. Excesses were no doubt committed, but there was, however, some regard for law and justice and the sentences were not as immoderate as during the August 1942 disturbances. Sometimes, heavy fines were imposed, but people did not mind them and gladly complied with the Mahatma's instructions not to offer any defence. But now the attitude of the Government seemed to have changed. Heavy sentences, including capital sentences, were the order of the day. The question, therefore, arose whether

Congressmen should now offer any defence or submit to such atrocities. I said emphatically that such cases must be defended. Some did not like my views and some were probably ignorant of them. Many, therefore, did not put up any defence and suffered heavy punishments. My friend, Jaglal Choudhury, was one of them and he was sentenced to ten years' imprisonment. His crime was that his son had been shot dead and he had gone to the police station to inquire of the whereabouts of his son's body! Instead of getting an answer to his queries be was arrested. I expressed myself once again in favour of offering defence when the revised Ordinance permitting appeals was promulgated. There were two arguments in favour of this course. First, if we started defending ourselves, it might make the magistrates less unscrupulous. Secondly, I saw that in the agitation were many people who had nothing to do with the Congress and wanted to defend themselves and there were also many Congressmen who wanted to do so. I said if such men were prevented from defending themselves, it might lead to discontent and in some cases defiance of instructions.

In the circumstances, the best thing to do was to allow everyone to defend himself. It was my conviction that most of us would be released at the same time, whatever the sentences awarded to us. It would be unthinkable to allow some of our workers to be condemned for long terms and to continue in prison when we ourselves were out. I was, therefore, gratified that, as soon as he came out of detention Gandhiji directed that defence should be offered in all cases. Our worry was about cases of capital sentences, because the others were bound to be released sooner or later. In Patna, quite a number were sentenced to death, but most of them managed to escape the gallows.

When Gandhiji was released, he began negotiations with Lord Wavell, the new Viceroy, on the capital sentences and he succeeded in getting all of them commuted. When Congress ministries were formed all these people were released. Unfortunately, in Muzaffarpur, Bhagalpur and Monghyr districts, some people were executed all of a sudden, before Gandhiji could intercede in there behalf. It is my conviction that this was how the people had come the conclusion that a destructive programme had been adopted by the Congress and began to act upon it spontaneously. Further, this programme seemed to be consistent with the ideas which used to occur to a section of the people even before, as I have said earlier, and so they took the Government at its word. I got sufficient proof for my argument even in jail. When Phoolan Prasad was arrested and brought to jail on the evening of the day I was arrested, he told me that, hearing of my arrest, some people had come and asked him what the Congress programme was, thinking that I would have told him. But he replied that he had not met me for long and he knew nothing about it. But the official communique had appeared the same morning and had attracted the people's notice. He referred them to that communique for the Congress programme. On account of these activities, the train services on the mainline between Moghal Sarai and Asansol were suspended for some time. This was followed by a suspension of traffic on the Patna-Gaya line. Only the Grand Chord line escaped damage and the train services on it were unaffected. In the areas north of the Ganga, the O.T. Railway (now North Eastern Railway) was so badly damaged that the train services remained suspended for several months. That was the reason why the people outside the province thought that the agitation was strongest in 'the eastern districts of the U.P. and in Bihar. Naturally, this area went through the severest repression.

A large number of people were killed in police and military firings Many houses were burnt and looted, and people had to undergo untold sufferings. The number of people sent to jail was beyond computation and to accommodate them ordinary convicts had to be let off Among such releases in Bihar were those of 30 or 40 dacoits who, people thought, had been let loose on the countryside so that the people might get fed up with the Congress. Instead, it would appear, some of these men joined the Congress agitation. One of them was sentenced to death and several others received heavy sentences. When I was released I spoke to the Governor about this. In the course of his investigation it was found that a number of criminals had been intentionally released before time. I also heard that, at the time when the agitation was at its height, no cases of thefts or dacoities occurred in the affected areas. The agitators raided many post offices and burnt some of them. In the early stages, they did not grab the money for themselves or for financing the agitation. Mostly they brunt the currency notes. But things changed later on. Some people started collecting money in the name of the agitation, so much so that even some dacoities were committed in the name of the agitation. No one knows where that money went and who made use of it. During the agitation, I should say that it was the Government official that incited the people to commit excesses, As for post office, those who manned them welcomed the arson and looting because, irrespective of the fact whether cash was removed or not, they could always say that they had been deprived of it. In the beginning, the police officials made common cause with the public whom they took to police stations, helped them plant national flags on them and then shouted slogans with them. Such officials were naturally treated well by the public.

In some cases, I was told, police officials were given hearty send offs as they left for the district headquarters and, in their absence, the people took possession of the police stations. Wherever, however, a police official was stiff, he was dealt with severely. In a few cases, police officials were killed. Some of the sub-inspectors of police were tyrants. With the arrival of the military, the attitude of the police officials changed. They committed excesses. Generally, it was the officers and not the constables who were responsible for the excesses. It has to be admitted that the people did considerable damage to railways and posts and telegraphs and also burnt down a number of Government buildings, but considering the tempo and extent of the agitation, it will be recognised that the agitators did not deal with Government officials harshly. Incidents of killing or even beating of officials were very rase. It seems that the general impression was that it was against the principles of non-violence to belabour or kill anyone, but that destroying property was not incompatible with non-violence.

Had the people so desired, they could really have killed a large number of officials without any difficulty, but they did not do so. In spite of this, the Government shot many people by way of reprisals. I believe the ratio would work out to be 50 or 60 men killed for every Government employee murdered but, in the absence of accurate figures, it is at best a conjecture. Nevertheless, it must be admitted that the agitation was not entirely non-violent and that the people lost restraint. The Labour Party came to power in Britain in July 1945, after the collapse of the Wavell Plan in June. In September 1945, Lord Wavell made a declaration reiterating the intention of His Majesty's Government to convene as soon as possible a Constitution-making body. The new Government announced in March 1946 that Lord Pethick-Lawrence, Sir Stafford Cripps and A.V. Alexander, three Cabinet Ministers, would come to India to hold talks with Indian leaders and the Viceroy to settle the country's problem. Clement Attlee, Prime Minister, gave the assurance that, while every effort would be made to safeguard the interests of the minorities, no minority group would be allowed to stand in the way of India's political progress. Britain was prepared to give freedom to India and would like her to remain within the Commonwealth but on that issue also India would be free to decide. On the surface, the announcement appeared satisfactory to us. On March 23, 1946, the three Ministers arrived in India and after preliminary discussions with the Viceroy, Lord Wavell, and his Executive Council, they began a series of talks with the various Indian political parties. They met Maulana Azad, the Congress President, and Mahatma Gandhi.

After protracted talks which seemed to take us nowhere, the British Ministers wrote to the Congress and the Muslim League to nominate four representatives each to carry on talks in Simla. The eight leaders and the Viceroy conferred with the Ministers, but their talks failed. Announcing the breaking-up of the conference, the Cabinet Mission said that they would put their plan before India in Delhi. On May 16 the plan was released to the press. The Plan was divided into three parts. In the first part, they gave cogent reasons for declaring the Muslim League demand for Pakistan as impracticable and said it-that could not be conceded. They proposed instead a Federal Constitution for India which the Princely States could also join. The Central Government would have three subjects under its jurisdiction, namely, Defence, External Affairs and Communications, with power to raise revenue to meet the expenses incurred under these heads. All other subjects would vest in the provincial Governments, as also all residuary powers not specifically mentioned. In the second part, the details of the Constituent Assembly which would frame the Constitution for the country were given.

The third part related to the immediate reconstitution of the Government of India. It also stated that India would be free to remain within the British Commonwealth or secede from it. The Constituent Assembly was to be formed in this manner : All provincial assemblies would return one member for every one million of its population, Muslims and Sikhs would elect their nominees on the basis of separate electorates. While Coorg and Baluchistan representatives would be elected afresh, those who had been elected to the.Central Assembly from Delhi and Ajmer-Merwara would be looked upon as representatives of these areas in the Constituent Assembly.

All these people would discuss with representatives of the Indian Princes on States' representation in the Assembly, and, in the case of States also, the basis of one member for every one million people would be maintained. British India would thus have in all 292 members, of whom 210 would be non-Muslims, 78 Muslims and four Sikhs. The provinces would be divided into three groups. In group one would be Madras, Bombay, the U.P., Bihar, the C.P., and Orissa. In group two would be the Punjab, the N.W.F.P., Sind and Baluchistan while Bengal and Assam would be in group three. In the first meeting of the Constituent Assembly, office-bearers would be elected and procedure determined. After that members of all the three groups would sit separately and frame Constitutions for their respective groups. Each group would decide whether it wanted to have a common Constitution for the country and, if so, what would be its form and what would be the subjects under its control. Finally, the Constituent Assembly would meet again jointly, with representatives of the Princely States also participating, and would frame the Constitution for India.

A separate committee would be constituted to consider ways and means to safeguard the rights of the minorities and its recommendations would be incorporated in the Constitution. Then, in accordance with the new Constitution, elections to the provincial assemblies would be held, each province having the right to remain in the group in which it had been placed or to break away from it. For the time being, the Viceroy would reconstitute his Executive Council on which, as far as possible, representatives of all Indian parties would be appointed. Although the Government of India Act, 1935 would continue to be 'in force and though, according to that Act, all powers would vest in the Viceroy, every possible effort would be made to carry on the work in consultation with, and according to the wishes of, the Executive Council. The Plan, while not accepting the demands of any political party fully, made an attempt to please all the parties by conceding something to each. Although the Muslim League demand for Pakistan had been rejected as such, the authors of the Plan hoped that the three-tier Constitution, consisting of a Union Centre, an intermediate authority representative of groups of contiguous provinces and finally, the provinces themselves, which permitted grouping of provinces and reduced the number of subjects with the Union to the barest minimum, would largely satisfy the Muslim demand of Pakistan. The opposition by other parties became all the more intense because the whole of the Punjab, Bengal and Assam had been placed in two groups likely to secede from the Centre, though parts of the Punjab and Bengal were Hindu majority areas and, in Assam, Muslims formed no more than one-third of the population. The Working Committee considered these proposal& for several days. During these meetings, the Congress President and other members of the Working Committee met the Viceroy several times to seek clarification of certain points of the Plan and to draw his attention to certain defects.

The Committee felt that the provinces should not be compelled to join the groups in which they had been placed. Although the Plan permitted any province to break away from its group after the Constitution had been framed, the Working Committee insisted that the provinces should have the freedom of secession even while the Constitution was being framed. The North West Frontier Province and Assam were opposed to joining the groups in which they had been placed and, on their behalf, the Working Committee claimed freedom to keep out of their groups from the very start. It thought that this was, after all, in consonance with the purpose of the Plan as a whole. The Cabinet Mission replied that it was not their intention to allow the provinces to keep out of their respective groups from the very beginning. But the Working Committee stuck to its view and decided that it would implement the proposals only according to its own views. The Muslim League, on the other hand, criticised the proposals because the demand for Pakistan had not been accepted unequivocally, but it saw in the Plan the seeds of Pakistan in the grouping of provinces, and so, as a step towards its final objectives, accepted the proposals. Discussions for the formation of an Interim Government were carried on for several days. The Viceroy Proposed a

Cabinet of 12 members composed of five Hindus, five Muslims, and two representatives of minorities.

The Congress opposed it, first, because it meant parity between Hindus and Muslims although Hindus were three times more numerous than Muslims. Secondly, the representation for the minorities had been reduced from the quota he had conceded during the Simla talks when a Cabinet of 15 had been proposed with five Hindus, five Muslims and five minority representatives, including two Harijans. It was, therefore, not merely a question of Hindu Muslim parity. The Congress had accepted the earlier proposals of Lord Wavell in view of the war situation, but now the situation had changed and it could not accept the new proposals which were worse than the earlier ones. The Congress thought that representatives of the minorities could be accommodated to their satisfaction only if the Cabinet consisted of 15 members." The Viceroy then increased the strength of the proposed Council to 13, with five Hindus, five Muslims, one Harijan and two other minority representatives. When this also was rejected by the Congress, the Cabinet Mission and the Viceroy announced the failure of their efforts to form a government acceptable to both the majority communities and, on June 16, 1946, they announced a list of 14 persons who had been invited by the Viceroy to form his new Cabinet.

The list included five Muslim Leaguers, five Congress Caste Hindus, one Congress Harijan, one Sikh, one Christian and one Parsi, which conformed generally to the list of 13 names given casually by Jawaharlal during discussions with the Viceroy except for the substitution of a non-League Muslim by a Leaguer, and a Congress Hindu by another. The name of a Parsi was added by the Viceroy. Meanwhile, the Working Committee met in Delhi and continued discussion of the Constituent Assembly proposals. With the exception of two or three members, the Committee was in favour of acceptance, although with some conditions. Mahatma Gandhi vigorously advocated acceptance of the May 16 proposals. Just at that time we received a telegram from a Congressman in Assam drawing our attention to one of the rules framed for the election of the Constituent Assembly of the eastern group according to which every candidate would have to sign a declaration agreeing to accept the grouping plan along with the other parts of the proposals.

The Assam Congressman interpreted the rule to mean that it demanded a commitment in advance on the grouping proposal. So misgivings arose and it was decided to study the rules governing the working of Constitution-making bodies more thoroughly. The discussions were postponed to the next day while the study was in progress. Meanwhile, at his prayer-meeting that evening, Gandhiji said that the Assam telegram had caused him concern. In the meantime, an A.I.C.C. session was convened in Bombay under the presidentship of Jawaharlal Nehru who had been re-elected Congress President. The meeting ratified the Working Committee decision on the Cabinet Mission proposals despite the opposition of the Socialists. Then followed the elections to the Constituent Assembly. The Congress followed the policy of getting even non-party persons elected whereas the Muslim League put up only League nominees. Jinnah himself was elected from the Punjab. The N.W.F.P. returned three Muslims, including Maulana Azad and Khan Abdul Gaffar Khan. The only non-League Muslims to be elected were Rafi Ahmed Kidwai from the U.P., Asaf Ali from Delhi and Fazlul Huq from Bengal. Most of the Congress leaders, prominent constitutional experts and patriots were successful. Dr. B. R. Ambedkar was returned from Bengal. After the conclusion of the elections, the Muslim League Council met and decided to reverse its earlier stand and reject both the May 16 and June 16 proposals. It also decided in favour of direct action for the attainment of Pakistan.

As a protest against the British attitude, it enjoined on its members to surrender all titles awarded by the British Government. Speeches in the Council were so intemperate, so full of illumination against both the Congress and' the Government that we thought the League Council was preparing to fight both. Meanwhile, the Congress Working Committee met in Wardha and adopted a resolution accepting the June 16 proposals for an Interim Government. In terms of para 8 of the June 16 plan, the Viceroy decided to form an Interim Government leaving out the Muslim League. He invited Jawaharlal Nehru and entrusted him with the task of forming a government. Nehru sent an invitation to Jinnah to join the Government, but he declined. Nehru, therefore, had no alternative but to form a Cabinet leaving out the Muslim League. After an interview with the Viceroy, he called a meeting of the Parliamentary Committee in Delhi to help him in the composition of his Cabinet. Sardar Patel, Maulana Azạd and I were members of this committee. While we were busy with the formation of the Interim Government, Calcutta was rocked by riots of a most unprecedented kind on August 16. That day had been fixed by the League as Pakistan Day. Muslims all over the country had been asked to observe a hartal in pursuance of that decision. In Bengal and Sind, the day was declared a public holiday by the Muslim League Governments. All offices and banks were forced to close down. This was an abuse of power by the Muslim League.

The Congress had organised successful hartals for 27 or 28 years in its struggles against the British Government but had never organised a hartal against the British since it assumed the reins of office in the provinces. But the League ignored protests and criticisms. In the Bengal Assembly, before the day of the hartal, opposition members vehemently protested against the declaration of a Government holiday on that day, saying that the hartal would render innumerable people idle and that processions and public meetings portended trouble. But Suhrawardy, Chief Minister, paid no heed to the protests and asserted that the holiday was in the interest of peace. On the morning of August 16, League volunteers started forcing people to close their shops. This naturally led to riots. Looting and arson became the order of the day. The Government did nothing to intervene till mid-Jay on August 17. But by then thousands of people had been murdered and thousands of houses looted and burnt down. Efforts to control the riots did not succeed till the city had passed through a four-day regime of terror. It is said that the conflagration claimed a toll of over 6,000. For days, dead bodies littered the streets. More than 3,000 bodies were collected. Many bodies, it would appear, were thrown into-underground sewers and the streets were said to be impassable because of the stench they emitted. The number of people charred to death in burning houses and those thrown into the Hooghly could not be counted.

The aged, women, or children; none was spared. This was perhaps the bloodiest carnage witnessed in India since the sacking of Delhi by Nadir Shah, although I am not sure that his armies could really have massacred so many people. A Muslim League leader, Feroze Khan Noon, had boasted a few days earlier that the League would create a situation which would make people forget the deeds of Chengez Khan and Halaku Khan. This was a sample then of the League's direct action presented to the country. Fracases did occur in some other places like Dacca, Banaras, Allahabad, Raniganj and Delhi on the protest day but they were completely eclipsed by the Calcutta massacre, and the situation in those places was quickly controlled. During this time, negotiations were going on for the formation of an Interim Government and the Viceroy and Jawaharlal made up their minds that the Calcutta happenings should not come in the way of their efforts to set up a Government at an early date. In consultation with us, Nehru finalised a list of names to be included in his Cabinet. I had been in Jaipur taking rest when I had received a telegram from Delhi to finalise the list. After the work was over I left for Pilani where I wanted to stay till the end of August, when the interim Government was expected to be sworn in. The Working Committee met in Delhi on August 27 and Gandhiji attended it. I returned front Pilani to participate in the deliberations. In the list of ministers, my name was also included. When during the Simla talks my name had been included in the Congress list, I was reluctant to agree since I was a conscientious objector. But now that the war had ended, that objection no longer held. At first, there were proposals that I should be nominated for presidentship of the Meerut Congress since Jawaharlal would be joining the Interim Government and he would have to vacate the office of President. There were also suggestions that I should be elected Chairman of the Constituent Assembly and not included in the Interim Government. Personally, I had nothing to say in the matter and whatever decision was taken would have been acceptable to me.

But if I may state my preference, either of the alternatives of Congress presidentship and chairmanship of the Constituent Assembly would have been more to my liking than a ministership. However, it did not depend on my likes or dislikes and the Working Committee decided that I should be in the Interim Government and I bowed to the decision. I thought we would now be working with a set of officers, many of whom would be those who sent us to prison and made our people suffer many hardships. But I had no prejudice against anyone and felt confident of enlisting everyone's cooperation. There were lots of difficulties before us. Who could say what the League intended to do and how the people would react to the League attitude ? I Was sure all would be well if we served the people sincerely and impartially. These were the thoughts uppermost in my mind. The Interim Government was formed on September 2, 1946. It consisted of twelve Ministers, namely, Jawaharlal Nehru, Sardar Vallabhbhai Patel, Sarat Chandra Bose, C. Rajagopalachari, Asaf Ali, Dr. John Matthai, Jagjivan Ram, Shafat Ahmed Khan, Baldev Singh, C. H. Bhabba, Ali Zaheer and me. The inmates of Birla House, where Sardar Patel, Jagjivan Ram and I were staying, gave us a ceremonial send-off that morning. We went to Gandhiji and took his blessings along with other colleagues and then proceeded to Viceroy's House to be sworn in.

7

Rajendra Prasad : His Achievements

First President of independent India; President of the Constituent Assembly; President of Congress in 1943 and 1939. Dr. Rajendra Prasad was the first President of independent India. He was the President of the Constituent Assembly that drafted the Constitution. He had also served as a Cabinet Minister briefly in the first Government of independent India. Dr. Rajendra Prasad was one of the foremost disciples of Gandhiji and he played a crucial role in Indian freedom struggle. Dr. Rajendra Prasad was born on December 3, 1884 in Ziradei village in Siwan district of Bihar. His father's name was Mahadev Sahay and his mother's name was Kamleshwari Devi. Rajendra Prasad was youngest among his siblings. Mahadev Sahay was a Persian and Sanskrit language scholar. Dr. Rajendra Prasad was greatly attached to his mother and elder brother Mahendra. At the age of five Rajendra Prasad was, according to the practice in the community to which he belonged, put under a Maulavi who taught him Persian. Later, he was taught Hindi and arithmetic. At the age of 12, Rajendra Prasad was married to Rajvanshi Devi. Dr. Rajendra Prasad was a brilliant student. He stood first in the entrance examination to the University of Calcutta, and was awarded a monthly scholarship of Rs.30. He joined the famous Calcutta Presidency College in 1902. Here his teachers included the great scientist Jagdish Chandra Ray and the highly respected Prafulla Chandra Roy. Later, on he switched from Science to Arts and completed his M.A. and Masters in Law.

Meanwhile, in 1905, Doctor, Rajendra Prasad was initiated into the Swadeshi Movement by his elder brother Mahendra. He also joined the Dawn Society run by Satish Chandra Mukherjee, and Sister Nivedita. The arrival of Mahatma Gandhi on the Indian national scene greatly influenced Dr. Rajendra Prasad. While Gandhiji was on a fact-finding mission in Champaran district of Bihar, he called on Rajendra Prasad to come to Champaran with volunteers. Dr. Rajendra Prasad was greatly impressed by the dedication, conviction and courage that Gandhiji displayed. Gandhiji's influence greatly altered Dr. Rajendra Prasad's outlook. He sought ways to simplify his life and reduced the number of servants he had to one. He started doing his daily chores such as sweeping the floor, washing the utensils-the tasks he had all along assumed others would do for him. After coming into contact with Gandhiji, Dr. Rajendra Prasad, immersed himself fully into the freedom struggle. He played a active role during Non-Cooperation Movement. Dr. Rajendra Prasad was arrested in 1930 while participating in Salt Satyagraha. He was in jail when on 15 January 1934 a devastating earthquake struck Bihar. Rajendra Prasad was released from the jail two days later and he immediately set himself for the task of raising funds and organizing relief. The Viceroy also raised a fund for the purpose. However, while Rajendra Prasad's fund collected over Rs.3.8million, the Viceroy could only manage one-third of that amount. The way the relief was organized, it amply demonstrated the administrative acumen of Dr. Rajendra Prasad.

Soon after this Dr Rajendra Prasad was elected as the President of the Bombay session of the Indian National Congress. He was elected as Congress President again in 1939 in the following the resignation of Netaji Subash Chandra Bose. In July 1946, when the Constituent Assembly was established to frame the Constitution of India, Dr. Rajendra Prasad was elected its President. Two and a half years after independence, on January 26, 1950, the Constitution of independent India was ratified and Dr. Rajendra Prasad was elected as India's first President. As a President, he used his moderating influence silently and unobtrusively and set a healthy precedent for others to follow. During his tenure as President he visited many countries on missions of goodwill and sought to establish and nourish new relationships. In 1962, after 12 years as President, Dr. Rajendra Prasad retired, and was subsequently awarded the Bharat Ratna, the nation's highest civilian award. He spent the last few months of his life in retirement at the Sadaqat Ashram in Patna. Dr. Rajendra Prasad died on February 28, 1963.

The first President of independent India, Dr. Rajendra Prasad was also the President of the Constituent Assembly that drafted India's Constitution. He had participated actively in India's freedom movement. Born on December 3, 1884 in the remote hamlet of Ziradei in Bihar's Siwan district, his father was a renowned scholar of Persian and

Sanskrit. He moved to Kolkata for his education. A brilliant student all throughout, he earned a Masters degree in Law, going on to complete a doctorate in law. He plunged headlong into the Swadeshi movement and was influenced tremendously by Mahatma Gandhi. Dr. Rajendra Prasad was arrested in 1930 for participating in the Salt Satyagraha. In January 1934, a devastating earthquake struck Bihar. Rajendra Prasad was in jail during this time, but was soon released. Upon his release, he devoted himself to the task of raising funds and providing succour to the people. He collected a large sum of money to provide relief to the affected people. He set up relief committees during the Quetta earthquake of 1935 too. He became the President of the Indian National Congress during the Bombay session in October 1934. He became the President once again when Netaji Subhash Chandra Bose resigned in 1939. He served as a Cabinet Minister for a brief period in the first government of independent India, before serving as the President of India for a period of 12 years from 1950 to 1962. He was awarded the Bharat Ratna in 1962. He left for his heavenly abode on February 28, 1963.

Major Events

3-12-1884 Birth, Jiradei, Saran, Sivan, Bihar **June 1896** Married (Dalan Chhapra in Baliya Distt) **March 1902** Passed Metric with First Division **March 1904** Passed F.A. from Kolkata University **March 1905** Graduated with First Division from Kolkata Unversity **December 1907** M.A. in Economy with First Division from Kolkata University **July 1908** Worked as Teacher at Bhumihar Brahman College, Mujaffar Nagar **January 1909** Worked as Principal at Bhumihar Brahman College, Mujaffar Nagar **March 1909** Went to Kolkata for Study of Law **July 1909** Worked as Professor of Economy in Kolkata City **1910** Graduated in

Law (B.L.) **1911** Started Practice in Kolkata High Court **1912** Became Secretary of Welcome Committee for Hindi Sahitya Sammelan, Kolkata Adhiveshan **1913** Became President of Bihar Chhatra Sammelan (Munger) **1914-15** Joined as Professor Kolkata College **1915** Passed M. L. with First Division **March 1916** Started Practice of Law in Patna High Court **1917-18** Visited Champaran with Mahatma Gandhi **1918** Published the famous English News paper "Searchlight" **1920** Published Hindi Saptahik "Desh" **1921** Established Bihar Vidyapeeth with Mahatma Gandhi and Maulana Majharul Haq **1922** Became President of Welcome Committee of Gaya Congress Adhiveshan **1923** Helped the Ganga flood affected people **1924** Became President of Akhil Bhartiya Hindi Sammelan, Kokinada Adhiveshan **1926** Became Sabhapati of Bihar Prantiye Hindi Sahitya Sammelan, Darbhanga **1923-27** Worked as Vice-chancellor or Bihar Vidyapeeth **1927** Visited Sri Lanka **1927** Became President of Sanyukt Prantiye Hindi Sahitya Sammelan, Kangri Adhiveshan **1928** Visited England & other European Countries. Attended meetings against War and gave message of peace. **6th July 1930** Arrested in Satyagrah Aandolan **4th January 1932** Arrested again in Sadakat Aashram **7th January 1932** Arrested as Dictator of Congress **17th January 1934** Released from Jail and helped Bihar Earth quake affected people **13th October 1934** Became President of Akhil Bhartiya Adhiveshan of Congress in Mumbai. **1935** Became President of Qveta Earth Quake Society **1936** Became President of Akhil Bhartiya Hindi Sahitya Sammelan of Nagpur Adhiveshan **14th December 1937** Received Degree of Doctor of Law from Allahabad University **May 1938** Became President of Ramgarh Congress Welcome Committee **1939** Became President of Contress after resignation submitted by Subhash Chandra Bose **9th August 1942** Arrested under Bharat Security Rules and stayed as Najarband in Patna Jail till 15th June 1945 **25th June to 14th July 1945** Attended Shimla Congress **2nd December 1946** Became Minister of Food & Agriculture **11th December 1946** Became President of Bhartiya Savindhan Sabha **17th November 1947** Became Congress President after resignation submitted by Aacharya Kriplani **1948** Became President of Gandhi Smarak Nidhi **26th January 1950 to 12th May 1952** Acting President of Republic of India **28th February 1950** Received Degree Vidyavachspati from Vidvat Parishad of Kashi University **10th April 1951** Received Degree Doctor of Law from Mysore University **30th November 1951** Received Degree of Doctor of Civil Law from Delhi University **13th May 1952 to 12th May 1957** Became First President of Republic of India **3rd January 1954** Received Degree of Doctor of Literature from Patna University **October 1956** Visited Nepal **3rd May 1957** Was re-elected as President of India **25th September 1958** Visited Japan **6th December 1958** Visited Malaya **8th December 1958** Visited Indonesia **15th March 1959** Visited Hind-China, Combodia, South Vietnam, North Vietnam and Laos **June 1959** Visited Sri Lanka **17th June 1959** Inaugurated Vidyalankar University, Colombo, Sri Lanka **25th January 1960** Elder Sister Smt. Bhagwati Devi Died **20th June 1960** Visited Russia **October 1960** Visited Badrinath **24th October 1960** Presented Abhinandan Granth to Rajrshi Purshotam Das Tandon in Prayag **19th July 1961** Took 5 month rest due to illness **20th December 1961** Resumed Duty **8th May 1962** Last Vidai Speech in Parliament **10th May 1962** Public of Delhi gave Vidai at Ram Lila Ground **13th May 1962** Retired from the post of President of India **14th May 1962** Reached and stayed at Bihar Vidyapeeth, Sadakat Ashram, Patna **June 1962** Delivered Inaugural speech at the conference of International Nuclear War (against) **9th September 1962**

Wife Rajvanshi Devi Died **October 1962** Donated Jewellary of his wife for the National secutiry Fund against China War **28th February 1963** Mahaprayan from Rajendra Smriti Sanghrahayala, Bihar Vidyapeeth, Sadakat Ashram, Patna, Bihar.

BIBLIOGRAPY

Andrews, C.F., *How India Can Be Free?* Madras, 1921.

Aziz, K.K., *All Parties' Muslim Conference, 1898-1935: A Documentary Record*, Karachi 1972.

Bakshi S.R., *Simon Commission and Indian Nationalism*, New Delhi, 1977.

Bakshi, S.R., *Bhagat Singh and His Ideology*, New Delhi, 1981.

Banerjea, Surendranath, *A Nation in the Making: Thoughts on Indian Discontents*, London, 1929.

Basu, Aparna, *The Growth of Education and Political Development in India, 1898-1920*, Delhi, 1974.

Bayly, C.A., *The Local Roofs of Indian Politics*, Allahabad, 18801920, Oxford, 1975.

Bipan Chandra, *Communalism in Modern India*, Delhi 1984.

Birkenhead, *The Earl of, Halifax: The Life of Lord Halifax*, London, 1965.

Birla, G.D, *In the Shadow of the Mahatma: A Personal Memoir*, Bombay, 1968.

Bose, S.C., *The Indian Struggle, 1920-1942*. New York, 1964.

Brockway, A.F., *The Indian Crisis*, London, 1930.

Bryant, J.F., *Gandhi and the Indianization of the Empire*, Cambridge, 1924.

Cadogan, Edward, *The India We Saw*, London, 1933.

Caveeshar, S.S., *India's Fight for Freedom*, Lahore, 1936.

Chintamani, C.Y., *Indian Politics since the Mutiny, Allahabad*.. 1947.

Chesney, George, Indian Policy: The System of Administration in India, Delhi, 1976.

Coatman, J., *Years of Destiny: India 1926-1932*, London, 1932.

Coupland, R., *The Goal of British Rule in India, London*, 1948. Graddock, the Dilemma in India, London, 1929.

Das, C.R., *India for Indians*, Madras, 1921.

Dutt, K. Iswara, *Congress Cyclopaedia*, Vol. I., New Delhi, Dutt, R.P., India Today, London, 1940.

Gandhi, M.K., *Hind Swaraj*, Madras, 1921.

Ghose, Sankar, *Political Ideas and Movements in India*, Calcutta, 1975.

Gopal, S., *Jawaharlal Nehru: A Biography*, Vol. I, London, 1975.

Gopal, S., *The Viceroyalty of Lord Irwin, 1926-1931*, Oxford, 1957.

Gordon, Leonard A., *Bengal : The Nationalist Movement, 1875-1940*, New Delhi, 1974.

Griffiths, P.J., *The British Impact on India*, London, 1965.

Halifax, *The Earl of Fullness of Days*, London, 1957.

Hasan, Mushirul, *Nationalism and Communal Politics in India, 1916-28*, Delhi, 1974.

Hoyland, John S., *The Case for India*, London. 1929.

Irwin, Lord, *Indian Problems*, London, 1932.

Iyengar, S. Srinivasa, *Swaraj Constitution*, Madras, 1927.

Iyer, C.S. Ranga, *India In the Crucible*, London, 1928.

Iyer, Raghavan N., *The Moral and Political Thought of Mahatma Gandhi*, New York, 1973.

Kamath, M.S., *The Home Rule League*, Madras, 1927.

Kenworthy, J.M., *India : A Warning*, London, 1931.

Kripalani, J.B., *Gandhi: His Life and Thought*, Delhi, 1970.

Liberal, A., *The Commission and After*, Bombay, 1928.

Mason, Philip, *The Men Who Ruled India*, Vols. I& II, London, 195354.

Mehrotra, S.R., *India and the Commonwealth, 1885-1929*, London, 1965.

Mehrotra, S.R., *Towards Indian Freedom and Partition*, New Delhi, 1979.

Menon, P.K.K., *The History of Freedom Movement in Kerala*, Vol. II, 1885-1938, Trivandrum, 1972.

Meston, Lord, *India and the Empire*, London, 1924.

Mitra, S.M., *Indian Problems*, London, 1901.

Mody, H.P., *The Political Future of India*, London, 1908.

Montague, E., *An Indian Diary*, London, 1930.

Moon, P., *Gandhi and Modern India*, London, 1968.

Moore, R.J., *The Crisis of Indian Unity, 1917-1940*, Oxford, 1974.

Nehru, Jawaharlal Glimpses of World History, Bombay, 1934.

Pal, B C., *The Spirit of Indian Nationalism*, London, 1910.

Pandey, B.N., *Nehru*, Delhi, 1977.

Panikkar, K.M., *The New Empire*, London, 1934.

Pat, B.C., *Swadeshi and Swaraj*, Calcutta, 1954.

Patil, V.T., *Nehru and the Freedom Movement*, New Delhi, 1977.

Paul, K.T., *The British Connection with India*, London, 1927.

INDEX